REFUSING TO FI
"GOOD WAR"

Conscientious objectors

in the North East of England

during the Second World War

Stuart Anderson

Tyne
Bridge
Publishing

First published in the UK in 2017 by

Tyne Bridge Publishing, City Library,
Newcastle upon Tyne, United Kingdom
www.tynebridgepublishing.org.uk
Copyright © Stuart Anderson, 2017

The right of Stuart Anderson to be identified as the author of this work has been asserted by him in
accordance with Sections 77 and 78 of the Copyright, Design and Patents Act 1988.

Edit/design by David Hepworth

Interview material courtesy of the Imperial War Museum, Tyne & Wear Museums & Archives and
the British Library.

ISBN-13: 9780993195679

Stuart did not enter the academic world until his retirement in 2007. He spent nearly forty years working in local government, mainly with the City of Sunderland, qualifying as an accountant in 1980. One of the many jobs he undertook was Managing Director of Sunderland Empire Theatre and later was the Project Manager for the £12million refurbishment of the theatre.

Stuart obtained his BA in History from Newcastle University in 2010 and his MA in British History in 2011. He completed his PhD thesis on Conscientious Objectors at Northumbria University in 2016. His previous dissertations have covered Crime in County Durham during WWII and the Loyalty of Northern Ireland's Loyalists during WWII.

His leisure interests include being a life-long supporter of Sunderland AFC, coaching swimming and playing Table Tennis, the latter showing a sharp decline as the years advance.

He has been married to Liz for forty-two years. They have two children and four grandchildren.

Contents

Abbreviations Used   7

Introduction: Pacifism and the North-East of
England in Context   9

Profiling Conscientious Objectors
in the North-East of England   25

Judge Richardson and the Newcastle Tribunal   77

Treatment of Conscientious Objectors
(Local Authorities)   111

Treatment of Conscientious Objectors
(Press, Public and Priests)   159

Treatment of Conscientious Objectors
(Prison, Land and Medical Experiments)   203

Women Conscientious Objectors   237

'You're in the Army Now"   263

Summary   295

Appendices   301

Bibliography   309

Index   318

PEACE NEWS

No. 156.   LONDON, FRIDAY, JUNE 9, 1939   2d.

CONSCRIPTION IN A NUTSHELL: TURNING MEN INTO ROBOTS!

LAST Saturday over 240,000 lads took the first step to being converted into automata: men into machines. They registered under the Military Training Act in the way the Government desired.

For four years they will be under the control of the Army Authorities. For six months they will be intensively trained.

Nearly 4,000 of these fellows stood firm for individual liberty of conscience; they registered as conscientious objectors.

It has been estimated that there still remain some 30,000 who have not registered at all. Who are they? Some are sailing the seas; some are ill; some have been careless. Many have refused to recognise the Act altogether. How many there are in this last category will only be shown by future events, by prosecutions.

What is certain is that the pacifist opposition to the Act by lads of conscript age is not confined to those who registered as conscientious objectors.

Number of men registered 234,172
Number of men registered as conscientious objectors 3,840

THESE are the latest available figures (as we go to press) of the registrations under the Military Training Act.

240,000 men, most of whom, it is safe to say, have never given any serious thought to the problem of peace, have now enlisted in the Army.

For four years they will be under military control. For six months they will be subjected to intensive training, directed to making them "good soldiers."

They will be taught how and when and whom to salute; how to drill; how to master their foreign tongues.

For six months they will awake to the bugle, parade to the bugle, eat to the bugle, retire to the bugle.

In six months they will have substantially lost their individualism; they will have become accustomed to obeying orders in units in a company, spontaneously, unhesitatingly, almost involuntarily.

Machines made out of men!

How Many Did Not Register?

SPECULATION is widespread as to the number of objectors who have refused to register (as too, 30,000 men in all have not registered).

An indication of what might be expected comes from Wales. The chairman of the Welsh Nationalist Party has calculated that 500 Welshmen refused to register. These included Nationalists, pacifists and members of the Independent Labour Party.

In Caernarvonshire a thousand men were

register, but the Nationalist Party organiser puts the figure at double that amount.

In Scotland an anti-war committee interviewed all intending objectors. Only 20 registered.

Intensive P.P.U. Activity

INTENSIVE activity by the Peace Pledge Union marked the beginning of registration under the Military Training Act last Saturday.

National and leading provincial newspapers carried prominent reports of demonstrations, meetings and leaflet distributions. There were some instances where pacifists incurred the displeasure of Labour Exchange officials and the police.

A leaflet distributed at Hastings was alleged by the police to be unsaleable. Mr. Kenneth Wray, Hastings PPU Group Leader, voluntarily gave his name to the police so that they could prosecute if they desired.

Over 10,000 copies of a special leaflet, entitled "Think Again!" were issued at exchanges throughout the country. Peace News and the Peace Service Handbook were generally on sale.

PPU members at Birmingham and West Bromwich had their names taken for obstruction.

Two offices of Peace News at Nottingham were asked to move on by the police. They obeyed, taking up their stance again several hundred yards away.

In an interview with the Nottingham Evening Post one of the sellers said: "When the police officer asked me to move, I

The "Thetis" Tragedy
A PACIFIST VIEW

THE loss of the submarine Thetis has shocked the nation as has no calamity of the kind since the destruction of the airship R101 nearly nine years ago.

Public reactions have been those of sympathy for the relatives of the lost and calls for a full and open inquiry into the circumstances of the disaster and the attempts at rescue.

Pacifists will join in the general and heartfelt grief of the loss of so many valuable lives, and in the expressions of violence to the bereaved. But does not this tragedy have a moral for the pacifist, a moral he will strive to bring home to the man or the people to whom it is not evident?

It was to this moral that the Rev. C. Plebland, minister of Westerham Congregational Church and a prominent pacifist, addressed himself in a sermon last Sunday.

Mr. Plebland said that it was wonderful to contemplate the unlimited eagerness to help the trapped men, and to do everything possible to bring assistance just to save

But there will also be a feeling of anger that such things as submarines should exist made so that men in order that man, urged from the dark depths of the ocean, might launch sudden and devastating destruction of some unsuspecting crew carrying hundreds of his fellow aboard.

With such a tragedy as that of the Thetis they could contemplate at one and the same time heights of nobility and the depths of depravity of which human nature is capable.

They saw humanity at its best, overflowing with love and sympathy and eagerness to help and save, and at its worst, in the form of a craft fashioned with incredible ingenuity and skill for one single purpose the silent, stealthy, cowardly launching of the torpedo, an unseen and invisible instrument of destruction and death.

There was no escaping the challenge of this tragedy when it said. "To what purpose are all these fine and noble impulses and thoughts of saving, when you severely tolerate vice and its preparation?

The ship in which the men were trapped represented an incredible amount of toil, energy and ingenuity devoted. We can, of course, rejoice. Yet in the hour of their noble bitter need, of salvation, human ingenuity to save was utterly inadequate to the situation and the despairing cry of the valiant mothers "Where are the experts now?" could receive no adequate answer.

Ex-Soldier, Turned Pacifist, To Be Court-Martialled

AWAITING court-martial is an ex-serviceman who became a pacifist before he left the Army recently, and who has refused to obey an order to report for further military training.

He is Mr. H. Daventry, of 112 St. John's Road, Highgate, N.6.

Mr. Daventry is determined to hold to his convictions despite what sentence the court-martial imposes and what subsequent steps the Army authorities may take.

ON OTHER PAGES

Philip S. Mumford on Palestine: 6
E. F. V. Collette on "False Reasons for War"   3
"Aren't You Ready to Defend Your Country?" by the Editor 4
CONSCRIPTION:

Abbreviations Used

AFS – Auxiliary Fire Service
ARP – Air-raid precautions
AWOL – Absent without leave
BUF – British Union of Fascists
CBCO – Central Board for Conscientious Objectors
CBE – Commander of the British Empire
CND – Campaign for Nuclear Disarmament
CO – Conscientious Objector
CPGB – Communist Party of Great Britain
FAU – Friends Ambulance Unit
FoR – Fellowship of Reconciliation
ILP – Independent Labour Party
JP – Justice of the Peace
KC – Knight Commander
MC – Military Cross
MP – Member of Parliament
NALGO – National Association of Local Government Officers
N-CF – No Conscription League
N-CL – No Conscription League
NCC – Non-Combatant Corps
NCO – Non-Commissioned Officer
NFU – National Farmers Union
NSO – National Service Officer
NUGMW – National Union of General Municipal Workers
NUPE – National Union of Public Employees
NYCC – North Yorkshire County Council
OBE – Order of the British Empire
PPU – Peace Pledge Union
RAF – Royal Air Force
RAMC – Royal Army Medical Corps
TUC – Trade Union Congress
UDC – Urban District Council
UK – United Kingdom
USA – United States of America
WILPF – Women's International League for Peace and Freedom
WRI – War Resisters International

Introduction:
Pacifism and the North-East of England in Context

In Tokyo in 1967 the acclaimed poet, James Kirkup, wrote *White Shadow*, reflecting on a photograph of the white shadow left by a man annihilated by the atomic bomb on Hiroshima.[1] The poem included the following lines:

> *Led by the ignorant and mad, we believe in worlds*
> *Where black is white, and white is black,*
> *Where leaders say peace cannot be found*
> *Except in continued bombing of the helpless.*
> *Where war is peace and peace is war,*
> *Where bombs are good and people bad,*
> *Where sleep is awake and eat I starve,*
> *Where live is die.*
> *Where love is kill.*

James Kirkup was from the North-East of England and was a conscientious objector in the Second World War. As an artist, he would have been seen by many of his contemporaries as the epitome of a conscientious objector - Mass Observation (see later) noted that objectors were typically in occupations requiring particular intelligence, and had intelligent and high-brow tastes in culture.[2] However, the industrial North-East would not have been seen as the typical environment for either a poet or a pacifist. Many histories have been written about the Second World War yet they have paid scant attention to either conscientious objectors or the North-East.

It has been noted that in total war, 'the nation's rulers, whether they liked it or not, depended on the willing co-operation of the ruled.'[3] This co-operation involved conscription, both military and industrial,

---

1 James Kirkup, *White Shadows, Black Shadows: Poems of Peace and War* (London: J. M. Dent & Sons, 1970), p. 9.
2 http://www.massobservation.amdigital.co.uk, Mass Observation File Report 312 – Conscientious Objectors, Summary, Item 2, June 1940.
3 Angus Calder, *The Peoples' War* (London: Jonathan Cape, 1969), p. 17.

and was accepted by the majority. It was not, however, accepted by all, and for the second time in less than quarter of a century the term, 'conscientious objection', was to be heard regarding the war effort. Official figures for the years 1939 to 1948 record 62,301 objectors appearing before tribunals nationally, of which 1,148 were in the North-East of England. This book shows the figures are understated.[4]

For the purpose of this book, the North-East of England is taken as the area covered by the conscientious objectors' tribunal, comprising of the geographic counties of Northumberland, Durham and the North Riding of Yorkshire (see map below). It examines the reasons for, and the degree of success, of those claiming conscientious objection, and it considers attitudes towards them, including their treatment by the tribunals, prisons, press, employers and public. The basis for this examination is a database of over 820 objectors from the North-East of England, compiled from a variety of primary sources. It, therefore, contributes to the national historiography on conscientious objectors as well adding to the social history of the region in the Second World War.[5]

Area Covered by the Northumberland and Durham Tribunal.

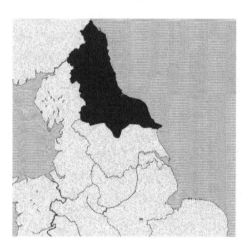

---

4 'Decisions of Local Tribunals up to December 31st 1948,' LAB 6/405, The National Archives, Kew, London.
5 Stuart Anderson, PhD Thesis, *Refusing to Fight the "Good War": Conscientious Objectors in the North-East of England During the Second World War*, Northumbria University, November 2016.

Literature on conscientious objectors nationally has become more prevalent in recent years. Prior to 1982 the only comprehensive volume on the subject in Britain was Denis Hayes' *Challenge of Conscience*, written in 1949.[6] Hayes was closely involved with the Central Board for Conscientious Objectors (CBCO) and therefore shows 'sympathy with Conscientious Objectors.'[7] Hayes does, however, attempt to be balanced, particularly regarding the operation of the conscientious objector tribunals set up to assess the integrity of objectors. His work is a well-written technical volume, with substantial statistical data for analysis, and essential for understanding of the mechanisms surrounding objection. Rachel Barker built on Hayes' contribution by drawing on primary source material other than the CBCO to assess the administration of the 'conscience clause'. Her work on the attitude of employers, particularly in the public sector, is informative and valuable.

Despite useful chapters on pacifism and conscientious objection by Peter Brock and Nigel Young in *Pacifism in the Twentieth Century* and Martin Ceadel in *Pacifism in Britain 1914-1945*, it is only in recent years that the literature has significantly expanded.[8] In *Twentieth-Century Pacifism*, Peter Brock contrasts the pattern of conscientious objection in the Second World War to that in the First World War.[9] The availability of Mass Observation records and oral testimonies, conducted primarily by the Imperial War Museum and Rena Feld at the British Library, has led to works by Lyn Smith , Felicity Goodhall , and Ann Kramer.[10] These new works are welcome additions, producing informative narratives of conscientious objection in the Second World War.

This additional material has also led to a number of articles on more specialist aspects of conscientious objection, most notably on the role of women, with articles by Mitzi Bales and Hazel Nicholson.[11] Bales'

6 Denis Hayes, *Challenge of Conscience* (London: George Allen and Unwin Ltd., 1949).
7 Rachel Barker, *Conscience, Government and War* (London: Routledge, 1982), p. 2.
8 Peter Brock and Nigel Young, *Pacifism in the Twentieth Century* (New York: Syracuse University Press, 1999) and Martin Ceadel, *Pacifism in Britain 1914-1945* (Oxford: Clarendon Press, 1980).
9 Peter Brock, *Twentieth-Century Pacifism* (New York: Van Nostrand Reinhold, 1975).
10 Lyn Smith, *Voices Against War* (Edinburgh: Mainstream, 2010); Felicity Goodhall, *We Will Not Go To War: Conscientious Objection during the World Wars* (Stroud: The History Press, 2010); Ann Kramer, *Conscientious Objectors of the Second World War: Refusing to Fight* (Barnsley: Pen and Sword, 2013).
11 Mitzi Bales, 'They Said "No" to War: British Women Conscientious Objectors in World War II', http://www.wri-irg.org/node/11902, ; Hazel Nicholson, 'A Disputed Identity: Women Conscientious

work, based on Hayes, Barker and the British Library Sound Archive, is a narrative of women's experiences, whilst Nicholson argues convincingly that the official statistics for conscientious objectors were understated, and explores how the definition of conscientious objection was different for women than men with regard to objection to military service. This different treatment of women is also analysed in an article by Tobias Kelly which examines the relationship between the obligation of the individual to defend the state and the holding of a conscientious objection to killing. He argues that this socially sanctioned form of dissent was only available to those who enjoyed the full rights and responsibilities of citizenship and produced exclusions based on nationality, race and gender.[12] John Pemberton describes medical experiments carried out on conscientious objectors from a medical point of view.[13] Perhaps the most significant recent contribution to the study of pacifism and conscientious objection in the Second World War has come from Richard Overy. Drawing on his recent research on bombing, he asserts that pacifism supplied an 'important dissenting discourse during a period when the government and media were united in presenting a common belligerent front and community solidarity in the face of a shared disaster'. Rather than divorce themselves from events, pacifists came to endorse the idea of service to the community as a way of demonstrating that a wartime social conscience, as well as displays of considerable bravery, were compatible with rejection of war and military service.[14] This book demonstrates that this social conscience, whilst displayed by many, was not displayed by all.

Overy was researching a facet of total war - where the whole of society, military and civilian, is organised for the prosecution of the war and where the numbers of people engaged on the home front exceeded those in the military. Angus Calder referred to this as the 'People's War',

---

Objectors in Second World War Britain', *Twentieth Century British History*, Vol. 18, No. 4, 2007, pp. 409-428.

12 Tobias Kelly, 'Citizenship, Cowardice, and Freedom of Conscience: British Pacifists in the Second World War', *Comparative Studies in Society and History*, 57 (3), 2015, pp. 1-29.

13 John Pemberton, 'Medical Experiments carried out in Sheffield on Conscientious Objectors to military service during the 1939-45 war', *International Journal of Epidemiology*, 35, 2006, pp. 556-558.

14 Richard Overy, 'Pacifism and the Blitz 1940-1941', *Past and Present*, 219, May 2013, pp. 201-236.

thus challenging the conventional wisdom of the time of wartime Britain, which has led to the war being studied as a period of British history and not just an event.[15] The concept of the 'People's War' has formed the basis of general histories of the War, including those by Juliet Gardiner and Felicity Goodhall, many of which are referred to in this book, and the use of oral testimonies of wartime experiences in compiling the BBC People's War project.[16] The 'People's War' also, however, had its dissenters.

As we move further away from the war, there have been changing public attitudes towards conscientious objection enabling the views and experiences of those regarded by many in their time as social pariahs are able to be published objectively. This, and the realisation that Britain's war had not entirely been one of everyone pulling together, has led to general histories of the Second World War in Britain including more than a simple passing reference to conscientious objection. Angus Calder had already exploded the myth of the blitz in 1991.[17] Sonya Rose, in *Which People's War*, contrasts the often-portrayed image of conscientious objectors, excluding Quakers, as lacking in masculinity to the popular perceptions that masculinity could only be enacted by military service; the latter presenting an image of good citizenship which the former did not.[17] This book provides some evidence to support this perspective on conscientious objection. The question of masculinity has also been explored in connection with men in reserved occupations in regional studies by Alison Chard, Juliette Pattinson and Linsey Robb, Robb recently undertaking research on men in Teesside.[18] In these studies physically fit

---

15 Angus Calder, *The People's War: Britain 1939-1945* (London: Pimlico, 1969).

16 Juliet Gardiner, *Wartime Britain 1939-1945* (London: Headline, 2004); Juliet Gardiner, *The Blitz: The British Under Attack* (London: Harper Press, 2010); Felicity Goodhall, *The People's War: Reliving Life on the Home Front in the Second World War* (Newton Abbott: David & Charles, 2008); *WW2 People's War*, BBC, 2006, www.bbc.co.uk/history/ww2peopleswar/categories/, Angus Calder, *The Myth of the Blitz* (London: Jonathan Cape, 1991).

17 Sonya O. Rose, *Which People's War?: National identity and Citizenship in Wartime Britain 1939-1945* (Oxford: Oxford University Press, 2006), pp.170-178.

18 Alison Chard, 'Conflicting Masculinities? Men in Reserved Occupations in Clydeside 1939-1945', *Journal of Scottish Historical Studies*, Vol. 32, Issue 2, 2014, pp. 218-236; Juliette Pattinson, Arthur McIvor and Linsey Robb, *Men in Reserve: Civilian Masculinities in Britain, 1939 – 1945* (Manchester: Manchester University Press, 2016); L. Robb and J. Pattinson (eds.), *Men, Masculinities and Male Behaviour in Britain during the Second World War* (Palgrave Macmillan, 2017).

men of conscription age, whilst having no choice but to remain in re-served occupation, felt emasculated by being undermined by the state and cultural representations in films etc., a situation made worse, asserts Martin Pugh, by the sudden rise in the status of women which was dis-orientating for men.[19]

A more mainstream coverage is provided by Juliet Gardiner in *Wartime Britain 1939-1945*, where 32 pages are devoted to the subject in a generally sympathetic manner. Perhaps indicative of the relaxation of attitude towards conscientious objection is the sympathetic coverage of the subject in television drama, such as *Foyle's War*, where a conscientious objector is maltreated and dies in a police cell, and even the comedy, *Dad's Army*, where Private Godfrey admits to being a conscientious objector in the First World War, being decorated for bravery when serving in the Royal Army Medical Corps.[20]

The recent works are welcome additions, but overall the literature continues to present a superficial picture of conscientious objection. This book, by examining one region as a case study, draws on new evidence to present a more detailed demonstration of how conscientious objection worked and how people responded to it in practice, thus giving nuance and depth to that picture.

Conscientious objection was, of course, not a feature unique to the Second World War. Peter Brock argues that it began with the refusal of many Christians to fight in the Roman Army.[21] This brief overview of pacifism in Britain starts at the end of the nineteenth century. It was part, but only a part, of a pacifist movement prevalent in Britain throughout the twentieth century and today. As this book shows, not all conscientious objectors were pacifists, and not all pacifists were conscientious objectors.[22] Apart from groups such as the Quakers, who had founded Britain's first peace organisation, the Peace Society, in 1816, there was no strong peace movement in Britain at the end of the nineteenth century. This was largely due to Britain being an island nation

---

19 Martin Pugh, *State and Society: A Social and Political History of Britain Since 1870* (London, Hodder Education, 2010) p. 257.
20 *Foyle's War*, 'A Lesson in Murder', ITV Television, 2002; and, *Dad's Army*, 'Branded', BBC Television, 1969.
21 Peter Brock, *Pacifism in Europe to 1914* (Princetown, 1972), p. 3.
22 Brock, *Pacifism in Europe to 1914*, p. 3; and Martin Ceadel, *Pacifism in Britain 1914-1945* (Oxford: Clarendon Press, 1980), p.18.

whose security was guaranteed by the world's most powerful navy: there was no need for a large conscript standing army. It seemed unlikely that Britain would be involved in a large scale European land war. This was to change with the emergence of a strong united Germany challenging Britain's naval supremacy and Britain's entanglement in the conflicting European power blocs. The resulting Great War, according to Martin Ceadel, marks the beginning of modern British pacifism with the founding of the No-Conscription Fellowship (N-CF) and the Fellowship of Reconciliation (FoR), both in 1914. The N-CF, founded by Fenner Brockway MP, had a national committee composed mainly of Independent Labour Party (ILP) socialists. The FoR's pacifist basis was Christian: predominantly, though not exclusively, Nonconformist and Quaker. Ceadel asserts that despite the introduction of conscription for the first time in Britain in 1916 which made pacifism a political issue, the First World War did not leave either a strong pacifist movement or a clear pacifist doctrine.[23]

The inter-war years saw a proliferation of peace and pacifist organisations, some of which were amalgamations of smaller organisations, including: The Council of Christian Pacifist Groups (1933); the League of Nations Union (1918); the No More War Movement (1921); the Sheppard Movement (1935); War Resisters International (WRI) (1923 in UK); and, most significantly, the PPU (1936). The PPU's founder, Dick Shepherd, asked people to write to him with the following pledge: 'I renounce war, and never again will I support or sanction another, and I will do all in my power to persuade others to do the same.'[24] Supported by prominent Labour figures such as George Lansbury MP, Lord Ponsonby and Ellen Wilkinson MP, it reached its peak in April 1940, with 136,000 members, although, as is shown later, its numbers dropped in the later war years.[25] During the war it was an umbrella organisation of religious and political pacifism, having become the British section of the WRI. in 1937. The FoR, WRI and the PPU are still in existence today.

---

23 Ceadel, *Pacifism in Britain*, pp. 31-35.
24 'Peace Pledge Union', *Sunderland Echo*, 2 July 1936, p. 8.
25 Martin Ceadel, *Thinking About Peace and War* (Oxford: Oxford University Press, 1989), p. 137.

These various peace organisations were not the exclusive property of the intellectual elite in London and elsewhere, as the considerable membership of the PPU suggests. Peace organisations had a significant presence in the North-East of England in the inter-war years. The FoR held a joint summer conference in 1935 with the Council of Christian Pacifist Groups at Bede College, Durham. One of its speakers was Canon S. D. Morris, later to be a leading figure in the PPU.[26] It also held meetings throughout the region, including Oliver's Café in Morpeth where on 2 June 1939, its Northern Area Secretary, Rev. Lloyd Phelps of Manchester, declared that during the Great War the world had paid such a terrible price that the futility of warfare should now be plainly apparent.[27] On the same day, it also reported that the Methodist Church in Ashington was giving war resisters the opportunity to sign a covenant to 'renounce war and all its ways and works.'[28] Earlier at Ashington, on Armistice Day, the Rev. P. S. Carden declared: 'I would like to build another Cenotaph, and on it I would engrave the names of the 71 men, who rather than sully their consciences, refused to fight; the men who preferred to die in prison – or shortly after their release – from the torture and hardship there received.'[29]

In Sunderland, where the Mayor, Alderman Summerbell, was a committed pacifist, the pacifist movement was particularly strong. The PPU held regular meetings in the Thompson Memorial Hall where, as the *Sunderland Echo* regularly reported, there were large attendances. Canon Morris was a regular speaker at these meetings, as was G. H. Bartram, a future conscientious objector. As well as discussing a wide range of topics, such as economic sanctions, non-resistance, and unilateral disarmament, the Sunderland PPU formed a drama group where one of its members, William Davey, a future conscientious objector, wrote a play called, 'None Other than Fighteth,' which prompted the *Sunderland Echo* to remind its readers that with propaganda plays 'the result is all too often a poor play.'[30]

The activities of peace organisations in Sunderland were not universally popular. The decision of Sunderland and District Peace Council

---

26 'We Can Never End War says Speaker', *Sunderland Echo*, 1 August 1935, p. 1.
27 'War and Peace', *Morpeth Herald*, 2 June 1939, p. 10.
28 'Peace Covenant at Ashington', *Morpeth Herald*, 2 June 1939, p. 11.
29 'Tribute to War Resisters', *Morpeth Herald*, 12 November 1937, p. 6.
30 'Peace Playwright', *Sunderland Echo*, 28 October 1938, p. 8.

to open a shop selling white and green poppies during the build up to Armistice Day led to George Cook of the British Legion describing it as 'a stab in the back for ex-servicemen'.[31]

The rise of pacifism in the inter-war years was no surprise given the horrors of the First World War, yet it was relatively slow to take off. The war weariness of all the participating nations and the establishment of the League of Nations provided an optimism that another war was not going to be allowed to happen. The pacifist surge occurred with the rise of the European dictators and Japanese militarism, and the resulting failure of arbitration attempts by the League of Nations. PPU and pacifist support for appeasement ensured that it maintained its impetus, but once it became evident that the policy had failed and war was inevitable, the political significance of the PPU declined to the point that only 1.8 per cent applied for conscientious objector status in June 1939.[32] Its decline was, according to Mark Gilbert, was assisted by the apologist tendencies among the leading intellectuals and writers of the PPU towards Germany.[33] To Ceadel, pacifism was not an uncomplicated social belief but one in which a number of distinct positions were taken to justify it.[34] Therefore pacifism in its various guises remained a strong motivator of many conscientious objectors during the Second World War, and, as this book shows, the activities of the FoR, WRI and the PPU were evident in the region. Despite its decline, Overy argues that the:

> ...pacifist argument during the Blitz about the futility and barbarity of retaliation bombing kept alive the idea of reconciliation with a defeated German people and the need for a renewed internationalism, and helps to explain how a country whose forces had spent four years obliterating German cities could generate amongst its people the will to help in their reconstruction, to ameliorate German suffering and to campaign against any renewal of total war.[35]

---

31 'What Our Readers Say', *Sunderland Echo*, 14 November 1936, p. 5.
32 Ceadel, *Pacifism in Britain*, p. 383.
33 Mark Gilbert, 'Pacifist Attitudes to Nazi Germany, 1936-45', *Journal of Contemporary History*, Vol. 27, No. 3, July 1992, pp. 493-511.
34 Ceadel, *Pacifism in Britain*, pp. 7-8.
35 Overy, 'Pacifism and the Blitz, p. 236.

A less complimentary view was taken by Richard Rempel who concluded that if pacifist views had prevailed then Britain would have been defeated but, however, it, 'says much for the tolerance of British society that pacifists could put forward unpopular ideas.'[36]

The decline of pacifism in many ways reflects the fact that, whilst the main protagonists remained the same (if not in the same alignment), the two world wars of the twentieth century were different in nature. Both were total wars, one affecting the civilian population by losing much of a generation in industrial trench warfare, the other bringing large-scale death and destruction directly to the population. The First World War introduced military conscription to Britain for the first time, and with it the conscientious objector. This much maligned, at the time, group of people received what is now considered treatment bordering on brutality in many instances. The Second World War brought a formal recognition of the right to conscientious objection. But the Second World War also brought with it a tacit acceptance that war was the only way of stopping Hitler, an acceptance which manifested itself in contrasting attitudes towards conscientious objectors. To the majority, it was a war for freedom and not of imperial dominance, which contributed to a degree of tolerance of conscientious objection. However, the majority public opinion remained firmly behind the view that everyone should be prepared to fight what was a clear evil. Tolerance was therefore not universal and neither was the view that it was not an imperialistic war. This book illustrates both the contrasts, and sometimes the similarities, between the treatment received by objectors in the Second World War and those in the First World War.

Another common feature of the current literature on the Second World War is that it under-represents the North-East of England. The region often appeared to be an inconsequential backwater to the London-centric establishment. Yet, it had been the powerhouse of the industrial revolution of the nineteenth century but as war approached the region was very much in decline. Characterised by the Jarrow Crusade of 1936, the traditional industries of coal mining and ship building were represented in 1939 by moth-balled shipyards on the rivers Tyne and

---

36 Richard A. Remple, 'The Dilemmas of British Pacifists During World War II', *The Journal of Modern History*, Vol. 50, No. 4, December 1978, pp. 213-229.

Wear and over 10,000 miners unemployed in the Durham Coalfield alone. Once war had broken out the emphasis was placed on the re-location of miners and skilled ship-builders, rather than on relieving the problems of those industries in the region. In December 1939 Sunderland Council requested the government to re-open the Wear yards to no avail in the short term.[37] This situation was not to last and soon the North-East of England was to be in the forefront of total war.

The country needed coal to power its war industries and merchant ships to bring food to prevent starvation and raw materials to produce weapons. Unemployment became a forgotten issue for the remainder of the war. Shipyards re-opened on the Wear, Tyne and Tees, and output increased substantially from the region's coal mines. The Liberty Ships, a major part of the Trans-Atlantic convoys, were built in the United States but based on a design by J. L. Thompson and Sons of Sunderland.[38] The industrial contribution to the war also included iron and steel production in Consett and Middlesbrough for the ship building and armaments industries, the largest armaments works being the Armstrong works at Elswick on the Tyne. Munitions production was carried out on a major scale at Aycliffe and Spennymoor, and the trains and wagons to transport vital goods, as well as millions of soldiers, were built at Darlington and Shildon.

The industrial contribution of the North-East was highly significant. However, the stereotypical image of the region fails to recognise that it is not only an area of industry. The rich arable lands of North Yorkshire and South Durham, as well as the livestock farms of Northumberland and the upland areas, provided a large proportion of wartime food. The region's contribution to the war effort was recognised by the German military which launched numerous bombing raids on Middlesbrough, Hartlepool, Sunderland and Tyneside. Whilst not coming to the public attention in the way that Coventry and the London Blitz did, the region suffered significant loss of life. Raids in the North-East and in Hull were referred to in the press and on radio simply as, 'a raid on a

37 Alan Burns, *Sunderland's War Diary* (Sunderland: Otterburn Publications, 2007), 6 December 1939.
38 Global Security.org, http://www.globalsecurity.org/military/systems/ship/liberty-ships-design.htm, accessed 6 March 2016.

North-East coastal town.'[39] Hard hit was Sunderland where 267 civilians lost their lives.[40] It is also an area with a long coastline and many ports, from which fisherman risked their lives to bring in more food. As well as building merchant ships, the merchant seamen of the North-East sailed them, primarily from South Shields and Sunderland. 330 Sunderland members of the merchant marine alone lost their lives to enemy action.[41]

This is a local/regional history, a form of study increasingly taken up by professional historians 'because of the opportunity it offers of straddling the conventional demarcations between specialisms'.[42] This study, rather than being an isolated one, has, through a detailed analysis, provided a proper social context to the broader national issues. By examining the diversity of the districts and localities within the (North-East) region it has provided 'a better understanding of the history of the nation at large.'[43]

Wartime histories of the region have been understandably localised, as many of their authors and readers had lived through the conflict and experienced the events depicted by the narrative and the photographs. They have therefore concentrated on the effects of the bombing and the stoic spirit of the blitz. Notable examples are *Sunderland's War Diary* by Alan Burns and *Wartime Teesside* by Bill Norman, which have a strong emphasis on the bombing experienced and their military and industrial contributions, but which make no assessment of conscientious objection.[44]

A sub-regional approach has been taken by Craig Armstrong in *Tyneside in the Second World War*. Armstrong provides strong insight into social aspects of the war but gives only limited attention to conscientious objection. He references the anti-war activities of the Jehovah's Witnesses and the Peace Pledge Union, which he describes as 'minimal'

---

39 Remembering the Terror the Luftwaffe's Butterfly Bombs Brought to the North, *The Guardian*, 21 June 2013; T. Geraghty, *A North-East Coastal Town: Ordeal and Triumph* (Howden: Mr Pye Books, 1989), p 7.

40 Geoffrey Milburn and Stuart Miller, *Sunderland – River, Town and People* (Sunderland: Borough of Sunderland, 1988), p. 184.

41 Burns, *Sunderland's War Diary*, Appendix – Roll of Honour.

42 John Tosh with Sean Lang, *The Pursuit of History* (Harlow: Pearson Education, 2006) p.139.

43 David Hey, 'Reflections on the Local and Regional History of the North,' *Northern History*, vol. 50, no. 2, 2103, pp. 155-169.

44 Burns, *Sunderland's War Diary* (Sunderland: Ouseburn Publications, 2007); Bill Norman, *Wartime Teesside* (Lancaster: Dalesman Books, 1989).

rather than 'infinitesimal' as some early reports had described.[45] Armstrong has gone some way to addressing the imbalance, but his work still emphasises the 'we can take it' attitude. It has perhaps been expedient not to concentrate on those for whom it was considered not to be their finest hour. This book does concentrate on them, showing that for some who served with distinction in non-combat roles in the Friends Ambulance Unit (FAU) and the Royal Army Medical Corps (RAMC) it was their finest hour. Whilst the suffering of those affected by bombing is all too plain to see and understand, nevertheless those who suffered for their deeply held beliefs can also be seen as war victims. This book fills a gap in the historiography of the Second World War in the North-East of England. It shows that conscientious objection, whilst a minority stance in the North-East, was nevertheless significant.

Even in the twenty-first century, there are conflicting memories of conscientious objectors in the North-East. These are illustrated in an article in the *Northern Echo*. In 2002, English Heritage planted 16 shrubs in Richmond Castle gardens to commemorate 16 conscientious objectors held in the castle during the First World War. This move provoked considerable local hostility, led by Major Ron Tyler, a retired Royal Military Police officer: 'Though many had come to recognise the real courage of the conchies' convictions, his comments echoed a century of venom. "They were cowards then, and they're cowards now," he said.'[46] The *Northern Echo* was not attempting to stir up old prejudices. The primary purpose of the article was to tell the story of two North-East conscientious objectors, Peter Leyland and Douglas Hardy, who had served in the FAU in the London Blitz and China during the Second World War, Douglas Hardy sadly losing his life. It tells of the reading of a poem, *Knight Without Armour*, written by Lily Hardy about her courageous uncle, at the inauguration of the FAU memorial at the National Arboretum in 2013. This book rediscovers other conscientious objectors from the region and, as with Peter Leyland and Douglas Hardy, tells their stories. It also demonstrates that it is a lot easier to be a pacifist in peacetime than in time of total war.

---

45 Craig Armstrong, *Tyneside in the Second World War* (Chichester: Phillimore & Co., 2007), p. 130-132.
46 'Matters of Conscience', *Northern Echo*, 7 May 2013.

To tell these stories, the book is structured around the preparation and analysis of the previously mentioned database of conscientious objectors. One of the most central sources for such an analysis, the records of the Newcastle Conscientious Objectors Tribunal, was destroyed in 1963, on the instructions of the government. Reasons for this decision are unknown, although they retained the records of the Midland's Tribunal in the National Archives for historians to examine. A similar decision was made regarding the records of the First World War tribunals in 1921 when the Ministry of Health decided that all papers relating to individual cases of exemption from National Service in the First World War and tribunal minute books (except those of the Central Tribunal), should be destroyed.

In the absence of official tribunal records the database has been prepared from a variety of sources, including: prison records; 18 regional and national newspapers; material compiled for the BBC People's War Project; Mass Observation records; central government records in the National Archives; and sound archives at the British Library (BL) and Imperial War Museum (IWM). Other sources include the database of objectors held by the Peace Pledge Union (PPU) and some objectors referred to in the secondary literature.

Regional newspapers were the most prolific source of data. These were chosen to cover all parts of the region, and all pages of the papers from May 1939 to September 1945 were examined wherever possible. National newspapers were accessed via the Database of British Newspapers (DBN). *The Times* digital archives and other on-line resources were also used. Some editions of the anarchist newspaper, *The Word,* was also accessed at Warwick University. *Peace News* and *Friends Ambulance Chronicle* were accessed at Friends House, London and *The New Leader* at the People's History Museum, Manchester. There was an awareness of press bias, so, for the purposes of the database, factual information was cross-referenced between newspapers.

Oral testimonies from local objectors were difficult to obtain at the time of writing the book, due to many having become deceased. Fortunately, such testimonies were available from alternative sources. The oral histories held by the IWM and BL added significant material. The IWM holds some 37,000 sound recordings of which approximately 200 are from conscientious objectors, from the First World War to post-

1945 conflicts. Those relating to the Second World War were collected between 1980 and 1996. The smaller BL collection relates to women conscientious objectors and were recorded in 1998 and 1999. Given that, to reference Valerie Yow, 'we construct narratives from our memories', it is important to recognise that oral testimonies have their limitations, therefore information obtained was cross-referenced where possible to other sources.[47]

One particularly significant source was the records of Mass Observation. Mass Observation was founded in 1937 by anthropologist Tom Harrisson and journalist Charles Madge. It consisted of a team of paid observers and a panel of volunteer writers, and in August 1939, with war imminent, it asked its panel to keep diaries to give details of their everyday lives. The diaries were sent in to Mass Observation on a weekly or monthly basis, and are 'a particular hybrid of private diary and public research journal.' Even though the respondents were self-selected they were a valuable source of opinion relating to conscientious objection. Between 1937 and 1950 they produced around 2,000 reports, including, in 1941, the only comprehensive report on conscientious objection during the war with was invaluable as a comparator for the analysis of the database.[48]

The book first considers who the objectors were and then examines how they were treated by the tribunal, their employers, the prisons, the press, the public, the churches and the armed forces. It devotes a chapter specifically to women objectors, a group traditionally understated in terms of numbers and significance.

---

47 Valerie Raleigh Yow, *Recording Oral History: A Guide for the Humanities and Social Sciences* (Maryland: Rowman and Littlefield, 2015), Chapter 2, p. 1..
48 Sandra Koa Wing, ed., *Our Longest Days: A People's History of the Second World War* (London: Profile, 2007), p. vii.

Chapter One

Profiling Conscientious Objectors in the North-East of England

Defining conscientious objection to military service proved not to be straightforward. Within the broad definition of an objection to killing and war, there are degrees of objection, which the government attempted to recognise in its conscription legislation. For some, however, there was an objection to the compulsion itself inherent in the legislation. This chapter examines how many objected within this legislative framework, or objected by ignoring it. It examines who the objectors were; their employment, social backgrounds and personal characteristics, comparing the region with national data. The reasons for conscientious objection are examined, and how these operated within families, often carrying forward the tradition of objection from one world war to another. This examination is undertaken referencing the experiences of individual regional objectors.

The Introduction of Conscription

To deal effectively with conscientious objection, the government had the experience, and the errors, of the First World War to draw on. The question in 1916 was whether, or not, to introduce legislation to provide for conscientious objection, and in 1939 the question was how to frame it.[1] The 1916 Military Training Act established tribunals, under the auspices of the War Office, to hear and test applications for exemption. This led to accusations that tribunal members, instead of acting impartially, were, through their reluctance to grant unconditional exemption, actively trying to recruit members for the armed forces.[2] Complete exemption was rare, and partial exemption normally meant non-combatant service in the armed forces. For many, this meant service in the RAMC,

---

[1] Barker, *Conscience, Government and War*, p. 114.
[2] Ibid., p. 115.

or as stretcher bearers where their life expectancy was extremely short. For those who would not accept the decision of the tribunal, the experience led to repeated terms in prison. Richmond Castle in North Yorkshire was the prison for 16 objectors who had refused non-combatant service and were secretly transferred to France where they received the death sentence only to be reprieved at the last minute as they faced a firing squad. Not so lucky were the 69 who died and 39 who went mad resulting from their treatment by the authorities.[3]

Introduced out of necessity in 1916, conscription was still alien to the traditional British method of warfare. It was one of the major political controversies of the war and fear of its introduction in Ireland was a major reason for the rise in popularity of Sinn Fein.[4] Despite the growing threat posed by Nazi Germany, Prime Ministers Baldwin and Chamberlain gave categorical assurances that conscription would not be introduced in times where peace prevailed.[5] However, the need to present some form of deterrent to Germany and achieve some level of preparedness led to Parliament approving the principle of conscription in the Military Training Bill of 27 April 1939. However, as Churchill states: '(this) did not give us an army...they still had to be trained and after they were trained they still had to be armed.'[6] The Bill required male subjects between the ages of twenty and twenty-one to register for military training, and made provision for conscientious objection. The *Northern Echo* commented that the 'last war was a painful lesson in this respect,' and hoped that there would be 'no loopholes left for outside busybodies to taunt any of these young men of shirking, who, on any valid grounds, secure exemption for reasons of conscience, health or any other circumstances.'[7] Prime Minister Chamberlain, who himself had served on a Conscientious Objectors' tribunal in the First World War, was equally emphatic:

---

[3] Caroline Moorehead, *Troublesome People: Enemies of War 1916-1986* (London: Hamish Hamilton, 1987) p. 10.
[4] David Stevenson, *1914-1918: The History of the First World War* (London: Penguin, 2004) pp. 202-204 and Arthur Marwick, *The Deluge: British Society and the First World War* (London: Macmillan, 1978) pp. 76-81.
[5] Hayes, *Challenge of Conscience*, p. 1.
[6] Winston S. Churchill, *The Second World War: Part 1, The Gathering Storm* (London: Cassell, 1948), p. 291.
[7] 'Editorial', *Northern Echo*, 2 May 1939, p. 6.

I want to make it clear that in the view of the Government where these scruples are conscientiously held we desire they should be respected and there should be no persecution of those who hold them.[8]

On 3 September, the Bill became the National Services (Armed Forces) Act (1939), the basic legislation covering the arrangements for conscientious objectors for the duration of the war. It introduced military conscription for specific age groups, and set up tribunals to hear applications for exemption from service. This time the tribunals were set up by the Ministry of Labour and National Service and did not include military representation. Those who disagreed with their tribunal decision could appeal to the Appellate Tribunal, which again had no military representative. The process was placed in the hands of the civil authorities, not only to create greater fairness but to allow the military to concentrate on prosecuting the war, relieved of the responsibility of dealing with dissenters in their ranks. However, there still remained, as Chapter 7 shows, some dissenters within the ranks.

Despite the experience of the First World War there was no common understanding in Britain of what a conscientious objector actually was. To the government, he was a man who objected to military service and the taking of life, who would, therefore, have no objection to carrying out civilian work as directed. As Peter Brock noted this was also the view of many tribunal members who saw non-combatant duties as humanitarian, but, to the conscientious objector was still a means of prosecuting the war. [9] It soon became apparent to those administering the process that many objectors did not comply with the expected norm, especially as compulsion was extended, mainly by the National Service Act (1941), to civil defence direction, to work direction and compulsory fire-watching. During the course of the war 575 men and 90 women were prosecuted for refusing fire-watching or other part-time civil defence duties:[10] The pacifist Duke of Bedford complained that there was no right to conscientious objection to work direction and fire-watching,

[8] 'Military Training Bill,' *Northern Echo*, 5 May 1939, p. 13.
[9] Brock, *Twentieth-Century Pacifism*, p. 159.
[10] Ibid., p. 161.

commenting: 'If the government don't want fires they should explore the possibility of a negotiated peace.'[11] The government did make some concessions when Ellen Wilkinson, Parliamentary Secretary at the Home Office, keen to avoid repetitive convictions for refusing to register, announced:

> that where a person is willing to do the job, that is, is willing to guard and save life and put out fires but is not willing to register, then, after his first conviction, he shall have deemed to have registered; so that as long as he goes on doing fire guard duties he shall not again be prosecuted.

She added the caveat: 'this does not mean, as some COs seem to think, that they can just go and fire-guard when they feel inclined. It means they have to go on the rota and do the job properly.'[12] These measures also applied compulsion to persons above the military call-up age and brought some First World War conscientious objectors back as objectors in the Second World War. Many of these were men in their forties who had objected to military service in the First World War and now objected to Fire Watching and Civil Defence duties. It was also to be applied for the first time, in 1941, to women.

Many objectors took the absolutist stand of refusing to do anything they considered part of the war effort. That included civilian work which they viewed as releasing someone else to participate in the war effort. Many absolutists objected to compulsion itself, leading to punishment for failing to carry out state-instructed roles which hitherto they had been doing voluntarily. William Albert Oxley was one of many jailed for refusing to sign the military register as a conscientious objector because it was compulsory.[13] This extended to fire-watching: John Thomas O'Connor, Bernard O'Connor, Donald Sutherland and Richard Gordon Paxton were each fined £10 for not registering for fire-watching duties. They had written to the Town Clerk stating they did not agree with compulsion and that they were doing voluntary fire-

---

[11] 'Pacifist Duke on Fire-Watching,' *Yorkshire Evening Post*, 2 March 1941, p. 1.
[12] 'Fire Watching,' *Peace News*, 29 October 1943, p. 4.
[13] 'Trade Exempt Claim: But Gateshead C.O. Will Not Register', *Evening Chronicle*, 5 March 1941, p. 3.

watching.[14] Absolutists, through their explicit rejection of the state's authority in this sphere, presented the greatest challenge to the authorities, a challenge which the First World War should have prepared them for. Absolutism produced strange bedfellows in the form of religious sects, including Jehovah's Witnesses, and political objectors, including socialists and anarchists. Receiving little sympathy from the tribunals or the courts they made a significant contribution to the population of Durham Prison. Therefore, the Second World War, like the First World War, saw the imprisonment of North-East conscientious objectors. It did not, however, reach the proportion of 30% of First World War objectors.[15] Instead, the flexibility of alternative service offered by the National Service Act resulted in only about 3% going to prison for failing to comply with the tribunal's decision.[16] However, as many absolutists ignored the tribunal system the percentage of objectors who went to prison was greater than 3% (see Chapter 5).

The government and the authorities did learn from the experiences of the First World War in dealing with conscientious objectors through its legislation. It still, however, faced challenges from the more intransigent objectors and only through the adoption of a pragmatic approach, albeit belatedly in some circumstances, were many of the excesses of the previous conflict avoided.

The Extent of Objection

Official statistics show that up to 3 March 1945, 66,811 out of 8,257,963 male registrations had provisionally been as conscientious objectors.[17] This represented 0.81% of the total registrations. This percentage considerably exceeded that in the First World War where 0.66%, or 16,500 of the 2,500,000 conscripted, registered as objectors.[18] It is not a marginal increase, as Rachel Barker has stated.[19] If the same percentage

---

[14] 'Objected to Fire-watching', *Northern Daily Mail*, 26 September 1941, p. 4.
[15] Calder, *The People's War*, p. 497.
[16] Ceadel, *Pacifism in Britain 1914-1945*, p. 302.
[17] *Number of men registering provisionally in the Register of Conscientious Objectors from 1939 to 1945 inclusive*, LAB 6/405, The National Archives.
[18] David Stevenson, *1914-1918: The History of the First World War* (London: Penguin, 2004), p. 275.
[19] Barker, *Conscience, Government and War*, p. 121

had objected in the Second World War as in the First then the number of objectors would have been in the region of 12,400 less. The main reason for this increase was the recent memory of the horrors of the previous conflict, reflected in the pacifist movements of the 1930s. It also reflects the availability of the CBCO to help objectors (see Chapters 5 and 7). To simply compare the number of objectors in both wars is misleading as the conscription period in the Second World War is three times that in the previous war. The Minister of Labour, Ernest Bevin MP, described the comparison as 'odious.'[20] The figures, however, do not give us the total number of objectors. They do not show the men in reserved occupations who would have registered as objectors if called up. Wendy Acres of Darlington stated that her father, John Acres, would have been an objector had he not been in a reserved occupation.[21] It does not include most of the men who chose to not even register, or the objectors to work direction who did not go through the military registration process. Some who simply went AWOL or managed to be invalided out of the forces, were likely to be motivated, in part, by an objection to combatant duties.[22] But the greatest omission is the real number of women objectors for whom, a different registration process was followed (see Chapter 6).

The percentage of male objectors decreased considerably from 2.2% in October 1939 to 0.45% in January 1941, eventually reaching 0.16% in March 1945.[23] The reasons for the decrease, though complex, are most probably reflecting what Mary Gamble referred to as a more pragmatic, though reluctant, pacifism felt by many. In the early days of the war, 'the vast majority would have backed any peace offer from any quarter,' but by late 1941 many pacifists, 'appear to think that because they can't trust Hitler a continuation of the war is better than a peace negotiated with the German Government.'[24] Sybil Morrison also considered that after Dunkirk it would have been damaging to pacifism to have continued campaigning for a negotiated peace.[25] Martin Johnson,

---

[20] 'Conscientious Objectors', *Hansard, HC Deb 09 July 1942 vol. 381 cc912-4.*

[21] Telephone interview with Wendy Acres of Darlington, conducted 28 October 2013.

[22] Tobias Kelly, 'Citizenship, Cowardice, and Freedom of Conscience: British Pacifists in the Second World War,' *Comparative Studies in Society and History* 57(3), 2015, p. 7.

[23] Hayes, *Challenge of Conscience*, p. 382.

[24] *Peace News*, 22 August 1941, cited in Ceadel, *Pacifism in Britain*, p. 298.

[25] Sybil Morrison, *I Renounce War: The Story of the Peace Pledge Union* (London: Shepherd Press, 1962), p. 45.

a Quaker, saw this view as the end, not of pacifism, but of 'absolutism' and there could be no justification for withholding help from a community whose 'Navy and Air Force guarantee our food by their sacrifice.'[26] For many, the Nazi actions in occupied territories and the invasion of the Soviet Union showed how unpalatable the regime was. It became more unpalatable as more evidence of Nazi atrocities emerged.

The official statistics do not give the percentages registering as objectors for each tribunal area. Locally obtained figures show that the percentage who registered as conscientious objectors in the North-East of England between December 1939 and February 1941 was considerably lower than the national average. (See Appendix A - Local Statistics of Conscientious Objectors, compiled from statistics published in local newspapers). In July 1940, when approximately 40,000 had registered as objectors, Mass Observation produced a major report on the subject. Whilst providing no direct comparison between tribunals the following Mass Observation statistics, covering the period when objection was at its peak, shows how the region compared with the rest of Britain. The Newcastle Tribunal is covered by the North-Eastern and Northern regions. These had the lowest averages of the three registration dates, suggesting Newcastle had one of the lowest percentages of objection in the country:

---

[26] 'Friends and "Absolutism",' *The Friend*, 25 May 1940, pp. 310-311.

Percentage of Men Registering as Conscientious Objectors

Region	21.10.39	09.03.40	25.05.40	Average
London	3.25	2.45	1.55	2.42
South Eastern	2.50	1.80	1.20	1.83
Eastern	3.00	2.00	1.18	2.06
South Western	2.70	2.15	1.30	2.05
Midland	1.90	1.40	0.90	1.40
North Midland	1.52	1.20	0.80	1.17
North Eastern	1.45	1.10	0.75	1.10
North Western	1.60	1.05	0.65	1.10
Northern	0.80	0.40	0.30	0.50
Scotland	2.00	1.70	1.06	1.59
Wales	3.70	3.10	1.50	2.77

The question is why? The answer is a combination of demographic factors, such as the employment mix in the region. This becomes more apparent when examining who the objectors were in the region. Mass Observation considered it unsurprising that there was a higher percentage in London and the South of England:

> there, people are more influenced by contemporary fashions in thought, and also centred in London is a higher proportion of intelligent people – and most pacifists who do not derive their convictions from particular religious beliefs do so from a highly intelligent and rational view of world affairs.[27]

This apparently condescending statement is evidentially supported by their analysis of who the objectors were.

---

[27] File Report No. 312, *Mass Observation*, pp. 28-29.

The Demographics of Objection

To ascertain who the objectors in the North-East of England were required an analysis of the complied database of 820 conscientious objectors from the Newcastle Tribunal area. In the absence of the official tribunal records the database provides the only major record of objectors from the region. Only persons whose conscientious objection could be evidenced were entered on the database. On this basis, some potential objectors were excluded. Although the amount of detailed information for individual objectors varies, there is enough for comparative analysis.

There are 389 objectors whose occupation is known. The objector with the most senior role was George Hylton Bartram, Managing Director of Bartram and Sons, shipbuilders. He did not, however, come from a pacifist background. His brother, Sir Robert Appleby Bartram, was Commanding Officer of the 79th (Scottish Horse) Regiment of the Royal Artillery from 1938 to 1940, having served with the regiment during the First World War. No information was found as to whether George served in the conflict. Up to April 1941 he continued in his role, as the yard was completing pre-war orders, but was then contracted to build ships to assist the war effort. This prompted him to resign, as did the requirement to do fire-watching, to which he also objected. As he was now unemployed he had registered under the Registration for Employment Order in July 1941. In interviews with Ministry of Labour officials he had indicated that he was only prepared to do welfare or social work, and obtained employment as assistant to the regional secretary of the Fellowship of Reconciliation. [28]

In December 1941, he appeared before Sunderland Magistrates Court for failing to obey a direction from the Minister of Labour to take up work on the land:

> If it had not been for the war I would not have been asked to do it. I have a conscientious objection to war and everything that appears to be connected with the further prosecution of the war.

---

[28] 'Prison for Sunderland Shipbuilder', *Shields Gazette*, 19 December 1941, p. 4.

> Simply that, as I see it, I am asked to do agricultural work because it will assist the government to prosecute the war. This conviction is based on a message sent by the Prime Minister to Norwich which read, 'you can release ships by growing more food and so bring nearer the day of victory'.[29]

> (My pacifist position is) based on an objection, not merely to the taking of life, but to war altogether....[30]

When asked if he was receiving benefit from the yard he said:

> I have no connection with the yard. I am not consulted by the directors and I draw no salary. It was expressly agreed between my brother and myself that should there be any profits distributed while I am in retirement that my share should not come to me, but should be held in trust for my children, or until I return to the shipyard or until I die. I do not benefit, therefore, in any way financially from the operation of the shipyard.[31]

He was represented, as were a number of objectors, by barrister John Harvey Robson, himself a registered conscientious objector. Mr Robson argued that it would be futile for the court to inflict punishment; Bartram was approaching 43 and his age group would soon be liable to register for military service when he could register a conscientious objection. The court disagreed and sentenced him to two month's imprisonment. He did achieve full exemption in September 1943.[32]

It can be argued that George Bartram had been prepared to make big sacrifices for his principles, particularly as at the time he did not know how the war would end, but, unlike many objectors, he was in a position of being able to resume his position at the end of the war until

---

[29] 'Ex-Wear Shipbuilding Director, now an "Objector," Sent to Prison', *Evening Chronicle*, 19 December 1941, p. 5.

[30] 'Wearsider's "No" To Land Work', *Sunderland Echo*, 19 December 1941, p. 4.

[31] 'Ex-Wear Shipbuilding Director now an "Objector." Sent to Prison,' *Evening Chronicle*, 19 December 1941, p. 5.

[32] C.O. Objects to H.G., *Sunderland Echo*, 3 September 1943, p. 8.

the company was sold in 1948. He was, however, consistent in his pacifism.

The occupations of those on the database have been categorised
by economic sector and job type. Despite a degree of subjectivity in the
categorisation, it provides a representative indication to compare with
the findings of Mass Observation (see Appendix B). The analysis indicates a broad range of over 100 different occupations, ranging from
George Bartram to a domestic servant, Constance Bolam. It also shows
49% coming from the managerial and skilled work categories and only
24% from the unskilled category. Of particular note are the relatively
high number of teachers (26) and persons employed in a clerical capacity
(43). Teachers are included in the 11% identified as being employed by
local authorities. As Angus Calder observed: 'They came disproportionately from the professions and the ranks of self-employed men providing
services such as barbers. Individualistic occupations, it seems, bred indi-
vidualist stances – few miners were conscientious objectors.'[33] Indeed
only 12 of the 389 were miners! Similarly, Juliet Gardiner commented
that 'there were fewer manual labourers and a preponderance of white-
collar workers – plus creatives and intellectuals'.[34] The database, as the
most comprehensive such database, allows for a more nuanced analysis
of who the objectors were in comparison with the general, less empiri-
cally grounded statements by Calder and others.

Mass Observation, using a smaller sample (96), analysed objectors who registered at six London Labour Exchanges. This also showed
a wide range of occupations and they commented: 'It is at once conspic-
uous that a large proportion if those registering as COs are in jobs requiring particular intelligence, intuitive or educational training.' They
noted a preponderance of clerks, civil servants and local government officers (including teachers). They also concluded that even in the mainly
working-class areas only a small fraction of the objectors could be called
working-class. Only 17% of the Mass Observation sample were in unskilled jobs.[35]

[33] Calder, *The Myth of the Blitz*, p. 76.
[34] Gardiner, *The Blitz*, p. 255.
[35] File Report no. 312, *Mass Observation*, pp. 33-36.

The Mass Observation findings are generally supportive of the analysis of the database with two notable exceptions. The high number of objectors among civil servants in London would not be repeated in the North-East where civil servants were far fewer. Secondly, whilst objection amongst unskilled occupations is low in both analyses, the higher proportion in the North-East is indicative of the greater proportion of this type of work in the region. The main correlation concerns the majority of objectors coming from occupations requiring education and skills training. Is this because they had 'a more intelligent and rational view of world affairs,' as Mass Observation implies, or, as some detractors suggested, is it because they had more in terms of salary and promotion prospects to lose?[36] These assertions are explored in later chapters.

Some answers as to why fewer objectors came from unskilled occupations can be found by examining Northern Ireland, where conscription was not introduced. Whilst the enlistment figures do not identify religious denominations, historians generally accept the *Irish Press* claim in June 1945 that the majority of those who enlisted in Northern Ireland were Catholic.[37] Nationalist Catholics made up the greater proportion of the economically disadvantaged for whom enlistment provided some financial security. Conversely, Loyalist Protestants had more to lose financially by enlisting. In the North-East of England, during the period of the greatest enlistment, unemployment was still high and the, albeit low, wages earned in the forces provided some financial security. A contributor to *Peace News* supported this view:

> a working man's mind is perhaps chiefly concerned with fighting for an existence. A man who has to work for what is just a living, with little or no margin, cannot afford to take risks, which even in peace time would endanger his living therefore in many cases he has to be ready to compromise in order to safeguard the bread and butter for himself and his family.[38]

---

[36] File Report no. 312, *Mass Observation*, p. 29.

[37] Brian Girvin, 'The Forgotten Volunteers of World War II', *History Ireland*, 6, 1 (1998), 184; Claire Wills, *That Neutral Ireland: A Cultural History of Ireland during the Second World War* (London: Faber and Faber, 2007) pp. 51 and 109.

[38] 'Pacifism and the Working Class,' *Peace News*, 29 September 1939, p. 7.

Appendix A shows the proportion of those who registered as objectors varied across the region. The districts with the greatest concentration of work requiring little education, i.e. the mining areas of Sunderland, Ashington and Durham, had the lowest proportion of objectors. This did not surprise a correspondent using the name, 'Registered 24':

> Most townspeople have collar-and-tie jobs, yet, compared with industrial districts, many have not got the courage to protect either their jobs or their families by registering for national service. Of course, the poor mining community who are looked upon as the curs of civilisation responded splendidly as shown by the following comparison of the figures for Ashington and Durham. Despite this proof of the miners' grit many of your correspondents, especially those living in Newcastle and Darlington, will continue to ridicule the working class, while these same critics are the shirkers when it comes to real service, unless they can buy a commission.[39]

Another, who supported Conscientious Objectors whilst not being one himself, using the pseudonym, 'Not a CO', reinforced the role of education, pointing out that the higher figure in large towns is, 'parallel with the number able to avail themselves of adult education of varying kinds.'[40]

Newcastle district, with the largest population, had the highest number of objectors by a considerable margin, though it did not have the highest proportion of objectors. Darlington, probably reflecting its Quaker traditions, had a marginally higher proportion, and Scarborough had the highest proportion by a considerable margin. Scarborough's high rate of objectors may be partially explained by a statistically small sample of only 3.8% of the region's registrations. Also, its population was concentrated in Scarborough and Whitby which did not have the

[39] 'Hear All Sides: Mining Areas Have Fewer Conscientious Objectors', *Northern Echo*, 14 March 1940, p. 4.
[40] 'Hear All Sides: More Conscientious Objectors in Large Towns', *Northern Echo*, 16 March 1940, p. 6.

unskilled labour intensive industries to balance the lower middle class occupations. Newcastle's percentage of objectors was significantly higher than the other major towns, Sunderland and Middlesbrough, reflecting the greater proportion of lower middle class occupations in the unofficial capital of the region.

The region's objectors were, therefore, a demographically diverse group largely comparable with, yet different in some respects, from the Mass Observation research sample. This regional sample confirms many of Mass Observation's conclusions whilst reflecting the region's distinctiveness. A greater understanding of these objectors is provided by examining the reasons for their objection.

Reasons for Objection

There are 374 persons on the database whose reason for objection is definitely known. The reasons are shown below:

Database of Conscientious Objectors - Reasons for Objection

Reason	Number	Percentage
Pacifism	22	6
Moral	46	12
Humanitarian	11	3
Religion	258	69
Political	20	5
Other	17	5
	374	

The reasons given are not mutually exclusive, although a Mass Observation report on conscientious objection in Scotland gave similar results.[41] Many objecting on moral or humanitarian grounds also had a religion, therefore the three categories are inter-changeable to a degree. Also, some smaller categories, such as anti-war and anti-militarism, could be placed in one of the major categories. The analysis is more re-alistic than that of a feature writer, who, following a visit to a tribunal, stated: 'I reached this conclusion – 80 per cent do not want to fight on religious grounds; five per cent on humanitarian grounds; the remain-der have just plain "wind-up".'[42]

Religious Objection

It is unsurprising that, as those with a strong religious belief would have an objection to killing, by far the most common reason given for objec-tion was religion. The table below shows the religious denomination of 334 objectors on the database compared to 258 who objected on reli-gious grounds. This demonstrates that belonging to a particular denom-ination does not always equate to having a religious conscientious objec-tion.

Two denominations where membership in all cases equated to conscientious objection were the Jehovah's Witnesses and the Quakers. This explains why two relatively small denominations had a dispropor-tionally high number of objectors compared to the major denomina-tions. It is where the similarity ends.

[41] File Report No. 312, *Mass Observation*, p. 30.
[42] 'London Letter: Romances end at Tribunals', *Evening Chronicle*, 20 April 1940, p. 8.

Table 3 - Religious Denominations of Objectors

Denomination	No.	Percentage
Jehovah's Witness	94	28
Quaker	63	19
Methodist	46	14
Church of England	25	8
Plymouth Brethren	21	6
Assembly of God	20	6
Roman Catholic	17	5
Presbyterian	7	2
Christadelphian	6	2
Other Denominations	35	10
	334	

The sincerity of Quaker pacifism had long been established. This was undoubtedly helped by their affirmation of the worth of every human being allowing many to volunteer to save life on the battlefield. In particular, the Friends Ambulance Unit (FAU), founded in the First World War and reformed in the Second World War, and run by the Society of Friends, allowed Quakers to save life without being under the control of the military. It played a major role in forming the public attitude towards Quaker objectors in both World Wars. It also presented Quaker objectors in a more favourable light to the tribunals. Judge Wethered of the South-West Tribunal, whilst not understanding the minority of Quakers who were absolutists, admired Quaker social-work activities and the FAU in particular.[43] Juliet Morland recalled that being accepted for a clerical position in the FAU meant she had no difficulty in getting conditionally registered by the Newcastle Tribunal.[44] At the Newcastle Tribunal 28 Quakers out of the 31 known instances were granted either complete or conditional exemption. Two of those served a prison sentence imposed by the magistrates for failure to do work as directed by the tribunal: Angus Earnshaw, a Gateshead student, received 12 months; and James Gale, a teacher, received 6 months. Gale, who

---

[43] Barker, *Conscience, Government and War*, p. 38.
[44] 'Juliet Morland, C880/12', Recorded 1998, British Library Sound Archive.

had been registered on condition he either joined the FAU or did hospital or land work, objected to compulsion.

The following 12 did join the FAU: Margery Asquith (Whittles) of Redcar; William Brough of Durham; Alan Dickinson of Darlington; K. E. Grant of Shotley Bridge; Peter Leyland of Wensleydale; Juliet Morland of Felling; Grigor McClelland of Gosforth; Michael Mounsey of Newcastle; Freda Wood (Smith) of York; Fred Wilson of Coxhoe; Douglas Hardy of Darlington: and Athol Johnson Wallis of Scarborough. In addition, Thomas Newby of Southwick, Matthew Johnson of Newcastle and Norman Taylor of Darlington, were registered on condition they joined the FAU and no evidence was found to say they did not.

Objection by Quakers therefore varied. Whilst many joined the FAU, others, such as Dennis Taylor of Durham, could not sanction joining as it was not an official Quaker organisation, nor could he take part in the construction of air-raid shelters as it was part of the military organisation.[45] George Winn of Acklam also objected to taking part in the construction of air-raid shelters.[46] Angus Earnshaw went further in stating that he would not help the war effort in any capacity, including civilian work on the land or in the mines, a view which led to him serving his time in Durham Prison.[47] Other Quakers were, however, prepared to do work of national importance. Kenneth Goom and Robert Pedley, teachers at the Friends School, Great Ayton, were examples. Pedley stated that he was not prepared to hide behind a reserved occupation to avoid his responsibility.[48] A. A. J. Wallis, a student from Darlington, showed the greatest flexibility, offering to give up his place at Armstrong College if the tribunal ordered him to work on the land. The tribunal duly obliged.[49]

Quakers were not neutral when it came to Nazism but saw war as being counter-productive to bringing about its demise. Maurice Rowntree elaborated, at a joint PPU and FoR meeting in Newcastle:

[45] 'Vegetarian Objectors "Progress" Religion,' *Evening Chronicle*, 13 October 1939, p.7.
[46] 'C.O. Had Not Time For Service,' *Evening Chronicle*, 18 September 1940, p. 6.
[47] 'Offered Body For Research,' *Evening Chronicle*, 28 March 1944, p.5.
[48] 'Judge Richardson Criticises Eppleby Conscientious Objector,' *Northern Echo*, 10 April 1940, p. 5.
[49] 'Pacifists Change Their Minds,' *Northern Echo*, 1 December 1939, p. 7.

Of course, it is necessary to destroy Hitlerism, but it is for the German people in their country, and we in our own, to do that. To make war has the result of establishing unity among the Germans and stabilising the very regime we detest. We can crush Hitlerism in Germany, not by starving and killing its men, women and children, but by convincing them that there is justice still in Europe and we are willing to co-operate in upholding it.[50]

Jehovah's Witnesses showed little flexibility which explains why they had 50% more objectors than Quakers and yet had considerably fewer members.[51] They invariably took the absolutist stance that any work, no matter how humanitarian, ordered in wartime contributed to the war effort. Unlike the Quakers, the organisation had only a short history of conscientious objection and could not point to the same longevity of involvement in humanitarian causes. Divorced from mainstream Christianity, its disregard for secular authority resulted in poor relations with both the UK and USA governments. Referred to by Peter Brock as 'the neglected victims of Nazism', they were also subjected to persecution and death by the Nazis.[52] Such poor relations, combined with their absolutist stand at a time of national peril, led to unsympathetic treatment by both the establishment and the press. The two denominations also differed in their members' occupations. The analysis of occupations showed 39% of Jehovah's Witnesses in unskilled occupations compared to only 13% of Quakers. Conversely, none of the Jehovah's Witnesses were from a managerial background but four Quakers were, including three members of the Rowntree chocolate dynasty, who were prominent in the organisation of the FAU along with the Cadbury family of Birmingham (After the war another Quaker objector, Athol Wallis of Scarborough, who served in the FAU in London and Glasgow, was to rise to be a director of Rowntrees). The fourth, Cyril Ward Chester, the son of a Teesside ship owner, argued to the tribunal that he was

---

[50] 'Maurice Rowntree at Newcastle,' *Peace News*, 24 November 1939, p. 6.
[51] Jehovah's Witnesses in Britain numbered 5,945 in 1939, rising to 11,622 in 1945. Corresponding figures for Quakers were 19,673 and 20,534. British Religion in Numbers, www.brin.ac.uk.
[52] Peter Brock, *Against the Draft: Essays on conscientious objection from the Radical Reformation to the Second World War* (Toronto: University of Toronto Press, 2006), p. 425.

doing all he could as a part-time member of a stretcher party and running his father's ships, an argument which got him conditionally registered for land work, subsequently changed to ambulance work.[53] Also recorded as a student was Grigor McClelland of Gosforth, whose family owned the Laws retail chain in the North-East. This social class distinction may have affected their treatment by the tribunal.

Women objectors were also present in both denominations. One-third of the identified women objectors and 69% of the women religious objectors were Jehovah's Witnesses. The latter percentage is well above the 28% for Witnesses as a whole. The majority appear to have been single women with no family connection to other Witness objectors, the exception being Dorothy Charlton of Haydon Bridge whose husband or brother, Clarence was also an objector. By contrast, known Quaker women objectors were small in number.

Other minority denominations well represented were the Plymouth Brethren, the Assembly of God, and the Christadelphians. Plymouth Brethren were not objectors on pacifist grounds, but on the grounds that their prime loyalty is to the preaching of the gospel, and they are quite clear that a nation must be defended and it is the duty of its nationals to do so.[54] The accepted tradition is that they accept non-combatant duty. Its members, and those of the Assembly of God, were generally willing to undertake work as directed. James Bell of Hartlepool, a member of the Plymouth Brethren, stated: 'I recognise that the country has a definite charge on citizens, and I wish to obey…'[55] Alfred Pitt of Sunderland, a member of the Assembly of God said he was willing to do civil work, such as agriculture, to help the country.[56]

Christadelphians were less compliant and many were absolutists. The most prominent case involving a Christadelphian was that of Kenneth Makin of Redcar, one of a number serving prison terms for their objection and whose case is discussed in Chapter 7. Their stance was somewhat damaged by John Wilson, a Sunderland shipping clerk, who

---

[53] 'Judge on Poisonous Christians,' *Evening Gazette*, 15 July 1940, p. 6.
[54] David, A. Martin, *Pacifism: A Historical and Sociological Study* (London: Routledge & Kegan Paul, 1965), pp. 189-191.
[55] 'Barton C.O.s Appeal Allowed,' *Northern Echo*, 7 May 1941, p. 3.
[56] 'Sunderland Men Registered,' *Sunderland Echo*, 26 January 1940, p. 8.

had arranged charters for armed merchant ships but did not think that was taking part in the war effort.[57]

Objectors also came from the established denominations: Church of England; Roman Catholic; and, Methodist. Methodists were better represented in a region where Methodism was strong. These denominations faced the dilemma of officially supporting the war effort with the Christian ethos of peace and love, and, how to deal with objectors to the war effort when their ministers were exempted from national service. They also had to be acutely aware that the majority of their congregation, or their families, were serving in the Forces. Some objectors, such as Charles Ramsay of Lowick, left the church because of its support for the war, although he later returned as a lay preacher.[58] Some ministers were themselves conscientious objectors. Royston Jones, a trainee Methodist preacher from South Shields, drew praise from the tribunal chairman on being granted conditional exemption: 'you seem to have done useful work building air raid shelters and have qualified yourself in rescue work and first aid.'[59] William Hodgson of Sunderland summed up the feelings of many of his colleagues:

> I am studying as a candidate for the Methodist Ministry and I do feel it would be impossible for me to preach the gospel of love while undertaking to shed blood…If it had not been for conscription I would undoubtedly have enlisted in the RAMC. It is the only way I can honestly serve in the war.[60]

He could, of course, on entering the Ministry have enlisted as a chaplain in the Forces, a genuine non-combatant role.

Religious objection, in line with the Christian pacifist tradition, was the most common reason given. There was, however, a considerable variance in the degrees of objection adopted not only between denominations but often within denominations. The majority of opinion

---

[57] 'Selfish Sort of Religion,' *Sunderland Echo*, 12 July 1940, p. 7.
[58] 'C.O. Tribunal Criticism of Applicant,' *Evening Chronicle*, 1 October 1940, p. 6.
[59] 'Shields Preacher an Objector,' *Shields Gazette*, 25 May 1940, p. 3.
[60] 'Gospel of Love v. Shedding Blood,' *Sunderland Echo*, 11 October 1939, p. 3.

within most denominations was catered for by the conscription legislation. Jehovah's Witnesses, were the exception and their difficulties are explored in the following chapters.

Political Objection

Objection on religious, moral or humanitarian grounds was understandable to the government and it legislated accordingly. It would not accept an objection on political grounds, especially an objection to a particular war. It was not willing to recognise that it was a matter of conscience, unlike the ILP politician, Fenner Brockway:

> The pacifist's supreme loyalty is to his conception of God or of the universe. The Socialist's supreme loyalty is to the workers of all lands, with whom he feels a unity which a patriot feels to his nation. To a political objector, it would be wrong morally to kill his fellow workers in the interests of the possessing class. It is a matter of conscience to him no less than to the pacifist.[61]

The major political parties had agreed to support the war effort. The Labour Party's foreign policy between 1932 and 1938 has been described as 'a long period of confusion.'[62] Between 1932 and 1935 its leaders in both Houses of Parliament, George Lansbury and Lord Ponsonby, were committed pacifists, a situation which, according to David Martin, may have created a superficial impression of a pacifist policy.[63] Yet, having been previously reluctant to accept conscription in peace-time, it was fully committed to the war effort. Because the Second World War was a different war, its supporters in the Labour Party included conscientious objectors and those sympathetic to objection in the First World War, such as Herbert Morrison, Home Secretary, and Durham miners' leader, Will Lawther. The Trade Union Congress

---

[61] 'Political Objectors' Claims Are Rejected by the Appeals Tribunal,' *Peace News*, 15 December 1939, p. 5.
[62] Andrew Thorpe, *A History of the Labour Party* (London: Palgrave Macmillan, 2015) p. 102.
[63] Martin, *Pacifism*, p. 133.

(TUC) had voted for the war as it being against fascism and not as solidarity with the ruling classes. At its Newcastle conference Lawther was asked why, when he been such an ardent advocate of conscientious objection in the last war, he, and the TUC, had condoned compulsory military service.[64] He replied that this was a war against Nazi aggression. As a former communist, and anarchist, his response when asked why French Communists were thrown in gaol was unambiguous: 'Because French trade union officials said they deserved it.'[65] However, support for the war was not unanimous within the Party. Councillor Ruth Dodds resigned from Gateshead Town Council and the Labour Party in protest at the Party's active support for the war: 'I cannot remain in the party, which is making the same mistake as in 1914, and again backing a war between rival imperialisms under the delusion that it is a war to end all wars.'[66] Ruth was also a Quaker, stating to the Durham Quarterly Meeting: 'in the North-East of England, after long periods of depression, the only people who welcomed the war were the poor who needed the extra money it brought them.'[67]

The Conservative Party were generally unsupportive of political objection. Lady Astor, speaking in the House of Commons made her position clear:

> I do not think that political COs, waiting to choose their own war, ought to get off scot-free and let men of this country go out and die for a country which they are waiting, when the war is over, to upset. I have not met a single soldier, sailor, or airman who wanted to go to war and I spend most of my time among them. I have seen the men return from the *Ajax* and the *Exeter* – do you think they like it? One thing that impressed me was that not one of them showed a touch of belligerence or bitterness in his heart. They hate their job but they do it. Is it fair to ask them to

---

[64] David Morgan and Mary Evans, *The Battle for Britain: Citizenship and Ideology in the Second World War* (London: Routledge, 1993), p. 13.

[65]'Mr. Will Lawther Questioned on Compulsory Military Service', *Northern Echo*, 15 January 1940, p. 5.

[66] 'Hear All Sides,' *Northern Echo*, 3 October 1939, p. 4.

[67] 'Quarterly Meetings: Durham,' *The Friena*, 12 April 1940, p. 222.

do it and let off the political CO who does not care a bit about his country? Let them do jobs, and darn disagreeable jobs. I do feel for Christians, but I have no sympathy with the ones who want to shirk.[68]

The chances of an objection on political grounds succeeding were therefore slim. The Appellate Tribunal ruled that: 'whilst the Act might cover religious, moral or ethical objections it did not cover political ones.'[69] *Peace News* expressed the fear that this would, in the words of Mr Chamberlain, lead to 'a new exasperating waste of time' and a new martyrdom, this time of the political objector. [70] As is shown in later chapters, this fear proved not unfounded. Only five political objectors on the database managed to achieve conditional registration at Newcastle, the remainder were removed from the register. Any North-East political objector appearing before the Leeds Tribunal would suffer a similar fate: 'At Leeds an objector who bases his case on Christian grounds and who has a minister to testify for him has a reasonable chance of conditional exemption; but the agnostic or free-thinker is treated with hostility from the start.'[71]

Objection to the war from the political left came mainly from the Independent Labour Party (ILP), which had split from the Labour Party in 1932, and, until Germany attacked the Soviet Union, the Communist Party of Great Britain (CPGB). ILP membership had declined during the 1930s, but in 1939 it still retained four active MPs, down from its peak of 37 in 1929. In the North-East it attracted a number of Trotskyites, who saw it as the only true socialist party, and its influence reached its peak in 1944 with the party offering its support to the Revolutionary Communist Party over the Tyneside Apprentices Strike.[72] As a socialist party, it shared many of the policies and ideals of the CPGB with which it suffered strained relations on the grounds of the latter's subservience

---

[68] 'Difficult and Unpleasant Task: Report on House of Commons Committee of Supply.' *Manchester Guardian*, 23 February 1940, p. 2.
[69] File Report No. 312, Mass Observation, p. 17.
[70] 'Few Political Objectors Get a Square Deal at C.O. Tribunals,' *Peace News*, 24 November 1939, p. 5.
[71] Ibid.
[72] Martin Upham, The History of British Trotskyism to 1949 (unpublished PhD Thesis, University of Hull, September 1980), 'Appendix F: Trotskyism and the ILP' (no page number).

to the Soviet Union.[73] ILP member Fenner Brockway, imprisoned as a conscientious objector in the First World War and a recruiter for volunteers to fight in the Spanish Civil War, elaborated:

> Communist Parties do not owe their first loyalty to the working-class movement as a whole, either in the country where they operate or internationally, but to their own organisation, to the Communist International, and to Russia. They do not regard their organisation as an instrument to be used for the working-class; they regard the working-class as an instrument to be used for their organisation.[74]

The ILP were clear on how they viewed the approaching war in April 1939:

> Britain's Imperialism finds expression in other continents where the colonial peoples are suppressed with a ruthlessness which is often indistinguishable from the methods of Fascism. Germany is expressing her Imperialism in Europe itself, no longer pretending that her interest is only in the German race, spreading her political boundaries over Czech and Slovakian people. Behind both Imperialisms is the Capitalist struggle for raw materials and markets. It is a Capitalist war for which the governments are preparing.[75]

They took a strongly consistent socialist and pacifist stand against the war, yet were not a pacifist party:

> ...we aim to establish a Socialist government which we would defend if it was attacked.
> Our policy is not one of absolute pacifism. We are prepared to admit into our membership absolute pacifists who otherwise accept the method of the class struggle and

---

[73] Matthew Brown, *ILP History 4: War and After*, 22 January 2012, http://www.independentlabour.org,uk/ilp-history-4-war-and-after.

[74] Fenner Brockway, *Inside the Left: Thirty Years of Platform, Press, Prison and Parliament* (London: George Allen and Unwin, 1942), p. 343.

[75] 'Lined up for War,' *New Leader*, 7 April 1939, p. 1.

the object of Socialism. We expect, however, pacifists who do join our ranks to refrain from misrepresenting the policies of our party.[76]

The ILP MP for Shettlestone, John McGovern championed the rights of political objectors, both in Parliament and in the Glasgow Tribunal. These included Kenneth Makin and Albert Foster (their cases are discussed in Chapter 7). Former ILP members included the Labour MP for Jarrow and wartime government minister, Ellen Wilkinson, who briefly was also a member of the CPGB. Wilkinson had been an active supporter of conscientious objectors during the First World War. In a letter to the wife of a First World War objector and future mayor of Middlesbrough, Albert Cocks, she expressed the following feelings:

> I think as a body of men COs have been treated about the worse. To me their suffering is worse than the soldiers although I am in full sympathy. Many have been lead and driven away without a thought. I know in trouble their minds and views have changed, one man 45 obliged to do munitions. I <u>am</u> a CO now....[77]

The Nazi-Soviet Non-Aggression Pact placed the CPGB in a particularly difficult position. Throughout the 1930s they had actively opposed fascism in Britain and abroad, most notably in the recruitment of volunteers to fight in the Spanish Civil War, and vociferously opposed appeasement. It was, therefore, no surprise that on 2 September 1939 the CPGB announced its support for the war, with the caveat that it was a war on two fronts: against Hitler abroad, and the imperialist Chamberlain government at home, whose policy of appeasement had bolstered fascism against the Soviet Union. Harry Pollitt, the party's General Secretary wrote: 'The Communist Party supports the war, believing it to be

---

[76] Fenner Brockway, 'The I.L.P. and the War,' *Peace News*, 6 March 1942, p. 3.
[77] Letter from Ellen Wilkinson to Mrs Cocks (Cox) and Mrs Beacroft, 22 September 1918, held in the private papers of the Cocks family.

a just war which should be supported by the whole working class and all friends of democracy in Britain.'[78]

The pro-war stance changed quickly and radically following the signing of the Pact, leading to Pollitt's removal as General Secretary. On 7 October 1939, the party manifesto was now stating: 'This war is a fight between imperialist powers over profits, colonies and world domination.'[79]

The policy of the CPGB, from 7 October 1939 until the German invasion of the Soviet Union on 22 June 1941, had been to stop the war, calling for the formation of a 'Peoples Government'. Its newspaper, *The Daily Worker*, was banned on 21 January 1941. Home Secretary, Herbert Morrison, claimed it was: 'striving to create in the reader a state of mind in which he will be unlikely to be keen to assist the war effort…calculated to have a bad effect on the morale of the people.'[80] However, their stance was not pacifist and they were not promoters of conscientious objection. In a *Daily Worker* article, John Gollan of the Young Communist League wrote:

> The idea that the imperialist war can be ended by refusal of military service is as illusory as to think that the exploitation can be ended by refusal to work for a capitalist exploiter…. Workers would not refuse to work in a big factory because it is non-unionist – in a like way they cannot refuse to enter the army because it is imperialist. They enter always remembering that they are members of the working class, fully convinced of the necessity for the workers' political aims to triumph.[81]

Mass Observation did, however, comment that the No-Conscription League (N-CL) were under Communist influence in their objection to compulsion rather than to war itself, on the grounds that conscription

---

[78] Harry Pollitt, *How to Win the War,* quoted in report to the War Cabinet, 13 March 1943, titled 'Communist Party of Great Britain,' reproduced in Attfield and Williams, eds., *1939: The Communist Party and War.*

[79] Communist Party of Great Britain, *Manifesto of the Central Committee: Peace or War,* 7 October 1939, reproduced as Appendix V in Attfield and Williams, *The Communist Party and War,* p.168.

[80] Memorandum from Home Secretary to the Cabinet, CAB 66/14, WP (40) 482.

[81] 'Boycott of War is a Stupid Phrase', *Daily* Worker, 27 March 1940, p. 2.

prepares the way for Fascism.[82] Objecting to the Military Training Bill, the N-CL stated:

> The net of Conscription has been thrown. Young men of 20 and 21 are enmeshed. They have no voice or vote in deciding the policy of the National Government, but they are to be its first victims. Others will follow.
>
> Life is to be conscripted at a shilling a day, while no action is taken to conscript wealth. Cannon fodder cheaply obtained will be cheaply spent. The military machine will squander it as it did at Passchendaele. Conscription is a further step towards a Totalitarian regime in which every citizen will be regimented by the Government for its Imperialist purposes....[83]

One communist with a conscientious objection was Raymond Featherstone of Stockton who said he would probably defend a Communist state if it was attacked by an imperialist power but was not prepared to fight in this war.[84] In appealing against his removal from the register, he said his use of the words 'capitalist war' and 'imperialistic war' gave the impression that his objection was political but his objection went deeper.[85] His appeal failed. Another Stockton communist removed from the register was Denis O'Neill, who told the tribunal that Fascism and Nazism were operating in this country.[86] The apparent lack of other stated communist objectors found was likely due to the entry of the Soviet Union into the war in 1941, and the decline in regional CPGB membership in the late 1930's as Labour strengthened its position.[87] The view of the Appellate Tribunal may have also created a feeling that political objection was futile.

---

[82] Mass Observation File Report No. 312, p. 45.
[83] 'A Call to Resist,' *The New Leader*, 12 May 1939, p. 1.
[84] 'Object to Fighting Hitlerism', *Sunderland Echo*, 13 October 1939, p. 6.
[85] 'N. E. Men Appeal Against War Service Decisions', *Evening Chronicle*, 20 December 1939, p. 3.
[86] 'Horrible Pacifists Teaching Boys', *North-East Gazette*, 16 August 1940, p. 6.
[87] Lewis Mates, 'A Most Fruitful Period? The North-East District Communist Party and the Popular Front, 1935-9', *North-East History*, 36, 2004, pp. 54-98.

The majority of political objectors in the region subscribed to socialist principles more akin with those of the ILP. Arthur Gregory Braithwaite, a motor driver from Richmond, declared that Socialist principles were against the present capitalist struggle and the Labour Party were not the real socialists. He conceded that socialism did not mean doing nothing against oppression, and this was probably, despite his willingness to do agricultural work, the reason for his unconditional removal from the register. In supporting his stance his elder brother, who he had served in the last war, stated that on a hunger march:

> I was felled by a policeman's baton and taken home to a dying wife. Hitler has done less to me than that. The National Government is the real enemy and Hitler is the child of the British and French Capitalist Governments...[88]

At his unsuccessful appeal hearing, he confirmed that he did not belong to any religious or pacifist body and, 'the hunger and suffering of the people around me brought me to these views.'[89] He maintained his stance, serving three terms in prison.

Others considering it to be a capitalist war included Mr Marshall of Wallsend, Frank Carter of Newcastle, and Douglas Bailey and Matthew Rutter of Billingham. Rutter claimed at his tribunal hearing:

> Hitler is merely a symptom of the real causes of the war. The cause is capitalist imperialism, and if we had wanted to remove that cause, we should have started a long time ago in our own Empire.

When challenged that the Empire was supporting the war, he replied that the people of India had not been consulted.[90] Joseph Baines of Darlington was not prepared to sacrifice his life for capitalists and Ernest Mounsey of Spennymoor objected to nations sacrificing life when they were not prepared to sacrifice property. Mounsey, who had been unemployed for 10 years, offered to do work without pay so that he

---

[88] *North-East Gazette*, 6 August 1942; *Yorkshire Evening Post*, 10 October 1939; *Sunderland Echo*, 10 October 1939.
[89] 'Socialist Influences World's Only Hope', *Northern Echo*, 20 December 1939, p. 5.
[90] *Northern Echo*, 7 December 1939.

would not make anything from the war, but this was rejected and he was jailed for six months.[91] Leonard Distance of York, at the Leeds Tribunal, applied his objection to a capitalist war in refusing to serve in the Home Guard, thereby extending his objection to defensive action.[92]

Some socialist objectors were prepared to stand by their convictions when it was not necessary. Mr Hepple of Gateshead, who could have gained exemption on medical grounds, chose to seek exemption as a conscientious objector:

> As a Socialist and member of the ILP I hold convictions which make it impossible for me to support this war in any way whatsoever. I consider it morally wrong for me to slaughter the workers of another country in the interests of Imperialism. I am totally opposed to the Capitalist system (the cause of this war) under which this country and the British Empire are governed. Therefore, I cannot assist in any way the war effort on the home front.
>
> In my opinion the government of a State should be based on humane, ethical principles, its duty being to create social conditions in which every individual is enabled to live the fullest, happiest life possible, everyone having according to their needs their fair share of the world's commodities. This life is impossible in the Capitalist State, which is not governed for the benefit of the masses, but of the ruling class, who exploit the workers under their control for their own mercenary ends, regardless of what this means in human misery and suffering.
>
> I believe in the strength and rightness of my convictions. I consider it my duty towards humanity to work for the abolition of the Capitalist system and so create a new world in which war, unemployment and all the kindred evils of the system will be abolished.[93]

---

[91] 'Conduct of a Hero', *Northern Echo*, 18 April 1940, p. 5, and, 'Prison for C.O.', *Durham County Advertiser*, 26 May 1944, p. 3.
[92] 'Woman C.O. "Seeking a Label"', *Yorkshire Evening Post*, 2 October 1942, p. 1.
[93] 'Gateshead Political C.O. Wins Exemption,' *The New Leader*, 5 January 1940, p. 4.

Unusually for a political objector, Mr Hepple was exempted from military service. Without the details of his tribunal appearance it is not clear whether his exemption was due to the sincerity of his convictions or whether the tribunal applied expediency in view of his medical condition.

A different interpretation of political objection was provided by Judge Richardson of the Newcastle Tribunal in the case of John Biagioni of Heighington. His father was Italian and interned on the Isle of Man. He did not wish to fight against his father's country and he stated that if he had been born in Italy, he would have fought.[94] Amelia Rossi of Bishop Auckland, British born of Italian parents, whose father had been interned, also objected on the grounds of her nationality, stating that she 'would not like to do anything against my own people'.[95] R. G. C. Torre of Berwick, also born of Italian parents, managed to gain conditional exemption.

Absent from the list of North-East objectors found were political objectors from the far right British Union of Fascists (BUF). Speaking to Hexham Rotary Club in April 1939, its leader, Sir Oswald Mosley, said:

> I am probably getting onto more controversial ground if I say that if we are not attacked, we have to look into what we are going to fight for when we are asked to intervene in some European quarrel on behalf of any state.[96]

This suggests a possible political conscientious objection, which did not become a reality as the government swiftly in interned BUF members, including Mosley. Many were released in 1941 and no record was found of any of them in the region objecting. Mosley himself was not released until 1943, further reducing the risk of fascists being a threat.[97]

---

[94] 'C.O. Son of an Italian', *Northern Echo*, 22 May 1942, p. 8.

[95] 'British Birth "Regret" by Woman: statement at C.O. Tribunal', *Evening Chronicle*, 28 October 1942, p. 4.

[96] Gordon Stridiron, *Blackshirts in Geordieland* (London: Blackhouse Publishing, 2013), p. 236.

[97] Nigel Copsey, *Anti-Fascism in Britain* (Basingstoke: Macmillan Press, 2000) p. 76.

Political conscientious objection was therefore limited in the region to minority left wing parties such as the ILP and the CPGB. There were considerably fewer than in the First World War, largely due to the prevailing view of the majority that this was not an imperialist war. However, those who did object did so with a determination which often led to repeated prison sentences. Many of these were members of Newcastle War Resisters, identified in the *New Leader* as members or supporters of the ILP.

Newcastle War Resisters

Not all political conscientious objection from the First World War ceased in the different circumstances of the Second World War. There was a particular concentration of political objection in Newcastle, particularly in the organisation Newcastle War Resisters. John Morley and Jack Sadler were the main inspiration behind the organisation, and their experiences, and those of their families, are detailed below.

The application of compulsion to persons above the age for call-up for military service brought some First World War conscientious objectors back as political objectors in the Second World War. This was the case with Newcastle brothers John (Jack) and Mark Sadler who each received three months in prison for refusing to register for fire-watching. Jack Sadler's life story is summarised here to demonstrate the continuity of objection, much of which is pertinent to the fate of serving soldiers detailed in later chapters.[98]

In 1914 Jack and his brothers, James and Mark, disillusioned with the pro-war stance of their Church, became attracted to the ideals of secular socialism found in the N-CF. In 1916 Jack applied unsuccessfully to the Newcastle Tribunal for exemption. The Northumberland Appeal Tribunal recognised him as a conscientious objector on condition that he undertook civilian work of national importance, but he considered that doing what the state ordered would make him part of the war machine. By refusing to comply, he became liable to full military service. He refused to put on a soldier's uniform and was sentenced to

---

[98] Peace Pledge Union, http://www.ppu.org.uk/cosnew/co_sadler.html, accessed 3 March 2015.

two year's imprisonment with hard labour, later commuted to six months. Whilst in prison Jack was adjudged by the Central Tribunal to be a genuine conscientious objector, and was offered a suspended sentence on condition he accepted work on a Home Office scheme. He refused, was returned to the Army and again refused to put on uniform and was sentenced to two year's hard labour, again commuted to six months. The same happened a third time and this time his sentence was not commuted. He then went on hunger strike before being released early in 1919 on health grounds. He maintained his view that true socialism was not based on military strength and did not support military intervention in the Spanish Civil War. He joined the PPU in 1934 and with others renamed the local PPU group as Newcastle War Resisters. The stance taken by Jack and Mark Sadler against fire-watching their premises was for the same reason that they had refused to do civilian work in the First World War.[99]

The research did not reveal any details regarding James Sadler, but did reveal Robert Sadler, a Newcastle Presbyterian, sentenced to three months in prison with hard labour for an offence against the National Service Act 1941.[100] Other members of the Sadler family falling foul of this regulation were Nancy and Cornelius. Cornelius had been unconditionally registered as a conscientious objector, but this did not exempt him from fire-watching. In court, he said he could not take part in war or in preparation for war.[101]

Jack Sadler's daughter, Dorothy, shared the political views of her parents. Dorothy was a teacher but it appears she was not troubled by the authorities, probably due to the different registration process for women and the shortage of teachers. She married Robert Morley, one of another family of Newcastle War Resisters. The Morleys were employed in the family business of coach building and cellulose spraying. John was the head of the family and had two sons, Alan and Robert. All three were sentenced to terms of imprisonment.

John Morley was 54 when war broke out. He had served sentences of 112 days and 12 months as a conscientious objector during the First World War. During the Second World War, he received further

---

[99] Ibid.
[100] 'Register of Male Prisoners, Durham Prison', P/1/27, Durham County Records Office, County Hall, Durham.
[101] 'Failure to Register: Objection to Fire-Watch Order', *Morpeth Herald*, 10 September 1943, p. 4.

sentences of 3 months in Durham Prison on 1 July 1941 and 1 May 1942. Both sentences were for refusing to make fire-watching arrangements at his business premises. *The Word* commented:

> British Law says: "No person shall be punished twice for the same offence." John Morley's offence is that he cannot conscientiously co-operate in this war measure......Technically, John Morley is guilty of continuous offence. This question was discussed fully during the last war. Everyone recognises that, in cases of conscience, one offence is committed.[102]

Robert Morley, 22 when war broke out, served three prison sentences for refusing to register and failing to submit to a medical examination. He served 20 days ending 8 January 1941, 56 days in February 1941, and 12 months in October 1942. The Ministry of Labour registered him provisionally as a conscientious objector, as they did with those they tracked down who did not register. He refused to attend the tribunal and was removed from the register unconditionally in his absence. *The Word* concluded: 'Thus the Morley family continues its magnificent stand for Socialism, Pacifism and anti-Militarism.'[103]

Alan Morley, 18 on the outbreak of war, also refused to register on pacifist grounds and on 11 November 1941 was sentenced to 12 months with hard labour in Wakefield Prison, for failing to submit to a medical examination, where he lost some prison privileges for refusing to undertake war work.[104] In April 1944 he was again sentenced, this time for refusing to obey a direction by the National Service Officer to take up forestry work. Writing to *The Word* his father said that, 'when he protested as a sincere anti-fascist he felt that he must refuse to obey a fascist direction from whichever source it originated.'[105] Alan was joining his brother, Robert, who in March 1944 received his fourth sentence, this time of 3 months with hard labour for failing to obey a direction to attend an interview with the National Service Officer.

---

[102] 'The Stand of the Morleys', *The Word*, October 1942.
[103] 'Newcastle C.O. Again Sentenced', *The Word*, December 1942.
[104] 'The Stand of the Morleys', *The Word*, October 1942.
[105] 'Morleys Again Sentenced', *The Word*, Vol. 5, No. 11, June 1944, p. 124.

Newcastle War Resisters, with their motto, 'The highest morality is the greatest expediency,' was one of the largest group of political objectors in the country. It met weekly in the Theosophical Hall and attracted an average attendance of around 60. *The Word* described its meetings as:

> Instructive, enthusiastic and convivial and its approach to pacifism as mainly political and humanitarian. The absolutist position was stressed but exponents of the 'alternativist' position, and even war supporters, were invited to speak and be given a 'critical, but nevertheless a keen and kindly audience.[106]

Whether such conviviality was actually evident is brought into question by John Morley when, in defence of the absolutist stance, he attacked the alternativists or exemptionists in *Peace News*:

> Fortunately, there are still many die-hards in the pacifist movement who see that the majority of C.O.s are not absolutists and they deeply deplore the fact. The reason for this is that the potential absolutists have been duped or doped by the casuistry and sophistry of the elderly writers and speakers who are looked on as leaders of pacifist thought. These persons, not being liable to the operation of conscription themselves are therefore inclined to advise others to adopt a more cautious approach than that which they themselves would probably have taken had they been personally involved....The predominance of absolutists in the last war was due to the fact that the organisation of COs was undertaken, in the main, by those vitally affected by the Conscription Act.
>
> It is undoubtedly true that "exemptionists" , both absolute and conditional, are placed in a position of privilege under the terms of the Act, and consequently their consciences must constantly trouble them until they can feel they are making some adequate return to society for the

---

[106] 'Newcastle War Resisters', *The Word*, November 1943, p. 46.

privilege they enjoy….Consequently we find many "exemptionists" are at pains to square their actions in assisting the operation of conscription, and a government at war, with their moral objection to war and conscription. This must be a great mental strain upon them; it probably accounts for the state of neurosis into which many of them have fallen. Such men you say are drawn (or should it be dragged?) to such "creative" work as the FAU, the PSU, ARP, Civil Defence and the Non-Combatant Corps, where they suffer a purgatory which must be more severe than the purgatory of the serving soldier…

This purgatory is suffered by many of those who attempt experimental methods of living, by segregating themselves from society to try and find new social foundations, not only within a capitalist economy, but by conforming to the requirements of the Ministry of Labour. These two conditions must make abortive any such attempts to establish new foundations for they are formed on the very basis of present society; that is Capitalism and Servitude.

(the Absolutists) prefer to associate themselves with the mass of humanity in the common bondage of conscription, and thus become truly conscientious objectors, and not merely conscientious with an object. For none can accuse the absolutist of using his conscience to obtain personal privilege.[107]

Morley was bemoaning what Ceadel refers to as the price pacifists had to pay for the acceptance of the right to conscientious objection: the simultaneous acceptance of the legitimacy of National Service.[108] To the absolutist registering meant legitimising the process of military and industrial conscription.

Newcastle War Resisters also held open air meetings in support of the PPU Negotiated Peace Campaign and against the alleged maltreatment of non-combatant conscientious objectors at Dingle Vale (see

[107] 'Case for the Absolutist,' *Peace News*, 28 May 1943, p. 3.
[108] Ceadel, *Pacifism in Britain 1914-1945*, p. 301.

Chapter 7). The list of members, in addition to the Morleys and the Sadlers, described as the 'Royal families of Pacifism,' includes: Albert Oxley, Alf Sharp, Jack Walton, Douglas Gordon Maitland, Harry Wood, Constance Wood, Constance Bolam, Kitty Alexander, Doris Philipson, John Potter, Frank Gillender (Secretary), Alma Gillender (*Peace News* distributor), and Edward Archbold. The occupations of members were also varied: businessmen, clerks, tradesmen, labourers, typists, and housewives. John Morley and Frank Maitland served on the PPU National Council and the PPU Negotiated Peace Committee. Up to November 1943 the group members had received 28 prison sentences, a number which increased significantly by the end of the war.[109]

Newcastle War Resisters were therefore significant both regionally and nationally. The statement made by Edward Archbold, who had volunteered to serve in the First World War, explained the absolutist position regarding civil defence:

> When I fill in a form for civil defence duties there is no limitation to what obligation may be ultimately thrust upon me. It is not true to say that the obligations are strictly limited to fire-watching…I am a pacifist and I am unconditionally opposed to armed force in any shape or form. I know from experience that war is absolutely futile, a negation of everything decent, and totally incapable of solving any human problems whatsoever. That is why I cannot cooperate in civil defence, which is a vital and integral part of the war machine. One of the main purposes of civil defence and fire-watching duties is to give a sense of security to people and to bolster the morale of the nation at war. To me it is the sugar coating that permits the Government to administer to the nation the bitter pill of war, and I am resolutely opposed to war.[110]

The Clerk to the Council disagreed with his interpretation of the Civil Defence (Compulsory Enrolment) Order, stating that its main objective was to procure additional manpower for fire prevention duties.

---

[109] 'Newcastle War Resisters', *The Word*, November 1943, p. 46.
[110] 'War Resister and Fire-Watching', *Morpeth Herald and Reporter*, 20 February 1942, p. 4.

Archbold, after refusing to pay a £5 fine, served one month in prison for refusing to register for fire-watching. He received a second sentence, 6 months in Durham prison, for refusing to submit to a medical examination. Before Newcastle Police Court on 22 April 1943 he stated his opposition to conscription:

> I am standing on trial to-day because I have refused to be medically examined for military purposes. I am uncompromisingly opposed to war because it is futile and insane and totally incapable of solving any worthwhile problem. I believe that our laws compare favourably with those of any other country, yet within our constitution there still remains much bad and inhuman law. I believe in law and order. My duty to society compels me to co-operate in all good laws and to resist all bad laws; I know that even the most humane of magistrates cannot cancel out an inhuman law. But I, from my privileged position here, can, by my resistance to this inhuman law, focus public attention and ultimately indignation on the matter; and therein lies one hope of its repeal.
>
> The purpose of conscription is to harness unformed and bewildered young men and women to the war chariot.
>
> I repeat, I believe in law and order. The tank, the tommy-gun and the bomber are the very antithesis of law and order; they are outlawry and disorder in their most abandoned and hideous garb.[111]

Unsurprisingly he again refused to be medically examined. Appearing before the court the following day, he eloquently expressed the effect that fighting in the previous war had had on his views:

> During the last war I voluntarily donned the King's uniform and served my country with the valour and nonchalance of youth, and they lauded me. To-day I serve her none

---

[111] 'An Ex-Service C.O. Speaks Out,' *Central Board for Conscientious Objectors Bulletin*, May 1943, p. 11.

the less valiantly in the wisdom and maturity of my forty-three years. I resist war because I now know that it can add nothing to human happiness - it can only take away. It may gain or lose us an inch of territory, but it always adds another mountain to that vast range of national prejudice.

You will probably disagree with me when I say that no Admiral or General, while pursuing his warlike job, has ever made a lasting contribution to his country...

My crime is that I have renounced war and will no longer fight against my fellow-men. More than twenty years ago I laid down my Lewis gun in despair; since then I have sought to rearm myself in the fertile minds of Newton, Lister...[112]

His speech must have impressed the court as he did not receive the usual twelve months.

Although not a Newcastle War Resister, Donald Henson, (referred to as Hersom in some newspapers), a Morpeth librarian, had a different view on the Fire Watching Regulations. Objecting on religious grounds, he condemned the blockade of Germany and the mass bombing of cities referring to the Fire Guard Scheme as: 'no more than their attempt to insure against retaliation, and I am determined not to be a party to it.'[113]

With political objection rooted in the First World War, Newcastle War Resisters were a major player in socialist and moral objection during the Second World War, both within the North-East and nationally. This somewhat contradicts Brock's assertion that 'the straight political objector was no longer an important factor in the pattern of conscientious objection.'[114] Newcastle War Resisters retained their absolutist stance, despite their refusal to comply with conscription legislation leading to many of them serving multiple prison sentences.

---

[112] Ibid., p. 11-12.
[113] 'Refused to perform Fire Guard duties', *Morpeth Herald and Gazette*, 21 January 1944, p. 1.
[114] Brock, *Twentieth-Century Pacifism*, p. 167.

Family Connections

Continuity of conscientious objection from the First to the Second World War was also evident within families of religious objectors, in particular, Quakers. An 18 year-old Quaker, Martyn Gaudie, given conditional exemption in September 1943, stated at his tribunal hearing that, 'He did not believe in war but felt that his place in life was to prepare himself for work on the continent after the war helping the reconstruction of Europe.' Judge Richardson reflected: 'If conscientious objectors are going to have anything to do with settling matters after the war, we will have another war in about 20 years' time.'[115] Gaudie reflecting on his experience: 'I found it very hard during the war when men were going away to fight the Nazis; how do you explain why you will not raise a hand against Hitler?'[116] It was not reported at the time that Martyn Gaudie was the son of Norman Gaudie, one of the Richmond Castle 16 from the First World War.

Norman Gaudie was an Accounts Clerk with the North-Eastern Railway and reserve team footballer with Sunderland AFC, his story being part of the 2014 'Football and the First World War' exhibition at the National Football Museum, Manchester. The son of a Quaker he objected to any form of military service, including non-combatant service, but the tribunal exempted him from combatant service only. On refusing to report to the army he was arrested, forcibly stripped naked, dressed in khaki uniform and locked in a cell and moved to Richmond. Transferred to France, Norman appeared before a Field Court Martial, charged with disobeying a lawful command given personally by his senior officer. He gave his reason for refusal as follows:

> My motive for refusing is because my religious convictions prevent me from taking any part in the military system whatsoever and I am therefore bound to disobey any military orders in loyalty to those convictions…

---

[115] 'C.O.s Would Cause Fresh Wars – Judge', *North-East Gazette*, 3 September 1943, p. 8.
[116] 'Prepared to Die…But Not to Kill', *Echoes Magazine: Northern Echo*, 8 January 1991, p. 4-5.

Released from prison in 1919, Norman was unable, because of long-term physical and psychological effects, to continue his football career.[117] His suffering after the war was not only physical. According to Martyn, Norman was barred from his local cricket team and shunned when he sought work: 'No one would touch them. They were the scum of the earth. Eventually a fellow at Whitburn gave him a job in insurance.'[118]

Norman Gaudie's case helps illustrate the extreme conditions faced by many objectors in the First World War, extremes which were not to be experienced in the Second World War. The chances of a Quaker being subjected to imprisonment were also considerably less in the Second World War. This is not to say that Quakers were not imprisoned or that non-combatant soldiers who refused to put on a uniform did not face imprisonment, and in some cases abuse.[119] It does, however, show that the greater range of options available to tribunals in the Second World War greatly reduced the likelihood of such cases arising. There was also a greater realisation that deeply held convictions were not going to be changed by brutality. But the greatest impact that the experiences of Norman Gaudie had, and the bravery he had shown, would likely have been his son continuing the Quaker tradition of conscientious objection. In the case of Martyn Gaudie the tribunal recognised his objection by conditionally registering him for land work.[120]

Another objector with a family tradition of pacifism was William Grigor McClelland. Born in 1922, his father and grandfather were Quakers and he joined the Society of Friends in 1941, having been an attender since the age of 14. He joined the FAU in London, having been a pupil at Leighton Park Quaker Boarding School in Reading, stating on his application that he had no objection to joining the Royal Army Medical Corps (RAMC) on the clear understanding that he would not be required to bear arms. He maintained this stance in his application to the London Tribunal, on 9 September 1941:

---

[117] 'Norman Gaudie – Footballer and Conscientious Objector', http://www.footballandthefirst-worldwar.com/norman-gaudie/, accessed 24 February 2015.
[118] 'Prepared to Die...But Not to Kill', *Northern Echo*, 8 January 1991, p. 4-5.
[119] See Chapter 6 for abuse of objectors.
[120] '"C.O.'s" Rebuked by Judge Richardson', *Evening Chronicle,* 2 September 1943, p. 2.

I believe:

- That it is my duty to God to try to follow in my life the teaching and example of Jesus Christ.
- That Jesus's message is of the brotherhood of all men, and his commandment to men is that they should love their fellow men and meet evil with good.
- That war denies these principles and is destructive of them.

I therefore refuse to take any part in war. I am, however, eager to help lessen the evil effects of war, but in no organisation in which my work would be identified with the war effort. I therefore joined the Friends Ambulance Unit on 1st January 1941.[121]

He was granted exemption on the condition that he stayed in his present occupation as a full-time member of the FAU or full time ARP or AFS work under the control of, or approved by, a local authority, or full time work in connection with the land. He continued in the FAU and served in Palestine, Egypt, Libya, Italy, France, and Germany. After the war, he founded the Manchester Business School and was awarded the CBE for his work as chair of the National Lottery Charities Board. He returned his CBE in 2003 in protest at the war in Iraq but requested it back in 2009 when British troops were withdrawn, conscious that the honour was held on behalf of other charity workers in Tyne and Wear.[122]

Douglas Hardy was another FAU volunteer who came from a family of objectors with First World War connections. He was the uncle of the previously mentioned Wendy Acres. The family were Wesleyan Methodists going back to the 1790s and held pacifist views in both World Wars. Her uncles were objectors in the Second World War: Frank Bishop of Darlington was sent to work in forestry and horticulture; Harold Bishop of Darlington volunteered for the medical corps.

---

[121] Ref. 5336, Archive of Grigor McClelland, Tyne and Wear Archives, Newcastle.
[122] 'Obituary: Grigor McClelland', *Guardian*, 14 November 2013.

Hardy, although a Methodist, attended the Quaker School in Great Ayton, hence his decision to join the FAU after he lost his job as an engineer for being a conscientious objector.[123] Things were not to end well for Douglas. As an engineer, he spent much of his time in China rebuilding petrol engines to work on charcoal because of the shortage of petrol. There he contracted dysentery and then typhus, resulting in his death. He was buried amid woodland nearby with a cornflower cross on his grave. The doctor wrote to his family in Darlington: 'He went home peacefully and triumphantly and with a smile on his face. Apart from dear old England, I'm sure he is in the most beautiful spot that you could wish.'[124] Accompanying Douglas to China was Peter Leyland of Wensleydale, his friend from the Quaker School. Peter's father, John, had been a conscientious objector in the First World War and had been awarded the Croix de Guerre for driving FAU ambulances under heavy enemy shell fire.[125]

Grigor McClelland, Douglas Hardy and Peter Leyland served in many parts of the world but the FAU, through its subsidiary The Civilian Service Corps, did relief work in many parts of Britain. They trained men to work on the land and placed men in hospitals as paid orderlies, attendants and porters.[126] The Northern Relief Section, based in Newcastle, worked in conjunction with the Ministry of Health, the Tyneside Council of Social Service and the Durham Community Service Council. Initially the work involved surveying the adequacy of rest shelters in towns most vulnerable to bombing. Later they undertook: welfare work with people made homeless by bombing; acted as an evacuation bureau in emergencies; and worked to prevent and treat scabies.[127]

Objection on religious grounds was not uncommon within families, even where there was no reference in the sources back to the First World War. Examples include: H. and Amos Almond; Clarence and Dorothy Charlton; George and Leonard Curry; Thomas and William Denny; H. M. and J. P. Hazel; John and Sydney Richardson; Fred and James Robinson; John and Robert Salkeld; Frederick, John and Robert

<hr>

[123] Telephone interview with Wendy Acres of Darlington, conducted 28 October 2013.
[124] 'Matters of Conscience', *Northern Echo*, 7 May 2013; and Telephone interview with Wendy Acres.
[125] 'Matters of Conscience', *Northern Echo*, 7 May 2013.
[126] 'Civilian Work for C.O.s,' *The Friend*, 8 November 1940, p. 618.
[127] 'Relief Work in Northumbria', *Friends Ambulance Unit Chronicle*, No. 43, 19 December 1942.

Shanklin; and, Kathleen, Thomas and Cecil Waring. Not all conscientious objection by siblings was for religious or political reasons. Paul and Louis Ronchetti were 2 of 4 children born near Redcar. Their brother, Thomas A. Ronchetti, was an officer in the army who died early in the war of pneumonia. Their father was a pharmacist. They worked as draughtsmen on the de Havilland Mosquito, a reserved occupation, in Hatfield, and both were in the Home Guard. Both were distressed at the area bombing of Germany and felt they could no longer work on airplanes, so they went home, leaving their Home Guard uniforms and rifles in their lodgings. Paul said that they had been uneasy about the bombing of civilians for some time but the bombing of Dresden was the final straw. In April 1945, they were each sentenced to six month's imprisonment in Durham Prison. They were not pacifists as such. Also, even though Paul had tried to join the fight against Franco when under 16, they were not political in their objections and were very proud of their brother in the army.[128]

Objection, both on religious and political grounds, was therefore often influenced by family members. What is also evident is that the suffering experienced by them for their beliefs did not deter other family members from following the same path. The family bond was most likely a comfort to those facing the experience of prison.

Practitioners of the Arts

In their 1940 report, Mass Observation concluded that, on the whole, conscientious objectors had highbrow and intelligent cultural interests, and to the conventionally minded, 'some appeared odd and arty.'[129] They also noted from their sample of 26, which they regarded as being of qualitative rather than quantitative value, that they were not interested in team games such as football and cricket.[130] The Mass Observation report therefore tells us more about stereotypes at the time than it does about conscientious objectors and their interests.

---

[128] Interview with Steve Ronchetti, son of Louis Ronchetti, on 30 October 2013, and telephone interview with Paul Ronchetti on 1 November 2013.
[129] File Report No. 312, p. a), *Mass Observation*.
[130] Ibid., p. 41.

No evidence was found to substantiate the conclusions of Mass Observation as the leisure interests of most North-East objectors are unknown. The analysis of occupations found nine employed in Arts and Entertainment and two students of music, one being the previously mentioned William Davey. This number is not significantly high, probably reflecting the region as being on the fringe of the national arts scene.

The poet James Kirkup is excluded from these figures as he is recorded as a student. His objection was derived from the stories of the Great War related to him by his father, a carpenter, of able-bodied men having to kill their fellow men.[131] He expressed his pacifism through his poetry, during and after the war. He told the Newcastle Tribunal that he objected on ethical and aesthetic grounds, believing, 'that modern warfare was the height of ugliness, both spiritual and physical, and that the claptrap of patriotic jargon spouted by politicians as well as the windy oratory of Churchill were defilements of the English language.'[132] In his statement to the tribunal he quoted Max Plowman's *The Faith Called Pacifism*, adding:

> I object as a poet, as a thinking artist, to methods of violence which are patently unaesthetic and degrading, and which constitute a negation of all beauty as men through have known it, a negation of cultural progress, a negation of all aesthetic appreciation, a negation of living soul. I therefore renounce this war, refuse to take part in or be even indirectly responsible for the mass slaughter of innocent men women and children by the ignoble methods of modern warfare.
>
> I need hardly add that I have held these views from the age when I was first able to think sanely and humanely without fear.[133]

His statement did not help his cause as he was removed from the register. By the time of his Appeal, he had moderated his views and was prepared to join the FAU or work on the land. He refers to the chairman,

---

[131] James Kirkup, *I, Of All People* (New York: St. Martin's Press, 1988), p. 50.
[132] Ibid., pp. 55-56.
[133] Ibid., *I, of All* People, p. 56.

H. A. L. Fisher, making demeaning remarks about his personal appearance, which Kirkup admits was strange and arty, and making cruel fun of his poetry. Nevertheless, he received conditional exemption.[134]

James Kirkup went on to claim fame as a poet and travel writer. In 1950, he won an award from the Rockefeller Foundation and was appointed Gregory Poetry Fellow at Leeds, becoming the first resident university poet in the United Kingdom. In 1956 he settled in Japan, where he became Professor of English Literature at Kyoto University. He won the Japan PEN Club Prize for Poetry in 1965 and later, in 1997, was invited by the Japanese emperor and empress to the Imperial New Year Poetry Reading at the Palace in Tokyo.[135] He became infamous in 1976 when his poem, *The Love That Dare Not Speak Its Name* was the subject of the last successful blasphemy trial in Britain. He considered the one good thing to have emerged from the war was the acceptance of his pacifism and bi-sexuality by his parents.[136]

The dilemma faced by many conscientious objectors was expressed by artist Miles Peter Richmond of London when interviewed in 2007. He was an Artist living in Northallerton at the time of giving his interviews at Northallerton Library. Objecting as a socialist, he questioned whether becoming a conscientious objector was an act of cowardice or of principle:

> I don't know? My brother said that many in the Army would have liked to have done the same but weren't brave enough. I was always a loner and did not mind being called a coward...I can't and don't want to defend my position...It increased my sense of being an isolated individual and it is still a problem to me that this generation saved the world from Hitler.[137]

Generally, those working in the field of arts and entertainment did not fare well at the tribunal. Basil Alfred Kilmourn, an Actor and

---

[134] Ibid., p. 57.
[135] 'Obituary: James Kirkup, *Daily Telegraph*, 12 May 2009.
[136] Kirkup, *I, of All People*, p. 55.
[137] 'Interview with Miles Peter Richmond', C466/263, British Library Sound Archive, Euston Road, London.

Stage Manager from Hartlepool, objected on religious grounds and was removed from the register without qualification. Responding as to whether he would do non-combatant duties he said: 'I refuse to have anything to do with the war at all. They will have to drag me in. I assure you they will have to shoot me.'[138] Major Lawrence Long, a variety artist from Newcastle, was removed without qualification, as was Ray Musgrave, an artist from Middleton–St-George, whose reason for objection was: 'It would be a hardship for me to be in the Army. I would not like the life and am conscious that I could not stand it. I am too sensitive.'[139] T. R. Carrick of South Shields also declared: I am the artistic type. I am not built for it.'[140] Such comments when reported in the press reinforced the stereotypical presentation of artists as 'sensitive souls'. It was unlikely to promote empathy with conscientious objectors.

Vegetarianism

Mass Observation also concluded that there was a tendency among objectors to vegetarianism.[141] This was a conclusion also arrived at by later historians. For example, James Gregory examines the relationship between peace, vegetarianism and other 'eccentric' causes in Victorian times, and Tolstoy's development of a moral philosophy which included pacifism and vegetarianism is examined by Charlotte Alston.[142] A *Peace News* observer of the Newcastle Tribunal, commenting on the difficulty the tribunal had in dealing with non-religious objectors, noted that to achieve exemption, 'a vegetarian diet seemed to be the deciding factor!'[143] Only one example was found of vegetarianism forming part of the reason for objection. George D. Smithson of Bedlington, objecting on humanitarian, pacifism and vegetarian grounds, stated to the tribunal:

---

[138] 'Will Have to Drag Me In', *Northern Daily Mail*, 23 May 1940, p. 4.
[139] 'Too Sensitive To Be In The Army', *Northern Echo*, 21 March 1940, p. 5.
[140] 'Happier on a Cannibal Island', *Evening Chronicle*, 11 March 1941, p. 3.
[141] Mass Observation, File Report 312, Summary, Item 2.
[142] James Gregory, *Of Victorians and Vegetarians* (London: Tauris Academic Studies, 2007), and, Charlotte Alston, *Tolstoy and his Disciples: The History of a Radical International Movement* (London: I. B. Tauris Ltd., 2014).
[143] 'Bias Shown at Newcastle,' *Peace News*, 20 October 1939, p. 5.

If Jesus Christ had had a knowledge of evolution before him, he too would have been a vegetarian. My only religion is that of human progress on humanitarian grounds. I would also refuse to do civilian work if it meant the fattening of animals for slaughter but would do work connected with the growing of vegetables.[144]

Before granting conditional exemption, Judge Richardson enquired whether he objected to the use of insecticides to kill slugs.[145]

One other vegetarian objector was found. George Sowerby, of Low Fell, on being registered as an objector, told the tribunal, 'a man who is in the Army is not human, he is a murderer.'[146] In the absence of other examples it is not feasible to attribute vegetarianism as a particular trait amongst North-East objectors.

Members of Pre-War Peace Organisations

Many objectors in the region were members of peace organisations. One was George Bartram. Prior to the war he had attended, and spoken at, meetings of the Sunderland branch of the PPU. He also put his name to a letter to the press from peace organisations in the North-East, offering assistance to conscientious objectors. The letter was from Thomas W. Large, Secretary PPU (Newcastle and District Branch); Lewis McLachlan, Chairman, FoR, with the following as supporting signatories: PPU – T. G. Anderson, Harold E. Berry, M. Hope Dodds, Rev A. H. Grant, Arthur W. Kay, Herbert W. Richardson, George Reavley (Sunderland chairman), G. Summerbell (Sunderland secretary), J. C. Swanton; FoR – Grace E. Arrowsmith, Rev R. G. Bell, Jean M. Cass, Marjorie G. Colman, Rev W. H. Goodall, Rev A. B. Hodgkins, Donald Ramage; Friends Peace Committee – Gerald G. Brown, W. Carr, Ruth Dodds, John Mitchell, E. Louisa Pumphrey, Arthur Raistrick, S. Elizabeth Raistrick, Nora Gillie; Methodist Peace Fellowship – Rev P. S. Carden, E. V. C. G. Udy; Unattached – Lady Trevelyan, Rev F. G. Berry, Rev Thomas

---

[144] 'Object to Fighting Hitlerism', *Sunderland Echo*, 13 October 1939, p. 6.
[145] 'Conscientious Objectors Tribunal', *Durham County Advertiser*, 20 October 1939, p. 8.
[146] 'Man who opposed his father,' *Sunderland Echo*, 5 December 1939, p. 6.

Litchfield, Rev P. M. Paton, G. H. Bartram, Stephen H. Wilson (member of ILP). The letter stated:

> We, believing that war in all circumstances is wrong, futile and destructive of the best in human relationships, have pledged ourselves to uncompromising opposition to war and to all preparations for war, including conscription. There must be many persons approaching conscription age, who are perplexed by the difficult confronting them. They are assured of sympathetic discussion if they are to communicate with any of the signatories of this letter.[147]

Bartram is an example of an active supporter of a pacifist organisation converting his pacifism into conscientious objection. Others who the sources showed declaring membership of the PPU before the tribunal were: Robert Harbottle, an articled clerk from Newcastle; Thomas Neil, a grocer from Newcastle; James Cecil Noble, a farmer from Hexham; Dennis Taylor, an advertising agent from Durham; A. Turner, a grocer's assistant from Middlesbrough; and, Joseph B. Willan, a farm worker from Durham. Given that PPU membership continued to grow at the beginning of the war, at its peak doubling the total number registering as conscientious objectors, it would seem reasonable to assume that many more objectors were PPU members. Yet Ceadel asserts that by the end of the war some earlier objectors had abandoned their pacifism.[148] Reasons he cites for this were the reluctance of the PPU to interfere in the conscription process because of the government's liberal approach to recognising conscientious objection, and, the military crisis of 1940.[149] The latter prompted the following comment by John Barclay in *Peace News*:

> If at the back of our minds has always been the comforting thought that in the end Allied Forces would win, our pacifism has never been more than an academic philosophy. I believe that this possibility of military defeat has come as a

---

[147] 'Hear All Sides: War and Conscription', *Northern Echo*, 22 May 1939, p. 4.
[148] Ceadel, *Pacifism in Britain*, p. 301.
[149] Ibid., pp. 296-297.

shock to so many people. Pacifism faced by military dictatorship and no longer sheltering behind it - this is something that may cause complete renunciation of previously
held convictions.[150]

Many who signed the peace pledge were outside the parameters
of the call-up. It was also one thing to sign a pledge expressing a senti-
ment and another to become a conscientious objector. Memories of the
treatment received by conscientious objectors during and after the First
World War were still fresh. In effect, it was easier to be a pacifist in peace
time than in wartime, especially when defeat was a possibility. This was
a conclusion also reached by Rena Feld after interviewing conscientious
objectors for the British Library. To not support a war that everyone else
supports is very difficult as there is no comradeship to be derived.[151] The
regional press, who had supported appeasement and shown no antagonism towards pacifists, began to exert pressure on pacifists once war became inevitable. Raymond Burns, the Political Correspondent of the
Northern Daily Mail, wrote:

> I have never had any sympathy for the pacifist. I regard pac-
> ifism as a combination of misguided, but nevertheless pro-
> found, sincerity and an element of exhibitionism…If ever
> Britain has to face an attack by those foreign armies one
> hopes that even some of the professing pacifists in this
> country would see the wisdom of uniting to protect our
> loved ones. What type of mind is it that, hating war, can
> nevertheless counsel pacifism once attempts to prevent war
> have failed?[152]

Once war broke out pressure on pacifists and conscientious objectors was not going to be limited to the press. The public, employers
and even Christian churches all had a role to play.

---

[150] 'What of Peace Now?', *Peace News,* 14 June 1940, p. 1
[151] Rena Feld, 'From the Interviewer's Perspective: Interviewing Women Conscientious Objectors,' *Oral History Review*, 31, 1 (Spring 2003), p. 38.
[152] 'Conscription and the Pacifists', *Northern Daily Mail*, 3 June 1939, p. 3.

Conclusion

The regional case study, has advanced the general understanding of conscientious objection in the Second World War by providing a detailed analysis of those who objected. It confirms the general conclusions reached by Mass Observation but, at the same time, it shows some regional variations which complicate the overall national picture. The North-East of England had one of the lowest percentages registering as conscientious objectors in Britain. Demographic reasons for this have been identified. Objectors came from over 100 different occupations, whose profile has supported the findings of Mass Observation, and provided a basis for confirming why the rate of objection was higher in Newcastle and Darlington, with their higher number of lower middle class occupations, than in the predominantly heavy industrial and mining centres within the region.

This chapter has also examined how the government learned the lessons of the First World War in legislating for conscientious objectors in the Second World War. However, total war brought about objections over and above that of a simple objection to bearing arms, which exposed the limitations of the legislation in dealing with objection to other forms of compulsion. There was little to which the absolutist objector could not object. This contributed to an understatement of the number of objectors. In the North-East of England there was the full range of objection.

It also showed the inconsistency in the treatment of political and religious objectors, as well as between different types of religious objectors. Two-thirds of North-East objectors were religious objectors, of which almost half were Jehovah's Witnesses or Quakers. There was, however, a sharp contrast in the form of objection shown by the two bodies, and the responses of the state apparatus to them. One was a body of 'respectable' objectors and the other was clearly not. To be a Quaker invariably meant being registered as a conscientious objector, to be a Jehovah's Witness would inevitably lead to prison.

Being a political objector inevitably led to prison. Political objectors, mainly of the ILP, were not to be shaken in their resolve to object, against the view of the majority, to an imperialist war. Jehovah's Witnesses were also found to be consistent in their absolute objection, whilst other religious objectors had theirs in varying degrees. How these variances were manifested in their treatment by the authorities is discussed in the following chapters.

For many their objection was following in the family tradition producing a progression of objection from the First World War to the Second World War, some objecting in both wars. Families whose members had been objectors in both wars, often imprisoned, were not uncommon. Many of these families were involved in peace organisations which, once war had been declared, continued to actively oppose war and assist objectors. Newcastle War Resisters, principally absolutist objectors, were a nationally significant organisation within this movement.

There was no single model to define who a conscientious objector was. Even within broadly similar groups it was individualism which dictated the reasons for and the extent of their objection. Vera Brittain got closer than most to explaining this:

> Pacifism is nothing more than a belief in the ultimate transcendence of love over power. This belief comes from an inward assurance. It is untouched by logic and beyond argument – though there are many arguments both for and against it. And each person's assurance is individual; his inspiration cannot arise from another's reasons, nor can its authority be quenched by another's scepticism.[153]

The numbers of conscientious objectors, whilst small in percentage terms, were nevertheless on a significant enough scale to be of interest to the public, press and authorities. How these groups treated the North-East's objectors is now examined.

---

[153] Vera Brittain, *Humiliation With Honour* (London: A. Dakers Ltd., 1942), p. 8.

The Moot Hall, home of the Newcastle Tribunal

Chapter Two

Judge Richardson and the Newcastle Tribunal

On 27 April 1939 parliament agreed for the first time to the principle of conscription in peace time and detailed consideration began on the Military Training Bill. Hayes describes as generous the provision for conscientious objectors which allowed them to sign up to a special register.[1]

Setting up the Tribunals

Once an individual had signed the Register of Conscientious Objectors, they would receive a summons to attend the local tribunal, where one of four outcomes would result: unconditional registration as a conscientious objector; conditional registration as a conscientious objector; deemed liable for military service but on non-combatant duties; or, unconditional removal from the register of conscientious objectors and registered for military service. The first three recognised degrees of conscientious objection, the fourth was a rejection.

In the North-East of England, the Northumberland and Durham (Newcastle) Tribunal was charged with determining the outcome in each case. Tribunal sessions were held at the County Court building in Newcastle, and were described by a *Sunday Sun* reporter:

> Picture a long dingy room, the walls of which are in urgent need of a vigorous wash and brush up. At the far end is a raised dais, under the Lion and the Unicorn, and here four elderly men are sitting. Directly in front of them is an enclosure reserved for Pressmen and behind the Pressmen about half a hundred people are scattered around on benches. This is the setting for the C.O.s Tribunal in Newcastle....[2]

---

[1] Hayes, *Challenge of Conscience*, p. 4-5.
[2] 'Lewis Ashley's Pageant: Dissenting Consciences', *Sunday Sun*, 28 January 1940, p. 2.

This grim and foreboding setting was where those who had an objection to military service would have the sincerity of that objection tested. In order for this to happen, the Prime Minister, during the second reading of the Military Training Bill, said: 'special care would have to be taken in choosing those who are to sit on these Tribunals.'[3] He was concerned that one of the main criticisms of the First World War tribunals had been their membership. To Barker the fundamental question was: 'what sort of person makes for the best judge of conscience, if indeed, such a task is possible.'[4] Given the experience of World War I, impartiality and civil control were the key factors in assessing conscientious objection. Sir Arnold Wilson (Conservative) MP recognised that this was not going to be easy, commenting: 'We are endeavouring in Clause 3 to try the mind of a man, and, I foresee, as in the last war, great difficulties.'[5] He was not wrong. George Lansbury MP (Labour), commented: 'I do not think that old men like me ought to be put on these tribunals to weigh up the judgement and conscience of much younger men, but persons much younger and persons with an appreciation of what conscience means.'[6] The older men on the tribunals, having either fought in the First World War or been sympathetic to its cause, would have created doubt among some of the younger generation of their ability to judge their consciences.

Where could the government find men capable of judging conscience? Leonard F Behrans, writing to the *Manchester Guardian*, asked:

Is it too bold to suggest that the tribunals should be largely selected from the leaders of pacifist opinion such men (or women) are competent to assess the sincerity of the applicants, and are sufficiently concerned for the reputation of those who share their convictions not to include shirkers and frauds among them.[7]

This was never given serious consideration by MPs debating the Bill. Only one, C. C. Poole (Labour), expressed the view that: 'You want someone who will be sympathetic and who will endeavour to put himself

---

[3] Hayes, *Challenge of Conscience*, p. 4-5.
[4] Barker, *Conscience, Government and War*, p. 30.
[5] 'Military Training Bill', *Hansard,* HC Deb. 8 May 1939, Vol 347, cc119.
[6] 'Compulsory Military Training', *Hansard,* HC Deb. 27 April 1939, Vol. 346, cc 1427.
[7] 'Letters to the Editor: Pacifists on Tribunals', *Manchester Guardian*, 5 June 1939, p. 7.

in the place of the person who is appearing, and not someone who calmly and dispassionately weighs up the pros and cons.'[8]

One former objector, T. Edmund Harvey MP (Independent Progressive), considered the absence of lawyers on First World War tribunals a serious omission and, whilst he considered that no machinery could be set up to satisfactorily judge the consciences of men, saw the judicial character of the tribunals as a matter of the greatest importance.[9] The government therefore had support when it decided that the necessary impartiality would be ensured by each tribunal having a County Court judge as its Chairman. In the early days of the war it seemed to be generally agreed that the 'atmosphere and attitude of these tribunals have been altogether different from the WWI tribunals,' due to 'the fact that the chairman is a judge, and trained to avoid at any rate an appearance of partiality.'[10] The Northumberland and Durham Tribunal was chaired by Judge Thomas Richardson, described by James Kirkup as a 'gruesomely patriotic old Tory.'[11] How did Judge Richardson and his tribunal respond to the challenges? It is not unreasonable to state that some difficulties were encountered. This chapter considers how his tribunal operated, what prejudices it exhibited and the criticisms levelled at it. It will do this by comparing its operation with that of other tribunals and by questioning the reputation that it, and, in particular, its chairman, has in the secondary literature. Did Judge Richardson's notorious hostility in his questioning of objectors mean that his was a particularly harsh tribunal in terms of its decision making?

Criticisms of the Newcastle Tribunal

Judge Richardson received much criticism from parliamentarians. Addressing the House of Lords in 1943 the Duke of Bedford, a well-known pacifist and sympathiser with conscientious objectors, stated:

> Several outstanding examples of unsuitable persons who have officiated on tribunals may be cited. Judge Richardson, head of the Newcastle Tribunal, has said publicly that

---

[8] 'Military Training (Money)', *Hansard,* HC Deb. 8 May 1939, Vol. 347, cc 206.
[9] 'Military Training Bill', *Hansard,* HC Deb. 4 May 1939, Vol. 346 cc2180.
[10] 'Striving to Judge Conscience,' *The Friend,* 10 November 1939, p. 901.
[11] Kirkup, *I, of all People,* p. 55.

conscientious objectors should be cold-shouldered after the war. The decisions of his tribunal show what little chance of justice a conscientious objector has under such a Judge.[12]

This was not the only criticism in Parliament of the learned Judge. As early as February 1940, Mr Kenneth Pethick-Lawrence (Labour), a conscientious objector in the First World War, commented that, whilst he understood the strain to which Tribunal members were subject,[13]

...The applicant has to face the members of the Tribunal, and they themselves have to do the cross-examining. I think that puts them somewhat in a difficulty, because they are both cross-examining the applicant and arriving at their verdict in the end; and, although some may succeed in maintaining judicial impartiality while doing so, the information which reaches me is that some do not. Three names were called out at the Newcastle tribunal. The names of Donald, Cameron, and Douglas were called out, and at once the chairman, Judge Richardson, remarked, "Good fighting names. I think the holders of some of these names would turn in their coffins if they could hear what some of these people are saying." That is a very improper remark for the chairman of a tribunal to make. The House of Commons has decided that it is not a crime, that it is not even contemptible, to be a conscientious objector if the person is genuine. Yet these insulting remarks are poured out by the chairman.[14]

Juliet Gardiner mentions that tribunals 'varied in the way they interpreted their brief,' and cites Newcastle as a 'notorious' example.[15] The brief for the tribunals to interpret was somewhat unclear. As Barker points out, the Act and guidance notes issued by the Ministry of Labour, whilst clarifying the functions and the procedure, left the manner in

---

[12] 'The Conscientious Objector', *Hansard,* HL Deb. 2 March 1943, Vol. 126 cc358-92.
[13] Hayes, *Challenge of Conscience*, p. 40.
[14] 'Ministry of Labour and National Service', *Hansard,* HC Deb. 22 February 1940, Vol. 357 cc1581-631.
[15] Gardiner, *Wartime Britain 1939-1945*, p. 105.

which they were to reach their decisions largely to tribunals themselves. She points to Judge Wethered of the South-West Tribunal complaining that none of the National Service Acts provided a definition of the term 'conscientiously objects,' and Judge Burgis of the North-West Tribunal affirming that, 'we receive no directions.' Judge Wethered further complained, along with Judge Davis of the South-Eastern Tribunal, that the Appellate Tribunal, which dissatisfied objectors could appeal to, offered very little guidance.[16] The Judges' expressed views did not result in further guidance from the Ministry of Labour. How the Newcastle Tribunal and its chairman interpreted this inadequate brief is examined here.

As mentioned earlier an examination of the tribunal proceedings was not possible as they were destroyed. However, a thorough examination of local and regional newspapers provides an in-depth qualitative picture of the operation of the tribunal and its critics. The newspapers were only too happy to report in detail the more controversial remarks made by Judge Richardson and the objectors themselves. As the press reported the sensational, it is possible that tribunal chairmen may have been sensational in turn to discourage the less sincere to register a conscientious objection. The local press, especially keen to record the details of hearings involving men, and later women, of their immediate locality, was a major source for compiling the Database of Conscientious Objectors. An analysis of the database's quantitative information, along with the statistical data held in the National Archives, assists in the critical examination of the operation of the tribunal.

The composition of the tribunal, consistent with that of the other tribunals, remained similar during the period. Only when conscription was extended to women were women required to be appointed to tribunals. The main members were: Alderman F. Nicholson CBE, JP; Professor James F. Duff M.A.M. Ed.; Sir Luke Thompson; J. Bowman; and, the chairman, Judge Thomas Richardson, OBE (see Appendix C for biographical information on members). One significant addition came in

[16] Barker, *Conscience, Government and War*, p. 16.

1943 when Rev. Dr E. L. Allen accepted an invitation to become a member of the tribunal. Dr Allen was a well-known pacifist and made his position clear before accepting the position.[17]

Judge Richardson's most telling biographical feature was revealed when he told an objector whose father had lost all his seven brothers in the last war: 'I am one of seven brothers of whom only two are alive. I lost five brothers in the last war and have a son going up next week.' His other brother was lost in a submarine disaster before war began.[18] One brother received a Victoria Cross at the Battle of the Somme.[19] If this had been known to W.L., an observer attending the first sitting of the tribunal, then he perhaps would not 'have been staggered that the Chairman, a Judge, should start by expressing his gratification that there was a relatively small number of Conscientious Objectors.'[20] To W.L. it did not seem to be the Judge's duty to express what he thought of conscientious objectors before hearing their cases. He would therefore not have been surprised if he had witnessed Judge Richardson commenting on two men who had requested their names be removed from the Register of Conscientious Objectors: 'It is very satisfactory to feel that so many people, on further consideration, are finding where their duty lies.'[21] In case some people were unsure where their duty lay, he pointed out, 'one of the most patriotic actions,' to come before him. A young man at Gateshead County Court wanted some compensation paid early to have an operation enabling him to join the Army, a request described by Judge Richardson as a 'magnificent contrast to the sort of thing I have to endure at the Conscientious Objectors' Tribunal. I hope it may shame some of them.'[22]

The Judge's sense of duty allowed him to sympathise with an objector's father who told the tribunal he was ashamed and shocked to come on such a mission as he had served in the last war and was proud of it: 'I am very glad to hear it. My own son is joining up tomorrow, and I should be sorry if he was like yours. I have every sympathy with you.'

[17] 'Pacifist on Tribunal,' *Central Board for Conscientious Objectors Bulletin*, No. 39, May 1943, p. 2.

[18] 'Judge's Son and Five Brothers', *Manchester Guardian*, 6 December 1939, p. 8.

[19] *Hexham Courant*, 26 September 1942, p. 1.

[20] 'North's First C.O. Tribunal: Age in Judgement on Youth', *Sunday Sun*, 15 October 1939, p. 9.

[21] 'Pacifists Change Their Minds', *Northern Echo*, 1 December 1939, p. 7.

[22] 'I Hope this may shame some C.O.s', *Northern Echo*, 7 August 1940, p. 5.

The objector was conditionally registered, as was another of whose father Judge Richardson stated: 'He is a very fine father. I can imagine what he feels like.' The Judge did, however, cause outrage at the same hearing when he responded to an objector saying that he would use an air raid shelter, but would not help build one: 'You are the biggest example of a coward I have encountered.' Following cries of 'shame' he added, 'Silence. I am giving my opinion. You would not help put up an air-raid shelter but would run like a rabbit into it.' Despite these remarks the objector, Geoffrey Rioch, was unconditionally registered.[23] Perhaps because of such decisions, Judge Richardson two days later denied bias against conscientious objectors:

> Every single decision the Tribunal had given has been unanimous. A lot of people have been given favourable decisions because we believed their motives were really conscientious. We don't decide on sympathies, but on the Act of Parliament, and whenever there have been any differences on interpretation we have always decided on that which is favourable to the man.[24]

Sir Luke Thompson explained, 'We want to find out the inner minds of the applicants.'[25] He was echoed by Judge Burgis at the Manchester Tribunal who hoped applicants would not resent their questioning or think they were persecuting conscience, which was something to be respected and revered, but, 'they had to ascertain the genuineness of applicants views and to plumb the depths of an applicant's convictions, and see that conscience is not made a cloak.'[26] In other words, the stiff questioning was to weed out the insincere. Unfortunately for Judge Burgis there was some resentment; he was stabbed, not fatally, by an applicant disgruntled at the decision of the tribunal.[27]

---

[23] 'Objector "Biggest Example of a Coward" –Cries of "Shame" at Newcastle Tribunal', *Northern Echo*, 15 December 1939, p. 7, and, 'Judge Calls CO a Coward, Protests from Gallery', *Manchester Guardian*, 15 December 1939, p. 3.

[24] 'Age Cannot Judge Youth: Quaker Condemns Comment', *Sunday Sun*, 17 December 1939, p. 5.

[25] 'Conscientious Objectors' Tribunal Held in Newcastle on Tuesday', *Durham County Advertiser*, 13 October 1939, p. 5.

[26] 'C.O. Applicants told "Don't Resent Questioning"', *Shields Gazette*, 13 November 1939, p. 6.

[27] 'C.O. Tribunal Chairman Stabbed In Back On Way Home,' *Northern Echo*, 6 April 1940, p. 1.

Judge Richardson's concern for the soldier resulted in controversy at the inaugural sitting of the tribunal with an event that went some way to establishing his reputation. Following a statement from an objector, D P Parry of Northallerton, that he would offer assistance to a civilian but not give first aid to a soldier or do nothing to relieve the suffering of anyone hurt in an air-raid, Judge Richardson retorted: 'I have never heard such a selfish, hard-hearted doctrine as some of these objectors seem to hold. I am certain, as sure as I sit here, that if Christ appeared today he would approve of this war.' People began to boo and hiss so the Judge ordered the court to be cleared, only for there to be a further outbreak of resentment when the Tribunal members returned.[28] The next day the Judge expressed contrition:

> I think I was carried away to say what was inadvisable in the circumstances when I said, 'I am certain, as sure as I sit here, that if Christ were here today he would approve of this war.'
>
> I agree that I am not here to express my views, but to listen to other people's views, whether I agree with them or whether I disagree with them. On the other hand, be it remembered that we had been sitting here all day listening to views of what Christ would do given by a great number of conscientious objectors.
>
> …. we were told not once but many times, that if Christ were here he would relieve the civil population but he would not stir a finger to relieve the sufferings of those in uniform. No doubt statements such as that irritated me as an individual. But, of course, we as a Tribunal are not sitting here to express our own views. If we are satisfied that an objector holds the view he expresses, whether we agree or disagree, we decide his case as we honestly believe it should be decided.
>
> The fact that no prejudice has entered into the decisions of any of the cases we have heard so far is, I think, demonstrated by the fact that in every one of those decisions by the Tribunal has been absolutely unanimous.

---

[28] 'Uproar at Tribunal', *Manchester Guardian*, 12 October 1939, p. 4.

I will say no more but to express my regret that I was carried away by something that was said at the end of a long and somewhat tiring day... [29]

There was no further need for the court to be cleared and Judge Richardson was no doubt heartened by the statement of George Lamb of Middlesbrough: 'Since my registration circumstances have arisen which make it impossible for me to adhere to my earlier decision. I feel in the present time of national emergency individual aims must be sacrificed for the common good.' The Judge responded: 'Rather like a breath of fresh air.'[30]

The tribunal incident caused reaction both locally and nationally. Perhaps surprisingly an observer from the Quaker newspaper, *The Friend*, reported that 'there was a great deal of provocation on both sides,' and:

> The Chairman, who had said he had a son who was a soldier, had listened to five young men say they would give aid to an injured civilian but not to a soldier. It was rather a stupid statement to make in support of Christian principles, but the applicants were being asked questions undoubtedly calculated to obtain some kind of admission that some form of army work was acceptable and to make it appear unreasonable for the applicant not to accept it.[31]

The same observer (noted by the use of identical sentences) was less generous when reporting to *Peace News*:

> It was clear in many cases that the introduction of conscription had started many boys thinking on pacifist lines for the first time. The tribunal seemed to regard anyone who had

---

[29] I am not here to express my views', *Evening Chronicle*, 12 October 1939, p. 1.
[30] 'Vegetarian Objector's "Progress Religion"', *Evening Chronicle*, 13 October 1939, p. 7.
[31] 'A Demonstration at Newcastle,' *The Friend*, 20 October 1939, pp. 852-853.

started thinking on these pacifist lines from the Munich Crisis as being a shirker and without exception were placed on the military register, usually without qualification.[32]

Locally, young people at a South Shields Congregational Church discussed the Judge's remarks, examining as impartially as possible the pros and cons of his position and that of the objector.[33] A.P. of Stockton wrote to his local paper: 'Based on his private convictions such a statement demands our deepest respect. Thousands will agree with him; many there are who will not.'[34] One who did not agree was the Rev. A. Bertram Hodgkins who wrote:

> I was caused spiritual agony as I witnessed young men losing their cases because they were unable to correct the gross misinterpretation of Scripture in the questions asked.
>
> It has been as wrong to omit from the personnel of the tribunal men with theological qualifications as would be to omit from a Medical Board men with medical qualifications.[35]

The aforementioned W.L. felt the decisions were conscientiously arrived at, giving Judge Richardson credit for publicly expressing his regret, and suggested a way of reducing misunderstanding, similar to that of George Lansbury:

> The tribunal, hearing the cases of young men, should have included some younger men. As the tribunal went on I could sense the gap between them all and the young men who came upon the stand. Even I, much younger than any of the tribunal, could feel that I was watching a new generation which I could never hope to fully understand. The older men should

---

[32] 'Bias Shown at Newcastle,' *Peace News*, 20 October 1939, p. 5.
[33] 'Shields Youth Debate Judge Richardson's Remarks', *Shields Gazette*, 24 October 1939, p. 3.
[34] 'Christ and War: Judge Richardson's Remarks', *Northern Echo*, 14 October 1939, p. 4.
[35] 'Readers Discuss – Tribunal Treatment of Objectors', *Evening Chronicle*, 16 October 1939, p. 12.

certainly stay but be supplemented by some people of military age.[36]

Mr Silverman MP (Labour), a conscientious objector in World War I, was moved to raise the incident with the Minister of Labour, Ernest Brown in Parliament, who responded: 'Yes I have been kept informed of the proceedings of local conscientious objectors' tribunals. My information does not lead me to suppose that the chairman referred to is not carrying out his duties in an impartial manner.' Mr. Silverman further asked: 'Does the minister consider that a chairman whose impatience with applicants in front of him is such that he makes remarks for which later he has to publicly apologise is displaying a proper judicial temper?' Mr. Brown responded: 'There was one display of irritability and what I thought was a very handsome apology the next day. I would point out that some of those giving evidence there are not themselves easy to deal with.'[37] The *Yorkshire Evening Post* viewed Judge Richardson's apology somewhat differently:

> …..It should be made clear that he did not apologise for holding such an opinion but for expressing it in a court whose business is to hear other people's views; a fine distinction in more than one sense of the words…..It scarcely needs reiterating that the mere existence of the tribunals, like the oratory in Hyde Park and His Majesty's Opposition, is a practical example of freedom of opinion, that factor in our civilisation which have been suppressed in the territories by those who have made themselves our foes. Our conscientious objectors at least can object. The more important point, however, is that this Newcastle tribunal itself displayed a conscience, so to speak. At the moment of the Judge's apology the tribunal became a microcosm of the British case for the rule of law. An arbitrator had the moral strength to submit himself to his own rules. In totalitarian eyes, which are psychologically as-

---

[36] 'North's First C.O. Tribunal', *Sunday Sun*, 15 October 1939, p. 9.
[37] 'Labour Critic of Newcastle Tribunal Chairman', *Northern Echo*, 20 October 1939, p. 6.

tigmatic, this would be construed derisively as weakness, degeneracy, or some other sign of democratic effeteness. Here, we can say with pride, it was to be supposed as inevitable. We not only let our objectors object; we keep the ring for them.[38]

Mr Brown's comments made it clear that the government were not going to interfere in the running of the tribunals. They had passed the 'conscientious clause' and set up the tribunals to administer it. To many with pacifist sympathies there were flaws in the set-up of the tribunals which negated a fair hearing for objectors. Echoing W.L.'s concerns regarding the age of tribunal members, Dr Arthur Raistrick, a Quaker conscientious objector in the previous war, stated:

It is difficult to see how men in late life, hardened by 40 years or more of political and social tradition and experience, can grasp and evaluate the ideas put forward by a generation born at the end of the last war. It is inevitable that many of the beliefs put forward will cut across the cherished beliefs of the members of the tribunal, and their constant reiteration will produce irritation, manifested in personal remarks. Is it right for a chairman to say: "I do not believe you"? Is this in the tradition of democratic justice? Is it the symbol of an impartial hearing that the chairman should call an applicant a coward, or state on many occasions that "Pacifism makes people intensely selfish"? We recognise the extraordinary difficulty of the service undertaken by the tribunal and we sympathise with their personal sacrifices and losses, both now and in the last war. Our young men are facing public scorn, the accusation of cowardice, the probability of prison and post-war retaliation (similar to the disfranchisement of objectors in 1919) in exactly the same spirit of sacrifice for the good of humanity as those serving in the military. The depth of their convictions is bound to make their testimony take on the colour of obstinacy, when placed before a tribunal. The men whose youth was passed in the pre-Boer War era, whose outlook is entirely different, and whose experience enables them

---

[38] 'Editorial: Tribunal Apology', *Yorkshire Evening Post*, p. 6.

to counter beliefs largely intuitively held by skilled debating methods that must inevitably lead the applicant into an illogical position. Would the general spirit of the country not welcome an attempt to reduce the enormous gap of age and experience between the applicant and his judges?[39]

Citing the low percentage of objectors being registered unconditionally and the variation between localities as evidence that the fault lay with the tribunals and not parliament, Rhys J. Davies, MP, wrote to the *Manchester Guardian*:

Parliament must be disturbed at the reports which appear in the press of the ugly performances of some chairmen and members of tribunals dealing with these very young people. It would seem that every objector is regarded by some tribunals as a felon and must be treated as such...

Those of us who sat through all the proceedings when this legislation was debated in Parliament are satisfied that the clauses covering these objectors are not being administered as the House of Commons intended.

Most of these young men come from humble homes, they are of working-class parents, and only a very few have enjoyed more than elementary education. They are often being catechised by highly educated persons, trained in the rules of evidence, familiar with dialects, and old and cute enough to know how to put awkward questions. There is an obvious unfairness in the disparity of age, education and experience between the parties to begin with, but this seems to have been forgotten by members of some tribunals.

Some chairmen adopt the French legal system, acting as judge and prosecuting counsel combined, demanding that the defendant prove his innocence, always with an eye on the

---

[39] 'Age Cannot Judge Youth: Quaker Condemns Comment', *Sunday Sun*, 17 December 1939, p. 5.

Bastille as it were. They proceed not in search of a man's conscience but in an endeavour to find that he does not possess
what to them is an "infernal nuisance."[40]

Concern that applicants were not being treated fairly was behind
Mr Pethick-Lawrence's criticism of Judge Richardson and others. It
prompted him to enquire if the Minister could review the personnel of
tribunals where; 'there are individuals who regard it as their right, and, I
suppose, their duty, to try and browbeat and bully the applicant.' The
Minister, Mr Ede, MP for South Shields, considered that, on the whole
the tribunals had done a good job and, 'have earned the gratitude of the
House, which placed a very heavy burden on them.'[41] One applicant
who claimed the Newcastle Tribunal had adopted a hostile attitude towards him was R. A. Featherstone of Stockton: 'The pronouncements of
this court have been the subject of national comment, and I feel I would
receive a fairer hearing from the Appellate Tribunal.'[42] His appeal was
dismissed.

Judge Richardson could be comforted by the comments of Mr
David Adams, MP for Consett, in his counter to Mr Pethick-Lawrence:

In so far as my experience in the North of England is concerned, regarding the tribunals to which reference has been
made, I would say that these have been conducted extraordi-
narily fairly and dispassionately, and, indeed, generously so
far as judgments are concerned. I happen to know the judge,
hailing from Newcastle, to whom reference has been made. I
can only conclude that his irregular observations were merely
a lapse, because he has a reputation for great fairness and consideration. We can only conclude that he was carried away.[43]

This was not the best defence of his behaviour. County-Court
Judges should not get 'carried away.' However, he could derive further
comfort from a report that of eight conscientious objectors who had

[40] 'Letters to the Editor – Rhys J. Davies, House of Commons', *Manchester Guardian*, 21 December 1939, p. 12.
[41] 'Ministry of Labour and National Service', *Hansard*, HC Deb. 22 February 1940, Vol. 357 cc1581-631.
[42] 'N.E. Men Appeal Against War Service Decisions,' *Evening Chronicle* 20 December 1939, p. 3.
[43] 'Ministry of Labour and National Service', *Hansard*, HC Deb. 22 February 1940 vol. 357 cc1581-631.

appealed against the previous decisions of the Newcastle Tribunal, seven had, at their own request, joined combatant or non-combatant branches of the services.[44] This led Judge Richardson to comment that some should carefully consider their position before appearing before the tribunal:

> One thing these decisions indicate is that members of this Tribunal are not severe in their decisions. Another is that a number of people seem to be finding that their objections are not so decided as they appeared before the Tribunal.[45]

He could perhaps have drawn the greatest comfort from the most unlikely source, *Peace News*. Previously critical, its observer commented in December 1939 that: 'the experience gained in previous sittings has produced an attitude of maturity, and tribunal and applicants appeared to meet with an improved understanding of each other's difficulties.[46] Of less comfort to him would have been the support offered to him from 'Cassandra', writing a letter to the press:

I had feared that the Tribunal dealing with COs was to have been an impartial and objective enquiry into the genuineness of the beliefs of the applicants. I was pleasantly surprised however to find that this is not to be the case. The object of the tribunal is instead to apply a moral censorship to the beliefs of the objectors and to bully these shirkers into joining the Services.[47]

[44] 'C.O.s Join the Services', *Manchester Guardian*, 5 December 1940, p. 10.
[45] Barker, *Conscience, Government and War*, p. 42.
[46] 'How Objectors are Faring Before Local Tribunals,' *Peace News*, 15 December 1939, p. 12.
[47] 'Will Conscientious Objectors Give Up Their Jobs After The War?' *Sunderland Echo*, 16 October 1939, p. 5.

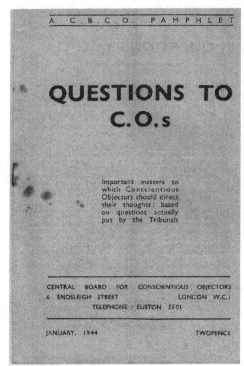

Questions To C.O.s, CBCO, January 1944

The editor of *Peace News* was concerned that many young men did not realise how deep their objection to war was, or, if they did they would express it so badly and give an unsympathetic tribunal an entirely wrong impression.[48] To reduce the apparent disparity faced by applicants, the CBCO issued a pamphlet, *Questions to C.O.s*. This contained a wide selection of over 100 questions from local and appellate tribunals, including Newcastle. The harsh questions were both general and technical and further demonstrate that they were a way of testing an applicant's resolve and strength of objection: Don't you think yours is a very selfish religion?; If you saw a wounded soldier in the street, would you help him?; Are you doing fire-watching?; Aren't you prepared to take all and give nothing?; Don't you know you are talking rubbish?; Do you eat food convoyed to you by the Navy?; What are you prepared to do for the community?; etc. The pamphlet also advised that by far the best way of getting to know the tribunal procedure was to attend one of its sittings.

A number of the peace organisations and groups offered assistance, mainly through the establishment of Advisory Bureaux for Conscientious Objectors, in most major towns in the North-East.[49]In addition, in South Shields a letter to the press from eleven individuals, from religious, political and other backgrounds, offered to assist objectors who were untrained in argument and unused to public appearance, to do justice to their case. Not all of them agreed on the

---

[48] 'From the Editor's Notebook,' *Peace News*, 27 October 1939, p. 3.
[49] *Peace News*, 6 October 1939, p. 4.

issue of pacifism but felt it important to maintain civil liberties in wartime. They considered conscientious objectors should receive the fair treatment stipulated by the government and that such a right was one of the main reasons for fighting the War.[50] Not all the paper's correspondents favoured the offer. R. Langley was concerned that their public-spirited offer could be misused by those whose only concern was 'saving their skins.' He considered:

> One must have a very deep-seated objection to war to out-weigh the moral duty of a Christian - to prevent in the only possible way a continuance of the atrocities committed in Germany in the last seven years... there have been numerous cases of so-called COs cloaking their real character behind the plea of conscientious objection, and, if anyone by reason of superior qualifications were to present successfully the case of one of the pseudo-moralists, it would be a most regrettable stigma on a democratic institution.[51]

The feelings of many were summed up by 'Parent':

> The clergy claim and get exemption from the fighting forces and they give their signatures to a letter offering to help the Conscientious Objector fight the tribunals camouflaging their action under the name of sympathy and help...On examining the list of signatories, we find that the majority are bachelors and childless married men. Our sons are having to do the fighting to protect these men so that they can be fed and sleep in their beds at night with every comfort, while our sons sleep on floors, and after that, what? How much of this conscience is evasion of service, as everyone has a conscientious objection to killing his fellow man? ...The clergy, like the French priests, have an obligation and should be in the fighting forces.[52]

Despite differing views held about and by conscientious objectors it remained the concern of the government that the tribunals were seen

[50] 'Letter – Conscientious Objectors' Tribunals', *Shields Gazette*, 22 January 1940, p. 3.
[51] 'Letter – Non-Conscientious Objectors', *Shields Gazette*, 23 January 1940, p. 4.
[52] 'Letter – Are Conscientious Objectors Genuine?', *Shields Gazette*, 29 January 1940, p. 4.

to be acting impartially, if for no other reason than to allow it to get on with the job of prosecuting the war free from criticisms in parliament.

How Did the Newcastle Tribunal Perform?

If the criticism of alleged bias against objectors, levelled specifically at Judge Richardson, was justified then it would be reflected in the statistics regarding the tribunal's decisions.

The tribunal's performance in its processing of objectors can be compared with other tribunals using statistics held in the National Archives.[53] The statistics are complete in detail in relation to the decisions made by local tribunals only up to the end of 1944 and again up to the end of 1948. No figures are available exclusively for 1945. Table 4 compares the Newcastle Tribunal with the national position regarding the categorisation of their decisions. The period up to the end of 1948 was chosen as it includes the whole war period and decisions made under both the 1939 and 1941 National Service Acts. Also, only 6% of the total registrations from 1939 up to the end of 1948 occurred after 1944.

The most advantageous decision to an objector was to be unconditionally registered. At the Northumberland and Durham Tribunal, this occurred at a rate of over twice the national average, and it ranked fourth highest in this respect of the nineteen tribunals. The equivalent figure for the nearest tribunal, the North Eastern at Leeds, was 2.5%. Equally the worst scenario for the objector was to be removed from the register. The national figure of almost 30% was approximately twice the percentage for the First World War, which Ceadel attributes to the flexibility of alternative service on offer encouraging marginal objectors to come forward, thus requiring tribunals to be stricter.[54] It was statistically less likely to happen at the Newcastle Tribunal than nationally, as it was for those liable to be called-up for non-combatant duties. 47.5% of objectors appearing before the Northumberland and Durham Tribunal were conditionally or unconditionally registered, compared to 42.6% nationally, a position bettered by only four tribunals.

---

[53] 'Ministry of Labour and National Services', LAB6/405, National Archives, Kew, London.
[54] Ceadel, *Pacifism in Britain 1914-1945*, p. 302.

Decisions of Local Tribunals to 31 December 1948

	Registered Unconditionally	Registered Conditionally	Non-Combat. Duties	Removed	Total
Northumberland & Durham	114(9.9%)	431(37.6%)	288(25.1%)	315(27.4%)	1148
National Average	2937(4.7%)	23638(37.9%)	17231(27.7%)	18495(29.7%)	62301
Highest	14.7% SW Scotland	65.1% Midlands	47.2% Cumberland	55.5% SW Scotland	
Lowest	1.1% London 1	15.3% N. Scotland	15% SW Scotland	11.5% SW England	

Source: Ministry of Labour and National Service, LAB 6/405, National Archives, Kew.

A tribunal member writing in *The Friend* noted that after Dunkirk many who would previously have been objectors had chosen to serve, while those who had persisted in their attitude were regarded with growing suspicion and resentment. The result was tribunals being less disposed to granting unconditional exemption, a claim which cannot be statistically verified.[55] The statement cannot be tested regarding the Newcastle Tribunal due to the lack of tribunal records and decreasing press coverage of the tribunal as the war progressed.

Another indicator of the effectiveness of the local tribunals would be the proportion of objectors who appealed to the Appellate Tribunals and the outcome of those appeals. There was no appellate tribunal specifically for the Northumberland and Durham Tribunal on which to make a statistical assessment. Appeals were initially heard in London and later by the Northern England Appellate Tribunal, which also covered the local tribunals at Leeds, Manchester, and, Cumberland and Westmoreland.

[55] 'What a Tribunal Member Thinks of C.O.s,' *The Friend*, 4 February 1944, pp. 69-70.

The Tribunal and Religious Objectors

Whilst religion was the most common reason given for a conscientious objection there was a wide disparity in the propensity of members of different denominations to apply for exemption. The greatest number of applications came from Quakers and Jehovah's Witnesses who suffered differing fates at the hands of the Newcastle Tribunal.

Eighty-eight percent of Quakers who went before the tribunal were registered conditionally or unconditionally, over 40% more than the average for the tribunal. Only one was unconditionally removed from the register and that was because he did not register for National Service. Some Quakers were also not required to attend the tribunal as they had already joined the FAU and notified the tribunal accordingly. The accepted Quaker tradition of pacifism and humanitarian war service was undoubtedly a factor, but the organisation's hierarchy were keen to ensure that its members presented themselves to the tribunals as reasonable:

> We would again urge every man who appears before a local or appellate tribunal never to forget that the exemption which he legally claims is in itself a secondary matter. He makes his application as a law-abiding citizen witnessing to a certain way of life, his fellow-countrymen having recognised that he is entitled to have convictions on the matter and he should not be compelled to do what he believes is wrong. Application for unconditional or conditional exemption is incidental to the giving of this testimony. All that is necessary being that the man should be certain to ask no more and no less than he can accept.[56]

Conversely only 19% of Jehovah's Witnesses who went before the tribunal were registered conditionally or unconditionally. 81% of Jehovah's Witnesses either removed from the Register unconditionally or registered for non-combatant duties, compared to the tribunal average of 52.5%. Only one Jehovah's Witness received unconditional exemption. This disparity is likely to be even greater as the tribunal decisions involving other Jehovah's Witnesses, whilst not known, are likely to involve being either removed from the register or be liable for non-combatant

---

[56] 'Commentary,' *The Friend*, 15 December 1939, p. 1003.

duties. When compiling the database of conscientious objectors, it was apparent that applicants who were doing, or expressed a willingness to do, work of national importance were more likely to receive a favourable decision from the Newcastle Tribunal, and indeed from the Leeds Tribunal. This was the case with the few Jehovah's Witnesses registered conditionally or unconditionally.

There is statistical evidence to suggest that there may have been an unfair bias against Jehovah's Witnesses in the tribunal decisions. This organisation presented the tribunal with specific problems. As an absolutist organisation, its members would not countenance any co-operation with the war effort. Their conviction was that a direction to any work was freeing up another man, or woman, for war service. Also, their general unwillingness to do work considered to be of national importance meant they were less likely to receive a favourable response from the tribunal. This record was highlighted by Mr Pethick-Lawrence referring to a case heard at Newcastle:

> … but possibly the Committee may be tempted to smile at the name of the society which the applicant claimed to represent. He said that he belonged to "Jehovah's Witnesses," and apparently, he had given up his work and had spent a month going round delivering tracts. The whole attitude of the tribunal was to try and deride what he was doing and to hold him up to ridicule…He had been a member for years, but he had been doing this work, I understand, for the last few months. I am not stressing that fact unnecessarily, but my point is that this man was, rightly or wrongly, quite clearly from the evidence, sincere. I do not put it higher than that, and the tribunal devoted itself to ridicule what this man believed to be his definite lot, and, not only that, they refused him exemption. The man who writes to me on behalf of this organisation says that in the other courts of the country the views of those who are definite members of the organisation have been accepted and their objection upheld, but in this particular court all the cases that have been brought forward have been turned down.[57]

---

[57] 'Ministry of Labour and National Service', *Hansard*, HC Deb. 22 February 1940 vol. 357 cc1581-631.

The remark regarding how long the applicant had been a member reflected a strong feeling in the country that many had joined the organisation only at the beginning of the war as a means of avoiding military service (Membership rose from 5,945 in 1939 to 11,622 in 1,945). This was a view consistently expounded by Judge Richardson: 'The incidence of members of Jehovah's Witnesses who have become whole-time servants of the sect since the outbreak of war, suggested an organised move to substantiate a claim of conscientious objection;'[58] also, 'That is the danger of this sect. anyone can come and join it, if just to show reason for shirking service;'[59] and, 'An easy refuge for those who wish to shirk their duty. It is remarkable how many young people have joined this sect since war broke out.'[60] To Judge Franklin at the Manchester Tribunal, they were also an anathema. He told one unemployed Witness, 'Isn't it time you took your coat off and kept the old lady instead of lounging about selling books on behalf of an American gang.'[61] Judge Stewart at the Leeds Tribunal, on the same theme, concluded that, 'A minister of Jehovah's Witnesses is nothing more than a pedlar's licence enabling the holder to purvey the publications of the society.'[62] They may have got some sympathy at the South-West Tribunal under Judge Wethered, who, according to Barker had a respect for Second Adventists as none claimed a total right of citizenship and were therefore logical in refusing to fight for a country to which they owed no loyalty.[63] Judge Richardson clearly had no such respect and reserved his most controversial remarks for them, describing them as a 'set of cranks'.[64] This was a relatively mild comment in comparison to some made later but nevertheless was enough to warrant a referral to the National Council for Civil Liberties.

The Judge's next comment to make the news led to the MP for Middlesbrough East, Mr Alfred Edwards, requesting that Richardson be removed from his position owing to his violent attack on Jehovah's Witnesses:

---

[58] 'Judge on "Poisonous Christians"', *North-East Gazette*, 15 July 1940, p. 6.
[59] 'Horrible Pacifists Teaching Boys', *North-East Gazette*, 16 August 1940, p. 6.
[60] 'Easy Refuge for Shirkers: Girl C.O. Left Land Work', *Evening Chronicle*, 18 March 1943, p. 8.
[61] 'Judge Told Not To Sneer', *Shields Gazette*, 17 August 1940, p. 6.
[62] 'Members as C.O.s', *Yorkshire Evening Post*, 17 January 1941, p. 5.
[63] Barker, *Conscience, Government and War*, pp. 37-38.
[64] 'Billingham Research Chemist Registered', *Northern Echo*, 7 December 1939, p. 5.

You people don't do a ha'porth of good to anyone in this world. I have the greatest contempt for you people. I think you must be mad. I don't believe that a man's full job is done if he does nothing but preach. He is not copying Our Lord if he does nothing but that.[65]

Mr Edwards found no support from the Parliamentary Secretary to the Minister of Labour, who whilst acknowledging two previous representations made regarding Judge Richardson, 'has received a number of tributes to his fairness and to that of his tribunal, in which he has every confidence.'[66] There was also little support in letters to the newspapers. One correspondent said: 'I and many others would like him to ask the House to give him more power to deal with conscientious objectors and make them take up stretcher-bearing in the RAMC or recall the last war methods of working camps.' Another suggested:

Mr. Edwards would be doing the public a greater service if he drew attention to the behaviour of some members of Jehovah's Witnesses. Their door-to-door visitations, expounding the virtues of their religion, are trying to the householder, who sometimes finds the Witness's foot within the door so that it cannot be banged in his face, while he says his piece. It gives me the satisfaction to know that certain of Jehovah's Witnesses have to listen to the intelligent criticism of Judge Richardson.[67]

Judge Richardson's criticism of Jehovah's Witnesses did not mellow as the war progressed, nor did he differentiate between male and female Witnesses. He responded to Dorothy Reeve's statement that she had made preaching the Gospel her life's work in typical style: 'In my opinion that is just rot and rubbish. You are not doing anything, just going about talking. You useless woman!'[68] In 1944 the Judge, in response to a statement that they could not fight, gave his view on Christianity: 'Thousands

[65] 'Judge's Contempt for Jehovah's Witnesses', *Northern Echo*, 12 April 1940, p. 4.
[66] 'Newcastle Tribunal, Minister's Confidence in its Fairness', *Manchester Guardian*, 4 May 1940, p. 9.
[67] 'Middlesbrough MP and the removal of Judge Richardson', *Northern Echo*, 19 April 1940, p. 6, and, 'Miner Critic of Jehovah's Witnesses', *Northern Echo*, 20 April 1940, p. 6.
[68] 'You Useless Woman: Judge to "Witness" C.O.', *Evening Chronicle*, 26 January 1943, p. 4.

of Christians are fighting in this war as a holy crusade, and I think they are truer Christians than those who believe in your nonsense.'[69] This was a view expounded on more than one occasion. When Raymond Bohenna of South Shields stated that taking up military service would be violating his conscience to God, Judge Richardson responded; 'Yes, but there are thousands of Christians fighting in this war and doing all they can for their country – treating war as a crusade.'[70] Similarly he described 'God fearing men, fighting the war as a crusade' to Joseph Dixon.[71] Also to Royston Jones who felt that the RAMC was part of the war machine: 'Part and parcel of a great crusade.'[72] He did not, however, go as far as Judge Franklin of the Manchester Tribunal: 'I want you and your Witnesses to leave the room. I don't want other people contaminated by your presence.'[73]

The question of what to do with Jehovah's Witnesses exercised all the tribunals. A tribunal member writing in *The Friend* referred to them as the 'outstanding problem for the tribunal,' and:

They are invariably aggressive and present their case in a stereotyped formula which smacks of mass production. One man will declare outright that he is not a pacifist, another will say that he has given years of service to the movement and yet profess ignorance of the most elementary matters connected with it, while a third will state he has no associations with any church or religious body and only admit after cross-examination that he is a Witness. It seems beyond the wit of man to devise a test of sincerity which would serve as a guide through such a labyrinth...... Is the subversive propaganda of the Jehovah's Witnesses the result of some influence behind it which is hostile to the state?[74]

---

[69] 'Objected to War Service', *North-East Gazette*, 28 March 1944, p. 5.
[70] 'Christians are Treating War as a Crusade', *Shields Gazette*, 18 January 1940, p. 4.
[71] 'Tees-side C.O.s Pleas: Tribunal's Decisions', *North-East Gazette*, 18 January 1940, p. 5.
[72] 'Shields Preacher an Objector', *Shields Gazette*, 25 May 1940, p. 3.
[73] 'The Smacking Judge Dead', *Northern Daily Mail*, 18 June 1942, p. 8.
[74] 'What a Tribunal Member Thinks of C.O.s,' *The Friend*, 4 February 1944, pp. 69-70.

Had this tribunal member expressed the reasons why Jehovah's Witnesses fared so badly at the tribunals, or was it the case, as Smithies observes, that: 'Jehovah's Witnesses did not possess the reserves of powerful political support (or any reserves for that matter) on which most pacifist and socialist objectors were able to draw.'[75] Trow goes further in speculating: 'it is probable that the large numbers of them in jail; - over 200 by April 1942 – resulted from their annoying habit of 'door-stepping' in peacetime.'[76]

Judge Richardson did not reserve his controversial comments only for Jehovah's Witnesses, commenting unfavourably on the views of members of other religious denominations. To Methodist Hazel Kerr he commented, 'If you carry your argument to its logical conclusion you should eat nothing and starve yourself to death. That might be the most useful thing you could do.'[77] A candidate for the Methodist Ministry who informed Judge Richardson that many Methodists were conscientious objectors was told, 'apart from the Methodists we have scarcely had a conscientious objector today.' The judge had previously commented: 'you are a very ignorant young man who thinks he has got a little knowledge. I advise that you read a bit before you join the ministry or you may do a tremendous amount of harm not only among your own congregation but outside.'[78] Members of the Plymouth Brethren, 65% of whom were recommended by the tribunal for non-combatant duties, were often the subject of strong comment. William Webb was told before he was conditionally registered: 'Yours is a horrible religion to my mind, but you are entitled to hold your views on it. It is not much good preaching the Gospel if you don't act it. You are entitled to your views, but they are poisonous.'[79] He was, however, prepared to praise a member when it was warranted. Regarding John Robert Boggon of South Shields, who had been a missionary in India for three years and, currently working full-time as an ARP ambulance worker, he declared: 'We feel in this case that Mr Boggan, in view of his history, will do everything he can for

---

[75] Edward Smithies, *Crime in Wartime: A Social History of Crime in World War II* (London: George Allen and Unwin, 1982) p. 19.
[76] M. J. Trow, *Underworld Britain in the Second World War* (Barnsley: Pen & Sword, 2008), p. 38.
[77] 'Judge's "Why Eat?" to C.O.', *Evening Chronicle*, 12 May 1942, p. 4.
[78] 'Judge Calls C.O. a Coward, Protests from Gallery', *Manchester Guardian*, 15 December 1939, p. 3.
[79] '"Poisonous Views" – Newcastle Criticism at Objectors' Court', *Northern Echo*, 20 March 1940, p. 7.

his country. He is as fine a type of conscientious objector as we have had in this court, perhaps the finest.'[80] Such praise, whilst rare was not unique, further illustrating that the tribunal was more sympathetic to those prepared to do war work. Objector Jack Tomblin was told, 'From the evidence of the letters here, what you have done today is the conduct of a hero. Thank you, Mr Tomblin.'[81] Controversial criticism was, however, rarely far away as he remarked: 'All Christadelphians should be put on a desert island and be left to stew. Middlesbrough seems one of the centres of this poisonous body.'[82] This led to the *Daily Mirror* commenting:

> For sheer bad tempered, bigoted recklessness, allow me to introduce Judge Richardson......This judicial swash-buckler regularly hits the news with his foolish and ill-timed jibes. His latest effort is well down to standard.[83]

Judge Richardson's earlier comments have to be placed in the context of a time when the country was in great danger and its armed forces and civilians were suffering more injury than they were able to inflict on the enemy. Many of the comments made were in response to statements which seemed unreasonable and uncompromising at such a time, and which caused disdain amongst many of the population. The most common of these related to the assisting of wounded soldiers, further examples being, 'I would not help my brother if he was wearing khaki,'[84] and, 'Christ would not have done so.'[85] Others related to a refusal to help their family if attacked, particularly women, such as the statement of Joseph Horton White that he would not defend his mother if she was attacked unless she was a member of Jehovah's Witnesses.[86] The comments which caused the greatest anger were those which gave the impression that conscientious objectors were prepared to benefit

---

[80] 'Shields Man "Finest Type of C.O.", *Shields Gazette*, 16 September 1940, p. 1.
[81] 'Conduct of a Hero', *Northern Echo*, 18 April 1940, p. 5.
[82] 'Tribunal Comment on Christadelphians', *Manchester Guardian*, 20 June 1940, p.9.
[83] Barker, *Conscience, Government and War*, p. 41.
[84] 'Uproar at Tribunal', *Manchester Guardian*, 12 October 1939, p. 4.
[85] 'Conscientious Objectors' Tribunal', *Durham County Advertiser*, 20 October 1939, p. 8.
[86] 'Shields Objector Taken Off Register', *Shields Gazette*, 20 May 1941, p. 3.

from the risks taken by others but give nothing in return. Such a comment was made by T H Carrick: 'I don't think I owe anything to the country for what it has done.'[87]

The questions from the members of the tribunal were often likely to elicit such unpopular responses. The *Sunday Sun* reporter whose comments opened this chapter reminded his readers: 'These courts have a great responsibility and a vital principle to uphold – the principle of liberty of conscience. We remain a great people only so long as we tolerate and protect minority opinion.' He perceived the operation of the Newcastle Tribunal as follows:

> I heard about a dozen cases and the abiding impression I took away was the strict impartiality and fairness of all the decisions reached, though I think objection could be taken legitimately to some of the type of questions put to the objectors. I disagree profoundly with the standpoint of the conscientious objectors, but at the same time, I draw the line at asking them whether they would give a cup of water to a dying man in uniform. It's not cricket and it gets one nowhere......
> ......Judge Richardson listens closely and courteously to all that is said, although he twice betrayed touches of irritation. I felt that whatever verdict he reached would be scrupulously fair and in accordance with the facts. Sir Luke Thompson took the closest interest in everything that went on. While I admired his determination to get at the facts, I could not always follow his reasoning, nor, on occasion, did I feel he was particularly happy in his Biblical research.
> To sum up, my impressions were that, with one possible exception, the applicants were honest and sincere and no possible fault could be found with the court's findings.
> ...... if I were an objector with a record of genuine religious conviction, I would go before these men confident that I would not be asked to do anything repugnant to beliefs I held precious.[88]

[87] 'Happier Born on a Cannibal Island', *Shields Gazette*, 20 March 1941, p. 1.
[88] 'Lewis Ashley's Pageant: Dissenting Consciences', *Sunday Sun*, 28 January 1940, p. 2.

His final comment presents a different impression to that conveyed earlier by the observer for *Peace News*. These comments do, however, further demonstrate the difficulty that the tribunal had in determining the sincerity of an applicant's conscience. The harsh questions, of a nature similar to those adopted by all the tribunals, may have been an honest attempt to filter out the insincere, but they were perhaps not the best way to establish the sincerity of religious belief. The reference to Sir Luke Thompson illustrates the point. Sir Luke, like many members of other tribunals, was a lay preacher, but no theologian. It was not the nature of the questions, however, which resulted in criticism of Judge Richardson but his response to some of the answers.

Not every observer was confident of conscientious objectors receiving fair treatment from the Newcastle Tribunal. E. Goddard, writing to the *Newcastle Daily Journal* on 28 August 1940 saw things differently:

I may say, as one who loves freedom of thought and expression, I was not enamoured in the least. The law was framed to grant exemption to those who had a conscientious objection to military service of any sort, but, the surprising thing to me was not one obtained that exemption, although they seemed to merit it. There were some fine intellectual young men who seemed very earnest and sincere in their beliefs, but members of the tribunal seemed to think it their duty to prevent exemption instead of granting it...[89]

Criticism of tribunals and the utterance of controversial comments were not reserved for Newcastle and Judge Richardson. Mr Pethick-Lawrence also referred to the unjudicial remarks of Sir Edmund Phipps at the London Tribunal referring to objectors as, 'these miserable creatures,' and their statements as 'tosh,' commenting:

I can quite understand that these people, whose views are peculiar, seem very odd, and naturally provoke a great deal of resentment in the minds of people whose attitude is more in accord with the majority opinion in this country; but people

---

[89] Reproduced in *The Wora*, Vol. 2, No. 4, November 1940, p. 45.

sitting in a judicial capacity ought to restrain themselves from giving vent to these unjudicial remarks.[90]

His chairman, Judge Hargreaves, was quoted in the *Daily Herald* on 2 November 1939: 'Pontius Pilate was the first pacifist because he did not resist evil': a remark the paper considered to be foolish, frivolous and cheap. The Mass Observation author conversely considered that it may have been humorously intended to jerk the conscientious objector out of easily repeating the well-worn Christian argument for pacifism.[91] Another challenger of tradition was Judge Stewart, chairman of the Leeds Tribunal. He was described by the *Peace News* observer of the first sitting of his tribunal as, 'wishing to be just to the objector but having no sympathy for his refusal to fight,' and his uncomfortable colleagues giving the impression that, 'the conscientious objector was to them a strange animal outside their personal experience.'[92] Stewart accused a Quaker member of the Halle Orchestra of being 'subversive' and of 'trying to put a spoke in the wheel of the national effort,' when he followed the Quaker tradition of refusing to serve in the RAMC or Pay Corps as part of the war machine.[93] Adopting a more bullying approach to an objector, he stated: 'I am not prepared to sit here and be talked to by an infant of twenty on these sort of lines indefinitely. It is unadulterated tripe and nonsense.'[94]

In dismissing the application of Percy Potter of York, he referred to his occupation as a credit check manager as, 'a parasitic growth which many people considered should not be permitted.'[95] When he asked a member of the Assemblies of God whose father and uncle had been conscientious objectors in the previous war 'Is it hereditary?' a fellow tribunal member added 'Is it infectious?'[96] With such comments it was inevitable that there would be complaints about him in Parliament. This came from Mr McGovern MP when the judge accused an applicant of, 'expressing the views of a traitor to the country's interests.'[97]

---

[90] 'The Conscientious Objector', *Hansard*, HL Deb. 02 March 1943 vol. 126 cc358-92.
[91] Mass Observation File Report No. 312, p. 162.
[92] 'First Session of the Leeds Tribunal,' *Peace News*, 3 November 1939, p. 5.
[93] Mass Observation File Report No. 312, Conscientious Objectors, p. 163.
[94] Hayes, *Challenge of Conscientious*, p. 43.
[95] 'I Cannot Kill Anybody', *Yorkshire Evening Post*, 24 June 1940, p. 4.
[96] Young Man Who Objected To Killing', *Yorkshire Evening Post*, 29 December 1939, p. 8.
[97] 'M.P. and Tribunal Judge', *Northern Daily Mail*, 22 February 1940, p. 3.

An attitude even more worrying to objectors was displayed by Sir James Baillee (London) who considered, 'that in his opinion many of the conscientious objectors really mean they are afraid of being killed themselves when they say that they don't want to kill other people.'[98]

Tribunal members were not afraid to express their views outside of the tribunal setting. Alderman Aveling of the North-West Tribunal informed the Chamber of Commerce: 'If you had to sit and listen to what we had to listen to, and not had a sense of humour, you would be worried to death and think we, as a country, were going to the devil.'[99] Alderman Nicholson, in his role as a member of the Agriculture Committee, addressing a dig for victory campaign meeting in Durham, expressed sentiments similar to many contributors to the press: 'The conscientious objector who was not prepared to dig in order to provide food, but considered he was entitled to consume the food produced by others, would not be allowed to exist in any other part of the world but Britain.'[100]

Judge Richardson made his views known when he addressed Hexham Rotary Club, suggesting firms and businesses who had employed conscientious objectors who had done nothing for their country during the present struggle should be 'cold shouldered', leading to the remarks, detailed earlier, of the Duke of Bedford:

> To my mind, all those Conscientious Objectors who have refused to do anything to help the war effort, should be made to take in their own washing after the war. Then their own selfishness towards this country in a time of emergency might be brought home to them. If Hitler came these people would not have their jobs, and because other people make it possible for them to be in comfortable positions at the end of the war, I don't see why they should be allowed to take advantage of the sacrifices which others have made for them. Many of those who had obtained total exemption on conscience grounds were doing nothing for their country at the present time, and a lot of them were keeping jobs in which they were earning promotion. I feel very strongly against this.

[98] Hayes, *Challenge of Conscientious*, p. 43.
[99] Ibid.
[100] 'Food For The Objector', *Sunderland Echo*, 8 January 1942, p. 4.

He said it had been his duty, he could not say privilege, to preside on the tribunal and see the sort of people who were conscientious objectors: 'The young women were more poisonous than the young men – they were so self-assertive.' Referring to objectors generally he said: 'The greater proportion were not genuine Conscientious Objectors at all, and were nothing more or less than shirkers, and there were those who used so-called religious societies as a cloak to make an endeavour to get out of doing anything for his or her country in the present emergency.' Referring to Jehovah's Witnesses he said that as far as he could see one of their chief things was that they must not fight or do anything for their country, but to wait and fight for theocracy, stating: 'How are you going to fight, or learn to do anything with such a selfish attitude towards your fellow men or women, I don't know. In the main those societies are composed of very ignorant, yet very dangerous people, who go about getting a hold on people who had not a great deal of brain.' He continued:

> Some Conscientious Objectors held most pernicious and selfish views, but if they were genuine, no matter how pernicious they may be, they had to have exemption. And I think it is right that we should have the right to conscientious objection, because after all it does show we are a free nation which gives freedom to the individual whatever views he or she may have. That is of course quite peculiar to this country, and I am not saying one word against it, but their arguments for conscientious objection, it seems to me, are very largely false.
> … I sometimes wonder how the Conscientious Objector would have justified the action of the good Samaritan if he had come by a little sooner while the robbing was taking place, and whether he would have called it a Christ-like thing to pass by on the other side"

But there were a few Conscientious Objectors, such as the Quakers, who, although they would not fight or wear uniform, were prepared to face danger in the front line as members of ambulance units. One cannot help admiring them for standing by their principles.

He also referred to those willing to work on the land, do forestry work, or any work to help the national effort in a positive light. He concluded: 'You will note from my remarks that I have not a very high opinion of the CO, yet sitting as chairman to the Tribunal, I try to the best of my ability to be fair, and above all I do try to keep my temper to the end of the day.'[101] It is poignant that the newspaper, on the same day, carried news that his son had been awarded the Military Cross for bravery in North Africa.[102]

To R.C. of Newcastle the Judge's comments were not welcome:

I am not a CO and have never seen Judge Richardson. The latter has come into prominence through his inveterate hatred of CO's. This is a dangerous attitude to adopt and the antithesis of our traditional administration of British justice. A great many of us don't agree with the CO mentally, but wish to differentiate between the genuine ones and the imposters. To Judge Richardson, they are all bad. He is obviously not the man for the position of chairman of the tribunal.[103]

Judge Richardson did of course continue as chairman of the tribunal and, one year after his speech to the Rotary Club, outlined his views in the tribunal of what the future should hold for conscientious objectors: 'You people who have got or may get exemption, it is hoped and trusted, that you won't get a job anywhere when the war is over, so long as there is one man who has done his bit at the front still unemployed.'[104]

Conclusion

Judge Richardson was the most criticised chairman, both at the time and in subsequent literature, an infamy which gives further justification for examining conscientious objection in North-East England. In assessing Judge Richardson's performance as Chairman, his regular apparently

---

[101] 'Few C.O.s Genuine: Most are Shirkers says Judge at Hexham', *Hexham Courant*, 26 September 1942, p. 1.

[102] 'Judge's Son Wins M.C. Emulates Godfather', *Hexham Courant*, 26 September 1942, p. 1.

[103] 'Judge and the COs', *Durham County Advertiser*, 16 October 1942, p. 4.

[104] 'C.O.s Rebuked by Judge Richardson', *Evening Chronicle*, 2 September 1943, p. 5.

outrageous comments have to be judged in relation to the decisions arrived at. They also have to be taken alongside the harsh questioning, the purpose of which was to provoke people to see that they were genuine in their resolve. He was not alone among tribunal chairmen in making such comments. Many of his more sensational outbursts were in relation to cases where exemption was given, suggesting that his manners did not often transfer to his decisions. That he was the chairman most criticised by Members of Parliament does not mean that the decisions of his tribunal were the least reasonable. He clearly was, as Juliet Gardiner claims, 'notorious,' yet his intemperance did not seem to actually affect the fairness of his decisions. The statistics of the Ministry of Labour bear this out when the decisions of the Newcastle Tribunal are compared with other tribunals, and, assuming, as both Barker and Hayes state, that the tribunals generally did a good job. The exception was the Jehovah's Witnesses who Richardson clearly, judging both from his comments and decisions, had no time for. There were certainly grounds to criticise many of his decisions regarding Jehovah's Witnesses but there were few outside the organisation having any sympathy for their beliefs, and few, including members of the tribunal, who understood the reasons for their absolutist stance. Newcastle was not the only tribunal where Jehovah's Witnesses were to receive harsh treatment.

It is also clear from his comments, especially those made to Hexham Rotary Club, that he was not impartial in his views of conscientious objectors. His partiality was undoubtedly influenced by the history and experiences of his family. Again, there is no evidence that this generally influenced the tribunal's decisions, apart from the previously mentioned attitude to Jehovah's Witnesses. His statement that exemptions were granted despite his personal views is most likely correct. The presence on the tribunal of a well-known pacifist from May 1943 may also have helped ensure that decisions were not influenced by partiality.

From reports, it would seem that many of the injudicious comments were provoked by the applicants, although this does not excuse him. Also, the remarks have to be judged in the context of the time in which they were made and not by the standards of today. There were more published letters to the press in support of Judge Richardson than against, and some of these contained comments more extreme than those made by the judge. An example of the emotions prevalent at the lowest ebb of the country's fortunes, is to be found in the following extracts from an article by B. C. McDonald and which provide a background to, but not an excuse for, many of the injudicious comments made by tribunal chairmen:

> Pacifism is a creed. It is a state of mind. If one reviews the statements made by pacifists before the Conscientious Objectors' Tribunals it is impossible to escape the conclusion that the pacifist suffers from some psychological ailment. Many are clearly moved by no more pious desire than to escape military service. But taking those who do evince a show of having some sort of genuine objection, there is an extraordinary conflict of consciences. This arises from the fact that the philosophy of pacifism is a retreat from reality, a mental cul-de-sac. It has been suggested that the conscientious objectors' tribunals are unfair. I do not take this view. It is true that remarks have been made that imply partiality. These tribunals have an onerous and disagreeable duty to perform. The morality of some of these so-called pacifists is so utterly warped that no normal man could listen to them without comment.
> I say without hesitation that these tribunals are not nearly stringent enough in their examinations. I will go further and say that only in very rare cases should complete exemption be granted. If considered desirable, exempt from combat service certainly...[105]

No matter how notorious he was, those in a position of authority did not think too badly of Judge Richardson. In April 1944, he was reappointed Chairman of Northumberland Quarter Sessions by the magistrates, and, 'he enjoyed the rare privilege of being the Chairman of both Northumberland and Durham Quarter Sessions.' [106]

---

[105] 'Is the Pacifist Sincere?' *Sunderland Echo*, 27 June 1940, p. 2.
[106] 'Chairman of Two Quarter Sessions', *North-East Gazette*, 13 April 1944, p. 4.

Chapter Three

Treatment of Conscientious Objectors
(Local Authorities)

At a meeting of Newcastle City Council on 19 June 1940, discussing a motion to dismiss conscientious objectors from its employ, Councillor Mowbray Thompson concluded his contribution to the debate:

> When history comes to be written I do not want future generations, when they turn up the Proceedings of the City Council, to say that on that day of June the Newcastle City Council drove liberty of conscience into the wilderness.[1]

The Councillor got his wish. His statement is, however, an indicator of the passion aroused by the relationship between local authorities and their conscientious objector employees. This, and equally passionate statements by those holding opposing views, are discussed in this chapter, which considers the attitudes of local authorities in the North-East of England towards those in, or wishing to be in, their employ. The picture is one of variations in attitude by both individual councillors and authorities as a whole; by employees towards their fellow workers; by trade unions, the defenders of the rights of workers; and, by tenants and ratepayers of councils. Beyond dispute is the depth of feeling on the question, displayed by those of differing opinions.

Discrimination against Conscientious Objectors

Most commentators accept that conscientious objectors suffered discrimination in the workplace.[2] Rachel Barker devotes a full chapter to the attitude of public employers and Juliet Gardiner refers to debates

---

[1] *Proceedings of Newcastle City Council, 1940-41*, p. 566, Newcastle Central Library.
[2] Kramer, *Conscientious Objectors of the Second World War*, pp. 157-172; and, Hayes, *Challenge of Conscience*, pp. 204-205.

that 'raged through council chambers throughout the land.'[3] In the private sector this was largely kept in the private sphere. Newspaper reports occasionally referred to someone losing their job, usually without naming the employer. One report referred to John Oates of Scarborough, a clerk in a solicitor's office, being dismissed for his pacifist views, he claimed, after being given one week to change his views.[4] In the public sector this was more overt. Barker cites the *Midland Counties Tribune's* reference to the Co-operative Society's extraordinary decision in 1940, given its pride in its tolerance, to dismiss conscientious objector employees, on the grounds that 'they are detrimental to the trade of the Society.'[5] The Manchester and Salford Equitable Society, after protests from its workers, considered any man persisting as an objector failed in his duty to the Co-operative movement.[6] Leicester Co-operative Society even decided not to employ the wives of objectors even though it still offered its objectors the choice of being dismissed until the war was over or to remain in their jobs at army rates of pay.[7] Kramer also refers to an Anti-Conscientious Objector League in Blackpool, in July 1940, sending letters to businesses threatening strike action if conscientious objectors were not dismissed.[8] For the public sector, and local authorities in particular, the regional press provided extensive coverage of their deliberations and editorial comment, usually anti-objector.

Local authorities in 1939 were not the monolithic bodies which developed after 1945. They were, however, still responsible for a wide range of public services, including education, public health, transport, libraries, parks, museums and art galleries, and highways. They were funded primarily by the local ratepayers, and were the largest public sector employer. They were also more 'local' and sensitive to the feelings of their electorate, if not always more responsive to them. This was an electorate of which 45.5% voted in 1938 compared to 31% in 2013.[9] They

---

[3] Barker, *Government, Conscience and War*, pp. 59-77; Gardiner, *Wartime Britain*, p. 123.

[4] 'Objector Says He Lost His Job', *Yorkshire Evening Post*, 11 October 1939, p. 7.

[5] Barker, *Conscience, Government and War*, p. 53.

[6] 'Co-op to Sack C.O.s', *Sunderland Echo*, 5 July 1940, p. 5., and 'C.O. Wives now threatened,' *Peace News*, 30 August 1940, p. 4.

[7] 'C.O. Wives now threatened,' *Peace News*, 30 August 1940, p. 4.

[8] Kramer, *Conscientious Objectors of the Second World War*, p.166-167.

[9] Sam Davies, R. G. Morley, Bob Morley *County Borough Elections in England and Wales 1919-1938: A Comparative Analysis, Volume 3* (Farnham, Surrey: Ashgate Publishing, 2006).

were particularly sensitive to the views of women, who, since the Representation of the People Act of 1928, had almost the same voting rights as men. Women were the mothers and wives of men serving in the Forces. Councillor Whitley of Salford, anxious to obtain the views of his electorate, sent out 3500 postcards asking whether electors thought conscientious objectors should be sacked.[10] In less than a week he had 152 returned saying yes and only 4 saying no.

Some local authorities responded to the pressure exerted by their electorate and the local press and took action against conscientious objectors, yet others did not. The moral dilemma they faced is displayed in their debates, played out in the public arena.

The North-East of England comprised three County Councils, ten County and City Boroughs, and approximately eighty Urban and Rural District Councils. The minutes of the County Councils and the County and City Boroughs have been examined as well as those of thirty-six small District Councils. The main priority, mentioned in the minutes of all the small authorities, was to retain sufficient staff to continue providing their services, for example, Boldon Urban District Council, on 5 June 1940, resolved to support a resolution from Bexley Heath Council:

> That in view of the additional duties which have been placed on local authorities by the government since the outbreak of hostilities, the Minister of Health and the Minister of Labour and National Service, be informed that this Council is of the opinion that all local authorities should be permitted to retain the services of essential 'key-men' in order that such additional and any further duties which may devolve upon them may be efficiently carried out.

However, some did discuss the question of their conscientious objectors.[11]

---

[10] 'Should C.O.s Be Sacked,' *Northern Daily Mail*, 6 May 1940, p. 6.
[11] UD.BO/2/18, Tyne and Wear Archives.

Local Authority Action Against Employees?

Rachel Barker conducted an analysis of how the sixty-three County and ninety-five County and City Boroughs in England and Wales treated their objectors.[12] Compared with the national figures, North-East authorities dismissed and retained the same percentages of employees. A notable exception is the two of the three County Councils who took some action against their conscientious objectors. A significant statistic, confirmed by examination of North-East authorities, is the one in three who declared no decision. As Barker states, it is unlikely that the press would fail to report the question being discussed given the strength of feeling on the matter.[13] Her assumption that this must be because they either retained them or had none to discuss, whilst likely with regard to small authorities, is probably too simplistic. Only by detailed examination of the records of the larger authorities can this figure be refined. This is where difficulties arise. Regional archival and local studies centres maintain the minutes of local authorities, however the availability of the minutes of sub-committees is inconsistent, due to the many reorganisations of local government and building of new headquarters since the end of the war, resulting in many documents being lost, or disposed of through administrative vandalism.

The decision-making process differed between authorities. Smaller authorities tended to be micro-managed by the Council itself whilst larger authorities delegated the management of functions and people to officers, within a policy framework. On occasions, minutes of sub-committees, where many of these issues are discussed, often with no press presence, were approved by councils without further discussion. Northumberland County Council, which dismissed objectors, decided at the Establishment Committee, 19 October 1939, item 13, that, 'The position of any conscientious objector be reviewed after the decision of the Conscientious Objectors' Tribunal has been received.' The published Council minutes contain only items 1-12.[14] Barker's analysis records Northumberland County Council dismissing objectors.[15] Also, the

---

[12] Barker, *Conscience, Government and War,* Appendix 2.
[13] Ibid., p. 69.
[14] Northumberland Archives, Woodhorn, CC/CM/CC/50-52.
[15] Barker, *Conscience, Government and War,* p. 140.

City of Durham Corporation, recorded by Barker as retaining its employees, but shown by Mass Observation as dismissing them, make no mention of conscientious objectors in their available minutes.[16] However, the *Durham Advertiser* reports:

> Members of the Durham City Education Authority have decided to inform the managers of non-provided schools that they do not consider the retention in the schools of any employee registering as a CO, or any member of other anti-war organisation, was desirable.[17]

This follows their editorial of 14 June 1940:

> Following the fearless and outspoken comment of the Mayor of Durham (Counc. S. Kipling) it seems very obvious that the City Corporation of Durham will not suffer gladly any conscientious objectors in its administrative or clerical departments, or in any other sphere of occcupation within the juridiction of the corporate body. His words are unequivocal. None could misunderstand their meaning or significance.
>
> It is not surprising to learn that, with such a lead from the civic chief, the City Education Committee is, it is reported, adopting a similar attitude and is determined to 'wash its hands' of COs wherever they may be...

These comments were made by Councillor Kipling at a meeting of the Council:

> There are many Councils who have taken a stand against conscientious objectors in their employ, and I hope this council will not shirk its duty by continuing to employ any

---

[16] Mass Observation File Report 312, p. 2.
[17] 'Conscientious Objectors', *Durham County Advertiser*, 21 June 1940. No minutes of the Durham City Education Committee were available in Durham County Archives.

person known to be a conscientious objector. As an ex-Serviceman, I am strongly against the employment of conscientious objectors, and will do anything in my power to upset anyone who has motives in that direction.[18]

Teachers as Conscientious Objectors

Roy Lowe has described the education system as one which in all countries 'faced the twin challenges of supporting economies which found themselves on a war footing, and of generating support for the war.'[19] As the war became increasingly seen as a conflict between democracy and fascism, Guy Neave asserts that education became a means of restating the goals for which both sides contended.[20] Whether it led to the increased sophistication of industrial technology being intimately dependent on the education institutions, which he claimed, is debatable, as the education systems in both Germany and Britain faced significant disruption. In Britain, as well as the disruption caused by evacuation, all male teachers over 25 were given reserved status but this was raised to 30 in August 1940 and 35 in July 1941, effectively rendering most teachers liable for call-up.[21] Attempts to plug the teaching gap by the use of retired teachers and married women were only partially successful. Prior to the war, it was expected that women in professions, or in clerical capacities, would leave their employment on becoming married. This applied especially to teachers who, except in exceptional circumstances, were required to leave the profession. Married women in the employ of local authorities were required to seek permission to stay on at work after they were married, and this was rarely granted. Inevitably, for most schoolchildren the war meant 'discomfort, shortages of books and materials, changes in the staffing of schools, and a struggle to sustain the curriculum.'[22] To Gardiner, 'education was the

---

[18] 'Objectors Not Wanted', *Sunderland Echo*, 6 June 1940, p. 2.
[19] Roy Lowe, 'Introduction,' in Roy Lowe, ed., *Education and the Second World War* (London: Routledge, 1982), p. 2.
[20] Guy Neave, 'War and the Educational Reconstruction in Belgium, France and the Netherlands 1940-1947,' in Roy Lowe, ed., *Education and the Second World War*, pp. 84-85.
[21] Roy Lowe, 'Education in England during the Second World War,' in Roy Lowe, ed., *Education and the Second World War*, p. 9.
[22] Ibid.

first casualty of the war for many children.'[23] Disruption was greatest during the evacuation period when less than half of elementary school pupils were receiving a normal education and 25% receiving no education at all.[24] This did not apply to the Public Schools who in some cases located to such glamorous surroundings as Blenheim Palace and Queen Margaret's School, Scarborough, to Castle Howard.[25] Yet all was not bad. Brian Simon noted that war conditions were when 'many of the more advanced techniques in our primary schools were worked out.'[26]

In Germany the teaching profession was also decimated by the call-up of teachers and the increased use of children in forced labour in the fields and factories, but this was a system where teachers were already held in low esteem, resulting from the Hitler Youth 'heaping derision on teachers and lauding its own style of education.'[27]

Nevertheless, the promotion of patriotism was a key long term function of the education system, however, as Bernard Porter contends, the Empire was of greater importance in public schools than in state schools, where it had a lower profile.[28] In class conscious Britain the public school system provided the officer class and the state system the other ranks. On his appointment as President of the Board of Education in 1941, R. A. Butler was told by Churchill that his job was to provide 'powder monkeys' for the war effort, and to see that the schools taught patriotism.[29] Nevertheless, Butler was the author of the 1944 Education Act which Calder refers to as:

> the most signal measure of social reform which became law during the war itself; indeed, it was potentially the most

---

[23] Gardiner, *Wartime Britain*, p. 32.

[24] Lowe, 'Education in England during the Second World War,' p. 9.

[25] Gardiner, *Wartime Britain*, pp. 18-19.

[26] Brian Simon, *Education and the Social Order, 1940-1990* (London: Lawrence and Wishart, 1991) p.35.

[27] Geoffrey, J. Giles, 'Schooling for Little Soldiers: German Education in the Second World War,' in Roy Lowe, ed., *Education and the Second World War*, p. 18.

[28] Roy Lowe, 'Education in England during the Second World War,' in Roy Lowe, ed., *Education and the Second World War*, p. 11, and, Bernard Porter, *The Absent-Minded Imperialists: Empire, Society and Culture in Britain* (Oxford: Oxford University Press, 2006).

[29] R. G. Wallace, 'The Origins and Authorship of the 1944 Education Act,' *History of Education*, 10, 4 (December) 1981, p. 289.

important gesture towards democracy in the twentieth century, a fitting product of the People's War. In practice, however it confirmed and legitimised the existence of class distinction in education.[30]

To Lowe it was hardly necessary to encourage children to instill patriotism. The country was 'engaged in total war which claimed widespread support, and few doubted that it could be counted on to continue to do so under the threat of invasion.'[31] This confidence was not felt by many local authorities who proceeded to dismiss teachers who were conscientious objectors.

The actions of North Yorkshire County Council (NYCC) demonstrate the vulnerability of their teachers and others who were conscientious objectors. The Education Committee carried the following resolution, of the School Management sub-Committee by 14 votes to 6:

> That teachers employed by the Committee who are or who have been placed on the register of conscientious objectors by the C. O. Tribunal should be given leave of absence, without salary, for the duration of the war; that, where necessary, managers of non-provided schools should be asked to take similar action against teachers employed by them; and that, on educational grounds, the consent of the Education Committee should not be given to the appointment of conscientious objectors as teachers in non-provided schools.[32]

The term, 'educational grounds,' is explained in a letter to the *Northern Echo*: 'surely the mothers of boys who are in a class where a conscientious objector is their teacher, will refrain from sending them to school.'[33] In proposing the motion, Canon A. R. Lee, asked the committee to:

---

[30] Calder, *The People's War*, p. 545.
[31] Roy Lowe, 'Education in England during the Second World War,' p. 11.
[32] 'Leave of Absence for C.Os. Without Salary', *Northern Echo*, 13 November 1940, Page 5.
[33] 'Taught by a Conscientious Objector,' *Northern Echo*, 5 February 1940, p. 5. Letter from 'Disgusted' of Darlington.

Imagine a man known to be a CO standing in front of a class of children whose fathers or brothers have gone to fight. Teachers, like others, have a duty to help keep up the morale and courage of the people. What influence would a teacher who is a CO have upon children in front of him and upon their parents, when it is known he was not willing to fight for his country? I am convinced we have taken the right action. We have not judged these men a second time. We are simply saying that for the duration of the war they will have leave of absence. We are not dismissing them; we are saying to them, 'Here is your opportunity. Go; prove yourself for your king and country.'[34]

He was supported by Councillor J. C. Eyles: 'I would rather see my son shot than be a conscientious objector', and Councillor W. B. Fairman who declared that if half of England were conscientious objectors then the country would indeed be in a bad plight. The only objections reported were from Alderman Booth who stated that a man's beliefs were not educational grounds, and Councillor Cunningham who disputed the right of any committee setting themselves up as a second tribunal.[35]

If not technically a dismissal, practically it was. The Education Chairman, Sir Bedford Dorman, said that if a teacher did not see his way to take leave of absence, it was obvious that his employment with the committee would cease and that seemed perfectly natural.[36] In its 1941 annual report, the Education Committee explained that it had at first found it possible to consider each case individually, but, as it was subsequently discovered that groups of conscientious objectors from other areas were applying for posts in the North Riding, it was found necessary to deal with the problem generally.[37] Its 1942 annual report demonstrated the policy in action:

---

[34] 'No Objectors as Teachers', *North-East Gazette*, 13 November 1940, p. 4
[35] Ibid.
[36] 'Leave of Absence or "Sack"', *North-East Gazette*, 10 September 1940, p. 5
[37] 'Annual Report of the Education Committee', North Riding of Yorkshire County Council Minutes 5 March 1941, County Archives, Northallerton.

The Managers of a Non-Provided school in the North Riding made a shortlist of men applicants from other areas for a vacancy in their school; all the applicants invited for interview by the Managers were conscientious objectors and the Committee refused to consent, on educational grounds, to the appointment of the candidate selected by the Managers. The Managers appealed to the Board of Education to declare that the action of the Committee, under Section 29 of the Education Act 1921, was invalid, but the Board, having received the observation of the Committee, determined that they were satisfied that the Committee had refused its consent to the appointment on educational grounds and that its consent had been validly withheld.[38]

It also dealt with existing teachers. The School Management Sub-Committee recommended that leave of absence be given, without pay, to George Pearson, an assistant teacher at Dormanstown Junior Council School, as he had been registered unconditionally by the tribunal.[39] It also decided that the services of J. G. Holroyd, a training college student, were not required after the tribunal rejected his application to be a conscientious objector and that J. Leaf, a teacher at the Sir William Worsley Senior County School, whose application had been rejected, have his position reviewed once he had received his call-up to H. M. Forces.[40] Another North Yorkshire teacher, Elizabeth Short of Leyburn, appeared before the tribunal in October 1942, although she is not specifically mentioned in the council minutes.

If the County Council desired support for its actions from the press, then the *North-East Gazette* obliged. Its editorial of 13 November 1940 included the following comments:

There are undoubtedly men whose conscience forbids them to take up arms even in defence of their own country. Possibly they are a very small minority, and there are strong

[38] 'Annual Report of the Education Committee', North Riding of Yorkshire County Council Minutes 4 March 1942, County Archives, Northallerton.
[39] 'NRCC and "C.O." Teachers' *North-East Gazette*, 7 September 1940, p. 5.
[40] '"Conchie" Teachers in North Riding', *North-East Gazette*, 6 July 1940, p. 6.

grounds for suspicion that a great many who seek the shelter of conscientious objection are merely shirkers who prefer other and braver men to figure in the fighting line......If, however, a certificate of exemption be granted there remains the further question whether these men should continue in public service. That is the point which has exercised the minds of the members of the Education Committee of the North Riding County Council.

In the judgement of the majority it is not desirable that men, in whose breasts the spark of patriotism has burned so low that they are unprepared to take any part in the fight for the preservation of a free democracy, should be entrusted with the moral and intellectual guidance of children at the most impressionable period of their lives. Their verdict, vigorously challenged though it may be, has the sanction of the overwhelming majority of public opinion. Fathers who have left their homes and their loved ones to take their place in the ranks of the Army, the Navy and the Air Force would strongly resent the idea that in their absence their sons should be under the direct and intimate influence of men whose warped mentality blinds them to the justice of Britain's cause.

The Council had chosen the course it wished to take. It is therefore ironic that Sir Bedford Dorman lamented in 1944: 'it is a pity that children have to be neglected because of a shortage of school teachers; it is serious.'[41]

The position of teachers also exercised the minds of Hartlepools Borough Council. The *Northern Echo* reported the Council approving a recommendation of the Education Committee that no conscientious objectors be considered for appointment as teachers, and that a motion to refer it back for further consideration was defeated. In proposing the referral Councillor Jaques stated:

---

[41] 'Shortage of Teachers is "Serious"', *North-East Gazette*, 12 December 1944, p. 4.

I am reminded of the axiom that eternal vigilance is the price of freedom. In this respect, I am not backing up any particular belief of my own. I am only putting forward the beliefs that have been put forward by a Conservative Government. The Conservative Government has agreed that every man has a right to a conscience. Therefore, without going into the usual preamble about freedom, dictatorships or Hitlerism, I move that this resolution go back for further consideration.[42]

The Chairman, Alderman H. Lightfoot, was, however, able to report that they had no conscientious objectors but the committee felt that if teachers had to leave to join the Forces they would not like their places taken by conscientious objectors.[43] The views of the Borough of West Hartlepool regarding teachers are less clear. The withdrawal of an item from the Council agenda, previously passed by the Education Committee, suggests an unsympathetic view. This had requested that in the event of Mr T. W. Oglesby, an assistant teacher, undertaking full time civil defence work in preference to service in the Armed Forces he be given re-instatement on return from war service.[44]

Whether governing bodies of schools appreciated the actions of authorities who took action against objectors is questionable, particularly as the shortage of teachers became more acute. The governing body of a school in the West Riding of Yorkshire, where the Council had adopted the same policy as NYCC, were anxious that a teacher faced with the dilemma of leaving his post, or being dismissed should he remain. A former governor said: 'There does not seem much point serving on a board of governors if their decisions are to be over-ridden in this way. I feel that when a unanimous view is expressed by a local administrative body, notice should be taken of it.'[45]

Sympathy for teachers by the tribunals was also not guaranteed. Nineteen teachers appeared before the Leeds Tribunal, and, after interviewing several of them, the Chairman, Judge Stewart, commented:

[42] 'Hartlepool Council: No Teaching Jobs for C.O.s', *Northern Daily Mail*, 29 November 1940, p. 4.
[43] '"C.O.s" Banned From Teaching Jobs' *Northern Echo*, 29 November 1940, p. 5.
[44] Minute of the Council 5 June 1941, Borough of West Hartlepool, Central Library, Hartlepool.
[45] 'Aireborough School C.O.', *Yorkshire Evening Post*, 21 January 1943, p. 5.

These people are teachers, but I find them more unintelligent than other men who come before us. I reflect that they are engaged and paid for the purpose of teaching children. One wonders how and why it can be so. They cannot answer questions. They come here and say they have profound consciences, then they go off into a series of mental processes. Some of them want minutes to answer simple questions.[46]

The Tribunal decisions in these cases are not known. The removal of J. G. Holroyd from the Register of Conscientious Objectors, drew further comments from Judge Stewart on the training of teachers:

How many students are there at St John's College, York? They manage to produce a very high percentage of pacifists. I don't know why it is, but it is a very amazing thing. Over and over again we have them here from the same place, and the conclusion it leads one to irresistibly conclude that there is an influence at work there which is producing this attitude of mind. He is not fit to teach either the young or anyone else. In my view, no educational authority should dream of employing a man who answers as he has answered this Tribunal.[47]

Teachers were the subject of questions raised in parliament, both favourable and unfavourable to their position. Lieutenant-Colonel Acland Troyte MP asked the President of the Board of Education (Mr Ramsbotham) to take steps to ensure that conscientious objectors exempted on condition that they remain in teaching are not employed in schools which receive state grants, as it was undesirable that patriotic citizens should be forced to send their children to be taught by them. He was reminded, as many questioners would be, by Mr Ramsbotham, that the appointment of teachers, and the termination of their employ-

---

[46] 'Teachers as Objectors', *Northern Echo*, 6 August 1940, p3.
[47] 'A York College as "Factory for C.O.s"', *Yorkshire Evening Post*, 1 July 1940, p. 7.

ment, were the responsibility of the local education authorities or governing bodies of schools. Mr Ramsbotham also had no reason to suppose teachers would fail to observe the principle that political propaganda should in no circumstances be introduced into schools.[48] He was also unwilling to state whether Staffordshire's decision to ask their teachers who were conscientious objectors to resign met with his approval, reverting to his standard reply as to the appointment and dismissal of teachers.[49] West Suffolk's appointment of a sub-committee to investigate the views of teachers and suspend where necessary elicited the same response.[50] It was the unequivocal position of the government that they would not interfere. When Professor Griffiths MP pointed out to the Minister of Labour that trained teachers sent to work on the land by the tribunals was a serious waste of national effort when there was a shortage of teachers, Mr Bevin responded that the prescription of work to be done rested with the tribunals and he had no power to vary their decisions.[51]

The Prime Minister, Winston Churchill, had previously said regarding conscientious objectors: 'anything in the nature of persecution, victimisation, and man-hunting is odious to the British people.'[52] Despite this, he expressed to the War Cabinet his surprise to learn that a number of conscientious objectors were running authorised youth organisations subsidised by the Board of Education, or were employed as teachers by local authorities. Whilst not suggesting that anything should be done to impair the statutory rights of conscientious objectors, he thought they might do great harm when employed as teachers of youth. The War Cabinet were advised that no cases had arisen of a conscientious objector teacher propagating his views among his pupils. They also agreed that if an attempt was made to debar all conscientious objectors from being employed as teachers of youth, controversy would be aroused and considerable difficulties result.[53] The War Cabinet view was not shared by Lord Elton who, writing in the *Northern Daily Mail*, commented: 'The conscientious objectors who have been allowed to crowd

---

[48] 'School Teachers (Conscientious Objectors),' *Hansard*, HC Deb. 10 April 1940, vol. 359, cc581-2.

[49] 'Teachers (Conscientious Objectors)', *Hansard*, HC Deb. 8 August 1040, vol. 364 c460.

[50] 'Teachers (Conscientious Objectors)', *Hansard*, HC Deb. 7 November 1940, vol. 365 cc1476.

[51] 'Conscientious Objectors (Teachers)', *Hansard*, HC Deb. 6 May 1943 vol. 389 cc277-8.

[52] 'Conscientious Objectors: A Case for Redress by Henry Carter', *Manchester Guardian*, 3 November 1941, p. 4.

[53] CAB/65/36/20, War Cabinet, 10 November 1943, Item 6, 'Conscientious Objectors Employed as Teachers of Youth', National Archives, Kew, London.

into the teaching profession – where they can hardly help indoctrinating some of their pupils with Pacifism – are a glaring type of war profiteering which must not be allowed to prolong itself after the war.'[54]

It was indoctrination by the media with its callousness which exercised one teacher, but his response, and that of pacifist teachers, was not to be dogmatic about pacifism. His answer was likely to be more worrying to Lord Elton:

> I don't think it matters that many school text books have a nationalist bias; provided that the master explains the bias and shows the other side of the picture. Indeed, it is often an advantage to use a prejudiced book, because it enables a teacher not only to make jokes at its expense, but to demonstrate the nature of propaganda.[55]

Lord Elton would no doubt have expected the Quaker schools, which did not dismiss their objectors, to be where pupils would have been indoctrinated. This does not appear to have been the case. A headmaster writing to *The Friend* complained that Friends schools were being criticised for not producing enough pacifists, an attitude he described as strangely authoritarian. As he pointed out, less than half the pupils in most schools were Quakers, and that whilst pacifism was the Quaker way, it was a view taught as one not universally held.[56]

Quaker Towns Dismiss Objectors

Teachers were not the only local authority employees to face sanction from their employers. Whilst NYCC teachers were promised reinstatement at the end of the war, other councils chose to simply dismiss their employees. The most publicised county boroughs which did so were Darlington, Middlesbrough and York. That two of the leading Quaker centres in the country, Darlington and York, should take this approach may be surprising.

---

[54] 'High Hopes & Some Doubts,' *Northern Daily Mail*, 27 February 1945, p. 2.
[55] 'Teaching Youth to Think and Act,' *Peace News*, 15 February 1944, p. 4.
[56] 'Friends Schools and Pacifism,' *The Friend*, 14 January 1944, pp. 28-30.

At a meeting of the York City Council sitting in Committee on 1 July 1940, Councillor J. H. Moore gave notice of his intention to move the following motion:

That immediately it shall have been ascertained by, or proved to the Town Clerk, that any person in the employ of the Corporation or any Committee thereof has, since 3 September 1939, declared himself to be, or has been registered as a Conscientious Objector or has appealed as a Conscientious Objector to any tribunal (whatever be the result of such appeal or whether or not it has been heard), then the minimum notice necessary to determine the notice of an employee with the Authority shall be given at once, or if the terms of the contract of employment permit pay in lieu of notice, such employee shall be subject to instant dismissal with such pay, and it shall be the duty of every chief official of the Corporation to bring such cases to the notice of the Town Clerk at the earliest possible moment.[57]

Conscientious objectors were to be dismissed as soon as possible and the findings of any tribunal were irrelevant to this decision. There was also no ambiguity as to the duties of Chief Officers in relation to the matter. The Council agreed that the Motion should stand, despite letters of protest from Mr T. H. Rowntree, Rev J. A. Hughes and the Society of Friends being read out, and referred it to the Finance Committee for consideration. This prompted letters to the press. The Clerk of the Preparative Meeting of the Society of Friends, Desmond Neill, stressed that it was against Parliament's express intention that conscientious objectors with proven sincere convictions should be protected from victimisation, and that adopting the resolution would encourage other local employers to adopt a similar attitude:

We regard it as a serious attempt to curtail the liberties of the individual that uniformity of opinion should be made a condition of employment by a public body. Leaders of every political party have stated that this struggle is being

---

[57] *Minutes of York City Council, 1939-40*, Research Section, Central Library, York.

fought for the principles of justice and freedom, and to penalise anyone on account of his sincere convictions in our
view violates these principles.[58]

Letter writer 'Recorder of 1848', stressing he was not a conscientious objector, commented on the contradiction of men elected to uphold liberty acting in a despotic manner because other men do not accept
their narrow class interpretation of freedom justice and fairness. To dismiss men who had won their case at a proper tribunal 'looks like Hitlerism gone mad.'[59]

The Finance Committee approved the Motion on 19 July 1940
and the Council ratified its decision on 29 July 1940.[60] The *Evening
Chronicle* reported that all conscientious objectors were to be sacked immediately, and that this decision also applied to those judged to be pacifists. They commented: 'No other local Council it is believed has so far
taken such a sweeping decision regarding "conchies" and peace propa-
gandists in their service.'[61] It also drew a letter to the *Northern Echo* from
11 Free Church Ministers residing in York, protesting that dismissal for
holding a conviction is an infringement of individual liberty and contrary to the freedom of liberty and thought that the country was fighting
for.[62] A response belatedly came from the Archbishop of York, Dr William Temple, who wrote in the diocesan leaflet that he regarded the decision of public bodies to be 'utterly deplorable and in the deepest sense
unpatriotic' when the State had recognised the reality of conscientious
objection in the fight for freedom, and freedom of conscience as its 'most
vital and sensitive element.' Whilst agreeing that an objector ought not
to benefit financially by his refusal to serve, 'to deprive him of employment is to frustrate the action of the State and destroy our most effective
witness to our cause.' [63] Similar condemnation was not forthcoming
from the majority of the press. However, *The Spectator*, one of minority
of newspapers that sympathised with objectors, commented: 'The York

---

[58] 'York City Council and C.O. Employees', *Northern Echo*, 5 July 1940, p .4.
[59] 'Dismissal of C.O.s: York Corporation Proposal', *Northern Echo*, 1 July 1940, p .4.
[60] By 26 votes to 19.
[61] 'Pacifists and C.O.s Sacked', *Evening Chronicle*, 30 July 1940, p. 5.
[62] 'York C.O.s: A Free Church Protest', *Northern Echo*, 2 August 1940, p. 4.
[63] 'Conflicting Views on Dismissal of Pacifists', *Durham County Advertiser*, 23 August 1940, p. 4

City Council is not an inherently wiser body, and it has certainly not shown itself a more reasonable or tolerant body, than the House of Commons.'[64]

Some Councillors attempted to reverse the decision. A Special Meeting of the Council on 12 August defeated a motion, 28-20, to rescind the decision and expunge it from the Minutes. The original motion stood and objectors were dismissed.

Support for one York objector came from the unlikely source of Judge Stewart. Regarding Geoffrey Lloyd Sowerbutts, an accountant with the Council, he cast doubt on the correctness, if not the legality, of the Council's decision: 'Being in a reserved occupation you could not join the army if you wanted to. It would surely be wrong for the Corporation to dismiss you in such circumstances.'[65] The Tribunal refused to deal with him until he was no longer reserved and adjourned his case *sin die*. Sowerbutts obtained alternative employment with Liverpool City Council, which had voted to retain its conscientious objectors.[66]

Davies and Morley emphasise the Quaker influence on the politics of Darlington.[67] They describe the council being an alliance of Independents and later Moderates, many, if not most, of which were supporters of the Conservative party. Quaker influence was particularly strong in the nineteenth century, when a number of prominent Quakers represented the town in parliament as Liberals. Most prominent were the Pease family.[68] It cannot be said that this influence was to the fore in the corporation's treatment of its conscientious objectors. Its decision to dismiss them was well reported in the Darlington based press, *The Northern Echo* and *The Darlington and Stockton Times*. 'Ratio', writing to the *Northern Echo*, expressed his sorrow that Darlington, with its fine Quaker traditions, should disgrace its heritage.[69] It was a rare example of support for conscientious objectors from public correspondents to the press. 'Briton' was pleased that the council had at last tackled the question of those who were unwilling to give or support patriotic service, and

---

[64] 'National Wisdom and Local Folly,' *The Spectator*, 1 August 1940, p. 3.

[65] 'Reserved C.O's Plea Rejected', *Yorkshire Evening Post*, 25 June 1940, p. 5.

[66] 'A "C.O.'s" Summons,' *Yorkshire Evening Post*, 21 October 1940, p. 6.

[67] Davies and Morley, *County Borough Elections in England and Wales 1919-1938*, pp. 222-225.

[68] Anne Orde, Religion, Business and Society in North-east England: The Pease Family of Darlington in the Nineteenth Century (Donington: Shaun Tyas, 2001).

[69] 'Darlington Town Council and the C.O.', *Northern Echo*, 4 July 1940, p .4.

wanted to remind councillors that the lads fighting and dying in France are not doing so to allow young conscientious objectors 'to preserve their jobs and save their precious skins.'[70] R. Rush commented that the ban should be extended to anyone known to be a Communist, a member of the Peace Pledge Union, a Fascist or engaged in any subversive activity.[71] 'Volunteer' considered there were very few genuine conscientious objectors, a recurring theme in comments by and in the regional press.[72]

The resolution passed by Darlington Council, having been considered twice by the General Purposes Committee, read:

> That any employee of the Corporation who has registered as a conscientious objector and, after appearing before the Tribunal, has not gone into any branch of the Armed Forces, should be given the notice required to terminate his services with the Corporation[73]

Strongly held views were expressed by councillors and aldermen during the process, especially by those opposed to the ban. This was after all supposed to be a war of democracy against fascism and for those who opposed taking action against objectors it was unbecoming to crush peaceful opposition within one's own democratic society. To this end, they argued that 'we are not going to defeat a barbarian by trampling on the consciences of a minority.' However, those who supported action against objectors argued that 'we will never defeat Hitler by conscientious objection.'[74] This rhetoric was played out in parliament and the press, as well as in local authorities, whenever there was disagreement on how conscientious objectors should be treated.

Alderman Best believed it impossible to win the war by stifling conscience:

---

[70] 'Darlington Town Council and C.O. Employees', *Northern Echo*, 13 June 1940, p. 4.

[71] 'Extending Darlington Town Council's Ban on C.O.s', *Northern Echo*, 9 June 1940, p.4.

[72] 'If C.O.s were put on Soldier's Pay', *Northern Echo*, 7 June 1940, p .4.

[73] *Minutes, Darlington Town Council*, 4 July 1940, item 6, page 420. Darlington Central Library.

[74] 'Employment of C.O.s still undecided', *Northern Echo*, 7 June 1940, p. 5.

During the last war many people went to prison for conscience sake. Many of these people proved their bravery by the extent to which they withstood the attempts at coercion at the time. Many of these men have suffered in health. They have suffered in many ways because of the imprisonment they underwent at that time. In this war, when the Military Service Bill was passed, there was a clause to the effect that if any person had a conscientious objection to military service, he was permitted by that Act to register as a conscientious objection to war, and if a tribunal was satisfied that he had a genuine objection to taking part in war service, then he is entitled to be excused on these grounds. We are fighting for democracy and Parliament has asserted that every person has a right to have his case heard if he has an objection to military service on conscience grounds. I claim that we as a Council have no right to attempt to override an Act of Parliament.[75]

Alderman Hardwick added that the right to exercise one's conscience was a vital principle which had been fought for and that the resolution had been passed in a 'gush of sentimental volatile patriotism.' Councillor Hildreth brought an element of pragmatism to the discussion:

I know really fine men who are not cowards, but who have an absolute repugnance to taking life in any way. If they are going to do useful work at home, I don't see any reason why we should get a reputation in this town for being bigoted, intolerant and narrow-minded, for the sake of the number who have been conscientious objectors among our employees.[76]

Less eloquent, but more forceful, was the view put forward which carried the vote for the resolution. Councillor Jackson, stressing that the country was fighting for its life, raised the often-stated view regarding

---

[75] 'No Decision on Employment of Objectors', *Darlington and Stockton Times*, 8 June 1940, p7.
[76] Ibid.

the genuineness of objectors: 'Why should a certain percentage get off because they have allowed themselves to contract a conscience they have never had before?' Councillor Gallagher expressed the view of many that it was the primary obligation of every man to defend what he was prepared to enjoy and subsist on, adding, that although the government had given conscientious objectors the right to appeal it did not insist that Darlington Corporation could not dismiss a man if it did not want him.[77] This was illustrated in Parliament by the Minister of Health, Ernest Brown, who stated he had no power to intervene between Dudley Council and their Medical Officer of Health over their decision to suspend him for the duration of the war for registering as a conscientious objector.[78]

An attempt to defeat the resolution, by moving an amendment that any employee who claimed to be a conscientious objector should not be given a cost of living bonus, was defeated. The contradiction was pointed out by Alderman Bates who stated that to claim a man has a right to a conscience and then penalise his wife and children by not giving him a war bonus was going about things the wrong way. He would not employ a man who would not defend his wife and children.[79]

The decision of Darlington Corporation was reported to the Joint Committee of Members of the Darlington Finance Sub-Committee and the Middlesbrough Salaries Sub-Committee on 7 August 1940.[80] This committee existed to apply a common approach to employee conditions of service. The onus was now on Middlesbrough to determine its position regarding conscientious objectors. It had already begun to do so. The Finance Committee, on 25 June, considered the case of Edgar Walker, an objector in the Treasurer's department, who had been instructed by the tribunal to take up work on the land, and ordered:

that the appointment of any employee of the corporation who, at the date of his registration under the National Ser-

[77] Ibid.
[78] 'Medical Officer of Health, Dudley', *Hansard*, HC Deb. 11 December 1941 vol. 376, c1703.
[79] 'No Decision on Employment of Objectors', *Darlington and Stockton Times*, 8 June 1940, p. 7.
[80] *Middlesbrough Town Council Minutes 1940-41*, p. 1965, Teesside Archives CB/M/C1/100

vice (Armed Forces) Act, 1939, declares himself to be a conscientious objector, whether before the date of this resolution or upon any date in the future, shall be determined in accordance with the terms of his employment.[81]

The resolution, which relieved conscientious objectors of their employment, was approved by the General Purposes and Parliamentary Committee on 16 July. The arguments for and against the decision, reported in the press, followed the familiar rhetoric of democracy versus fascism and the victimisation of individual opinion versus the abhorrence that an objector could stand aside while his family are butchered. Alderman Spence also expressed the view that conscientious objectors should be prepared to pay the price of their convictions by refusing to take money which came directly or indirectly from the war, citing members of the Peace Pledge Union and other pacifists in Middlesbrough who were doing more business because of the war.[82] In response to Alderman Spence, Henry Daley of Middlesbrough again raised the issue of what we were fighting for, asking whether he was proposing that they be starved to death, and if so he could not have any objection to Nazi concentration camps.[83] Prior to Edgar Walker, Alfred Peter Cox had appeared before the tribunal in December 1939, although no reference to him was found in the minutes. Mr Cox, the articled clerk to the Deputy Town Clerk, was given unconditional registration following a written statement from his housemaster at Harrow stating he was confident that he would find himself work of national importance.[84] Perhaps social class was still a factor in assessing sincerity.

Prior to the full Council confirming the resolution, the Bishop of Whitby entered the discussion. In an open letter to the Town Clerk, he stressed the importance of freedom of conscience and urged that the resolution be referred back for further consideration:

Now in wartime it is inevitable that the individual's freedom of action must be greatly curtailed, and this readily tends to blur the real distinction between our position and

---

[81] Ibid., pp. 1588 and 1724.
[82] 'C.O.s to lose their jobs at Middlesbrough', *The Northern Echo*, 17 July 1940, p. 5.
[83] 'Voice of the North: Conscientious Objectors', *North-East* Gazette,18 July, p. 4.
[84] 'Middlesbro' Man Who Refused an Army Career', *North-East Gazette*, 5 December 1939, p. 7.

that of our opponents. But in recognising the rights of the individual to follow his own conscience, even in a matter so vital as his participation in its defence, our country has done something of supreme importance towards maintaining this distinction unimpaired. It has given its formal allegiance to the doctrine that there is a higher loyalty even than that which is owed by its citizens to itself, and that the loss of a certain number of hands from its war effort is less important than the preservation of the sense of the supremacy of loyalty to conscience.[85]

The bishop was not totally against changes regarding the employment of conscientious objectors. He argued that any genuine objector would support bringing payments in line with emoluments paid to those serving in the Forces. He was supported by a registered objector, J. A. B. Gale of Redcar, who agreed that no one would wish to gain financially by reason of his objection and many were contributing to charity the difference between their own remuneration and a serving soldier's pay.[86] Council members were also prepared to write to the press to express their disagreement with the bishop. Describing the bishop as behaving as though he were in a debating class, Alderman Spence expressed the frequently-held view that the arguments put forward by objectors were cowardly and unworthy, and:

>...that the tribunals amply prove that so-called called conscientious objectors stand for evasion of duty and lack of ideals. No wonder Hitler believed that conscientious objectors, Peace Pledge Union members and pacifists made up a very considerable number, and he counted them on his side...We shall win the war because we know the mighty things which are at stake. Their glorious deeds of valour are a happy contrast to the spineless lot who find every conceivable excuse to keep out of the Army and retain their jobs.[87]

[85] 'Dismissing C.O. Employees,' *The Northern Echo*, 29 July 1940, p. 4.
[86] 'C.O. and the Scales of Justice', *North-East Gazette*, 31 July 1940, p. 2.
[87] 'The Bishop of Whitby and the C.O.s', *Northern Echo*, 1 August 1940, p. 4.

The bishop's intervention was temporarily decisive with the full Council voting to refer the matter back to the Salaries Sub-Committee and General Purposes Committee. In moving the motion Alderman Brown was concerned, not with the bishop's moral arguments, but with the likely legal implications of the dismissal proposal.[88] To seek legal clarification, the council wrote to the Minister of Labour who responded that he deprecated any victimisation of conscientious objectors by their employers and was considering whether it was practical to require that the difference between the remuneration of a conscientious objector and the value of a soldier's pay and rations should be paid into a central fund and devoted to some special purpose.[89] The suggestion was, of course, impractical, as he stated to parliament on 6 February 1941: 'it would arouse acute controversy and would require disproportionately elaborate and expensive administrative machinery for its effective operation. I have decided not to proceed further in this matter.'[90] His opposition to victimisation was an admission that it was not illegal for objectors to be dismissed. The letter from the minister did, however, result in an amendment to the wording of the resolution by the General Purposes Committee:

> If any Corporation employee was called-up and objected he could express his opinion before the Tribunal, and whatever the Tribunal decided the Corporation would act accordingly. If a man failed to observe the directions of the Tribunal, if he failed to register or appear before the Tribunal, his appointment would be determined in accordance with the terms of his contract.

In supporting the resolution Alderman Spence stated that other people in the town were taking the same step and he did not see how anybody who refused to fight for his country could remain in the council's service and receive pay. To the alderman there was no conscience at

---

[88] 'Dismissal of C.O.s: Middlesbrough Thinks Again,' *Northern Echo*, 31 July 1940, p. 3.

[89] 'When C.O.s may be dismissed: Middlesbrough Recommendation', *Northern Echo*, 25 September 1940, p. 5.

[90] 'Conscientious Objectors', *Hansard*, HC Deb. 6 February 1941, vol. 368, c1054.

all in the objections. Religion did not enter into the question at all and these people were nothing other than friends of Germany.[91]

Newcastle and South Shields Retain Their Objectors

In Newcastle and South Shields, the stance adopted by the respective Council differed from that taken by the Aldermen of Darlington, despite the pressure to adopt a similar hard line. The passion and indignation felt by many was expressed in a petition, signed by 139 residents, to Newcastle Corporation:

> We, the undersigned, who are residents and ratepayers of the city, and loyal members of the British Empire, beg to protest against the action of the Corporation of Newcastle-upon-Tyne in employing persons who refuse to perform national, military or naval service during the stress of war and the crisis in our nation. Many of us have relatives undergoing hardship and suffering, and facing death in the perils of sea, land and air, so that we consider it unfair and unpatriotic that money paid by us in rates should be spent on salaries or wages to support those who refuse to help the country. We suggest there should be purge from the Corporation staffs of anyone not prepared to give of their best in some form of national service in this time of anxiety when so much is at stake.

The petition was referred to the Finance Committee on 6 June 1940. Members were advised of three conscientious objectors, one of whom had received unconditional registration and two who were yet to go before the tribunal. The committee agreed to present the facts to the Council for a full discussion.[92]

At the meeting of the Council on 19 June, Councillor Sword moved an amendment that all conscientious objectors be dismissed, declaring, with regard to men who would not register for military service:

---

[91] 'When C.O.s may be dismissed: Middlesbrough Recommendation, *Northern Echo*, 25 September 1940, p. 5.

[92] Finance Committee Minute, 6 June 1940, *Proceedings of Newcastle City Council, 1940-41*, Newcastle Central Library.

'The man who has the time and does not come forward to answer these various appeals is a traitor.'[93] The debate was certainly passionate and unsurprisingly covered the points raised in the other council debates previously detailed. A number of views were, however, uniquely expressed in this debate. In supporting the amendment Councillor Mole referred to objectors as 'spineless parasites sheltering under the cloak of sheltered occupations' and opined that the whole question is 'wrapped up in Nazi secret agents and other despicable bodies', requiring that the Council 'should take all means at our disposal to clean our own stables.' Referring to Councillor Mole's speech as one of the saddest he had he had listened to, Councillor Pugh took moral objection to the amendment and reminded them that a sincere and convinced pacifist, George Lansbury, had recently been entered onto the roll of Freemen of the City. He also emphasised that 'the duty of a city councillor is not simply to follow popular passions and prejudices, but also to defend the rights of minorities,' and as such 'we should not follow all the petty little boroughs in this matter.'[94]

One "petty little borough" was Lytham St. Annes in Lancashire. Its resolution that 'all conscientious objectors should be compelled to carry out work of national importance at rates of pay no higher than and under conditions no better than those of His Majesty's Forces,' was supported as a middle option by Councillor McKeag.[95] He questioned whether the objectors had a conscientious objection to being paid a war bonus, 'which is only being paid because of the very thing to which they have a conscientious objection.' Whilst Councillor Sword's amendment was defeated he took up Councillor McKeag's suggestion and proposed to the Finance Committee on 3 July, 'that in no case shall a war bonus be paid to any employee who claims to be a conscientious objector.'[96] Prior to the motion being discussed by the Council on 31 July, the Finance Committee were advised on the 17 July that one of the objectors had refused the bonus and the remaining two, whilst receiving the bonus, were in occupations regarded as reserved until 1 August 1940.

---

[93] 'Hysterical Council Speeches', *Newcastle Journal*, 20 June 1940.

[94] Council Meeting 19 June 1940, *Proceedings of Newcastle City Council, 1940-41*.

[95] Council Meeting 15 June 1940 – Enemy Aliens and Conscientious Objectors, *Proceedings of Newcastle City Council, 1940-41*.

[96] Council Meeting 19 June 1940, *Proceedings of Newcastle City Council, 1940-41*.

The Newcastle-based *Evening Chronicle*, obviously aware of the council's decision not to dismiss objectors and of its upcoming debate on the payment of a war bonus, applied a degree of pressure. In an article of 5 July 1940, they referred to a steady stream of protests received by them and criticisms voiced at local authority meetings regarding the privileged position enjoyed by a large number of conscientious objectors in the public services:

> Resentment that such persons should be maintained in high paid and sheltered jobs promises to culminate in a campaign to secure firmer control over "conchies". A number of local authorities on Tyneside have one or more conscientious objectors and there is a growing feeling that action must be taken to prohibit their employment. Darlington have taken steps to dispense with their services and other Corporations are showing a tendency to discontinue any special privileges they may enjoy. [97]

To allay any fears that strong action would meet with trade union resistance the *Chronicle's* enquiries found they would support a member dismissed as a result of registering as an objector. If, however, his colleagues objected to working alongside him and threatened to cease work unless he was dismissed, then the union would not support him in any way but would respect the feelings of the majority.

The Council debate on 31 July was again a passionate one, involving many of the protagonists from the earlier debate. Despite both camps claiming that a person's right to have a conscience was not under discussion, the merit or otherwise of conscientious objection featured in the debate. The number of employees affected had already been established as being small, and as Councillor Pugh pointed out that they could safely be relied on to decline the bonus, the motion was accepted by 23 votes to 16, correctly amended to a cost of living and not a war bonus.[98]

---

[97] 'Action Calls Against C.O.s: Firmer Control Demand', *Evening Chronicle*, 5 July 1940, p. 1.
[98] Council Meeting 31 July 1940, *Proceedings of Newcastle City Council, 1940-41*.

The employment of conscientious objectors by Newcastle City Council was therefore secure. There does, however, remain the anomaly of one objector, Walter Rutherford, who declared to the North of England Appellate Tribunal that he had been dismissed by Newcastle Corporation for being a conscientious objector.[99] Rutherford, a fire-watcher of Charlotte Square, Newcastle had been registered for non-combatant duties. He was supported by his mother who claimed: 'I have been dismissed from my employment because my boy was a conscientious objector, and the Newcastle Corporation dismissed him because he was one.....The Corporation kept four Conscientious Objectors in their employment but saw fit to get rid of my boy.'[100] One objector kept on was referred to by 'A Ratepayer' writing to the *Evening Chronicle* as a 'very fine character.' More expected was the comment from 'Son Fighting':

> I was disgusted to read about the CO who kept his job on Newcastle Corporation. It is not a matter of conscience at all with some of these. They just object to Army pay. Where would we be today if all our sons acted in this way? It is high time COs were put on solders' pay. Then this racket would almost vanish. The people of Newcastle should demand their removal at once.[101]

The security of conscientious objector employees was again threatened in July 1942 when Councillor Frame moved for consideration by the Council on 3 September 1942:

> The Council immediately suspend for the duration of the war all employees who are avowed conscientious objectors. Also for the same period all contractors whose partners or directors are avowed conscientious objectors be excluded from tendering for any Council contracts.[102]

Also at the same meeting a motion from Councillor McKeag submitted:

---

[99] 'Appeals against Service' *Durham County Advertiser*, 9 May 1941, p. 1.
[100] 'Widow's Appeal for her Son', *Manchester Guardian*, 6 May 1941, p. 2.
[101] 'Readers' Letters', *Evening Chronicle*, 20 May 1940, p. 4.
[102] 'Newcastle Ban on C.O.s Suggested' *Evening Chronicle*, 11 July 1942, p. 8.

Conscientious objectors should not derive any benefit by means of promotion or increase in salary during the absence of their colleagues on service.[103]

The crisis of 1940 and the blitz of 1941 may have given way in 1942 to a more positive outlook to the war's ending. The involvement of the United States and the Soviet Union in the war ensured that Britain was not alone in opposing Nazism, and, as the war progressed, it was not going to be lost. But, feelings towards conscientious objectors remained strong. The two motions were more far-reaching than those proposed in 1940 and prompted a renewed flow of letters to the *Evening Chronicle*. The wider rhetoric of the war as a struggle of democracy against fascism was evident when A. J. S. Croasdale described the motion 'as savouring more of Fascism than democracy.' He considered that all the council had to decide was whether their employees carry out their duties in an efficient manner and not whether they agree with their conscience.[104] Most correspondents were, however, supportive of Councillor Frame. A. B. of Castleside asked 'how much more precious time and money are we going to waste on these so-called conscientious objectors,' whilst 'Is It Worth It' wondered when 'something is going to be done about these people who can sleep in their beds at night while the RAF protect them from air raids.'[105]

Both motions were defeated and the security of employment of conscientious objectors in the largest county borough council in the North-East was not raised again. One beneficiary was Robert Handyside, a bricklayer with the Council. He was a Seventh Day Adventist who successfully appealed to be registered as a conscientious objector on the grounds that the national services did not allow Saturday to be the Sabbath. His registration was conditional on him remaining in his current occupation which the Council policy allowed him to do, although he could not work on Saturday mornings.[106]

[103] 'City Council's Attitude Towards C.O.s', *Evening Chronicle,* 3 September 1942, p. 5.
[104] 'Letters to Editor', *Evening Chronicle*, 16 July 1942, p. 6.
[105] 'What our readers are saying', *Evening Chronicle*, 18 July 1942, p. 2, and, 'Letters to the Editor', *Evening Chronicle,* 22 July 1942, p. 2.
[106] 'Adventist and the Sabbath', *Shields Gazette*, 11 August 1943, p. 2.

The majority of local authorities made their initial decisions on the employment of objectors in 1940 or 1941, South Shields County Borough took the unusual step of addressing the issue before war broke out. On 8 May 1939 at a Special Meeting of the Town Council the following resolution, proposed by Alderman Pearson and seconded by Councillor Newman, was passed 30-19:

> That this meeting of the County Borough of South Shields views with serious apprehension the proposals of the Government to introduce immediately a measure for the compulsory training of young people for military purposes. This Council pledges its unqualified support in the fight now being waged against the complete shackling of the workers by the chains of conscription, both military and industry. As an expression of its good faith in the matter, the Council do resolve that volunteer, conscript and objector within the service of the Council shall, if occasion arises, receive the same treatment without any differentiation.[107]

Why the Council should make this unprecedented decision is unknown. That one of its most influential Labour councillors, Aaron Gompertz, had been imprisoned during the First World War as a conscientious objector may have been a factor. The *Shields Gazette* was of the opinion that council workers viewed the resolution as being of doubtful standing and probably unworkable. Councillors interviewed by the *Gazette* were in some doubt about its operation. They said a conscientious objector would have to convince the Council that his grounds were really just and sincere. One member said:

> We know the views of one or two members of staff who, it has emerged, will apply for exemption. Those views cannot be classed as of conscience but only as politic and we should be very diffident about treating them in the same

---

[107] Special Meeting of the Town Council (Military Bill 1939), 8 May 1939, *Proceedings of the County Borough of South Shields*, Local Studies Section, South Shields Central Library.

way as volunteers and conscripts if they were granted exemption. I might go further and say that the views of one or
two are definitely pro-Nazi.[108]

Another councillor commented: 'the object of the resolution was
to protect those who were really opposed to military service on conscientious grounds – a belief that to kill is to commit the greatest sin.'[109]

In the opinion of the *Gazette*, as most members of the staff held
the opinion that Britain was fighting a just war to defeat Nazism, any
employee applying for exemption because he believed in the German
policy would be strongly opposed, but the complexity of the issue meant
it was likely that the Council would discuss the matter again for the purpose of clarification.[110] The Council did not discuss the matter again and
it appears security of employment was enjoyed by conscientious objectors in their employ. One employee was Patrick Shiel, a surveyor, who
successfully appealed to be registered as a conscientious objector on condition he remained in his current employment.[111]

The *Gazette's* actions were clearly designed to put pressure on the
local authority to take action against its objectors. A similar tactic was
employed by the *Morpeth Herald*, which also raised the familiar issue of
the genuine conscientious objector:

Resentful whisperings about conscientious objectors in
sheltered positions are now being heard in Ashington. It
was bound to come. The stress and strains of war upon the
civilian population, the unavoidable and avoidable inequality of sacrifice, the anxiety and fear, are all contributing to
the creation of a mood of resentment against those who
claim they have a conscientious objection to taking life, especially if the objector happens to occupy a congenial, sheltered and well paid post.

---

[108] 'What's The Position of C.O.s Who Work for Shields Council,' *Shields Gazette*, 10
April 1940, p. 1.
[109] Ibid.
[110] Ibid.
[111] 'Objection to Taking Life', *Shields Gazette*, 1 May 1941, p. 3.

The general opposition to the conscientious objector is neither philosophic nor religious. It is based upon the argument that the objector is a person who refuses to take the rough with the smooth, a person who accepts the good things in life while being unwilling to share in the fight to preserve them. It is a purely materialistic viewpoint, but one that finds favour with the majority.

The problem is one of extreme difficulty. I know a pacifist or two in these parts, for whose attitude I have deep respect, and I know they are not cowards. I know that if the supreme test came they would display as much bravery as the men who march away.

But there are others. Public opinion, however, is not constructed for grasping the niceties of human conscience, and therefore the conscientious objector, be he false or true, cannot do other than face up to the resentment of men and women who give their sons in the country's service.[112]

An Objector is Appointed and then Dismissed

Unlike in South Shields, job security seemed uncertain at West Hartlepool Borough Council. Whilst they had decided not to appoint any objectors as teachers, their Health Committee did appoint a conscientious objector in July 1943.[113] He was the only applicant and was working his one-month notice from his previous post. Moving that the appointment be terminated, Councillor F B Magee said they had heard a lot about uniformity of action in municipal affairs, and some time ago, after considerable debate, had declined to employ a conscientious objector. He felt that they should refuse again in this instance. Citing the difficulty in getting sanitary inspectors Councillor P M Williams was of the opinion that, as the man had been exempted by the tribunal, and:

…while in the opinion of the majority of us this man's ideas are not the right ones, he has a right to hold these views, and I don't think we should refuse to employ him, with the

---

[112] 'Ashington Window,' *Morpeth Herald*, 31 May 1940, p. 4.
[113] 'Committee's Decision Negatived', *Northern* Daily Mail, 30 July 1943, p. 2.

proviso that he does not try to force his views down other people's throats.

Speaking against his employment, Councillor T W Pinkney, 'didn't see why West Hartlepool should be saddled with any of these people,' and, that, 'the town he is coming from won't be sorry to lose him.' Councillor Harbron felt that:

…the towns-people would not applaud in any way the appointment of a man who has escaped service to his country by the laws that allowed him to do so. I say it is wrong indeed to appoint any individual who deliberately shirks the responsibility nationality has placed on him. The question is, is he fit to be in our employ? I say no.

The Council decided to terminate his appointment. The issue was still a real one after nearly four years of war.

Some Small Local Authorities

Security of employment was also not guaranteed in some smaller local authorities. Easington Rural District Council, at a Special meeting of the Council on 20 June 1940, agreed the motion of Mr Peart: 'that any employee of the Council who claimed to be a conscientious objector when he registered for military service, be given notice to terminate his employment with the Council forthwith.' The *Durham County Advertiser* reported that there was no discussion.[114] Seaton Valley Council in Northumberland may also have had a poor opinion of conscientious objectors in their employ as they voted to fully support the Lytham St. Anne's motion, although there is no mention in the sources of them dismissing objectors.[115]

Other objectors were found who had been dismissed by unknown local authorities, which highlights the difficulty in establishing a full list of authorities which took action against them. In view of the

[114] '"Conchies" to be sacked Durham,' *Durham County Advertiser*, 28 June 1940, p.7.
[115] 'A.R.P. Petrol Misuse Allegations,' *Morpeth Herald*, 31 May 1940, p. 6.

almost total reliance on public transport to get to work it is assumed they worked for an authority close to their home. In his tribunal statement Oswald Dover declared he had lost his job with the local authority because his conscience would not allow him to do work normally done by a person called up for military service.[116] Mr Dover lived at Langley Park, between Durham and Lanchester, and his probable limited transport options would suggest he worked for one of the small district councils in his locality or for Durham County Council. The available records for these authorities do not show the dismissal of conscientious objectors.

For some the decision was taken out of the hands of the local authority. For example, Fred Wilson of Durham Rural District Council and K. E. Grant, a librarian from Shotley Bridge, joined the FAU, which satisfied the tribunal conditions. The National Association of Local Government Officers (NALGO) applied for Wilson's pay to be augmented for the period of the war but this was refused.[117] For others, such as Joseph Dixon, a teacher from North Shields, the tribunal determined his future employment by registering him for non-combatant duties.[118] For a further five on the database of conscientious objectors their local authority or their future employment beyond the tribunal is unknown.

The Response of Fellow Workers

In other parts of County Durham, a different attitude was taken to that of Easington. Jarrow Housing Committee were told the men objected to working with a man who had appeared before the conscientious objectors' tribunal and women tenants were complaining. When Councillor Scullion enquired whether such grievances should not come from trade unions, Councillor Warwick said the matter was outside the trade union movement and doubted if any union would take it up. The councillors, generally unsympathetic to the objector, commented: 'I am sure there would be no conscientious objectors in this country if they could hear the stories the men of Belgium have to tell'; 'if he was not proud to be British he should not be getting his living here, and particularly not from a public authority'; and, 'I have yet to see the difference between

---

[116] 'Richmond Man's Protest at Tribunal,' *Northern Echo*, 15 October 1939, p. 5., and 'Hear All Sides,' *Northern Echo*, 13 October 1939, p. 4.
[117] Durham RDC, Council Minute 6 July 1942, RD/Du/55, Durham Records Office.
[118] Registered as Objector, *Shields Gazette*, 6 May 1941, p. 1.

the Fifth Column and a conscientious objector.' Councillor Scullion did however state that, 'If he is sincere in his views we have no right to interfere, although I disagree with him.' Rather than make a general policy decision the Council, on hearing the man was likely to be called up in due course, decided to transfer him from repair work and let matters take their course.[119]

A similar situation arose in Stanley Urban District Council, where a dispute arose between members of the Electricity Department over the appointment of an alleged conscientious objector. One said:

> I and several of my mates objected to working with a "conchie" for patriotic reasons. We sent our complaint to the chief electrician, Mr George Blackmore. It was considered by the Council and a decision taken that the men who refused to work with the conchie would be suspended until the September meeting. In other words, we are being intimidated by the Council.[120]

A motion that the men be dismissed was amended: if the men could not give satisfactory reasons at the September 1940 meeting then they would be dismissed. The amendment was carried by two votes. Many councillors expressed the view that they had no sympathy with the conscientious objector, but the men were employed by the Council and, as their first duty was to the ratepayers, they should be dismissed if they were not prepared to discharge their duties. The men agreed to work under protest.[121] The available council minutes make no reference to the dispute. No identification of the objector is provided but the database of conscientious objectors records a council worker from Stanley, James Cornell, attending the tribunal in May 1941.

Similarly, Sunderland Transport Department employees passed a resolution protesting against being asked to work with conscientious objectors. Their position was explained by Mr T. Caygill:

[119] 'Jarrow Council Tenants Object to C.O.', *Evening Chronicle*, 5 June 1940, p. 5.
[120] 'Stanley men object to C.O.', *Evening Chronicle,* 5 August 1940, p. 5.
[121] 'Trouble About a C.O. at West Stanley', *Durham County Advertiser*, 8 August 1940, p. 1.

We believe that this is a just war in which everyone must do their part and that there is no room in our job for men who are shirking their duty. So far only one man from the Transport Department has appeared before the Conscientious Objectors' Tribunal and he was registered for non-combatant duties. We have taken this decision in anticipation of future action, and hope to save trouble and friction by making our position perfectly clear. We recognise that we have to accept the decision of the Government so far as the registration of objectors is concerned, but we don't want them working alongside us and using the fact that they are engaged in municipal transport to escape military service.[122]

No evidence was found of the men taking future action. Significantly, in this particular case the letters to the *Sunderland Echo*, whilst reflecting both sides of the argument, were marginally un-supportive of the action of the workers, for reasons both of freedom of thought and the desire to avoid creating martyrs.

The cases of the Stanley and Sunderland men do not appear to have been repeated on a major scale in the North-East. The *Evening Chronicle* reported that feelings ran high but the number of cases was low. The protest of Sunderland Tramway workers was a situation not repeated in Newcastle and Gateshead Transport Authorities neither of which received any applications for employment from Conscientious Objectors.[123] This was perhaps evidence that the stance taken by the National Union of General and Municipal Workers Union, the blue collar council workers' trade union, to encourage restraint by their more violent anti-objector members, for fear of creating martyrs of objectors, was having a degree of success.[124] They also reminded councillors who had voted for reprisals, or were thinking of doing so, that they were going against the expressed wish of the Prime Minister.[125] The Sunderland meeting was not held under the union's auspices.

---

[122] 'Wearside Transport Men Won't Work with C.O.s', *Sunderland Echo*, 1 April 1940, p. 1.

[123] 'Little Trouble in North over C.O.s in Jobs', *Evening Chronicle*, 3 April 1940, p. 1.

[124] Mass Observation File Report 312, p. 127.

[125] 'Reprisals Against Objectors Condemned', *Daily Herald*, April 1940.

Skipton's Unique Approach

Skipton Urban District Council, currently in the County of North Yorkshire, was not in the North Riding of Yorkshire during the Second World War. It is included because of its unusual, if not unique, approach to its conscientious objectors. At a meeting of the Council on 18 June 1940, Councillor Daley enquired how many men in the employ of the Council were conscientious objectors. The chairman replied that there were none to his knowledge, a statement which it transpired was inaccurate.[126] The Council passed two resolutions ensuring that there remained no objectors. On 13 May 1941, the Finance Committee resolved that no conscientious objectors should be appointed as substitutes for men called up for National Service, and, on 10 June 1941 resolved that when advertising for temporary staff it must be only for men over 41 or otherwise ineligible for National Service.[127]

The conscientious objector in their employ was Mr R. C. H. Jones. He had been directed to undertake duties as a hostel warden by the Leeds Tribunal. Councils collectively undertook to maintain the superannuation payments of staff called up for National Service for the duration of the war and to reinstate them to their current posts on demobilisation at the end of the war. Skipton UDC agreed that a letter be sent to the Minister of Health requesting:

> In view of Mr Jones having registered as a conscientious objector, and having been given an appointment as warden of an agricultural hostel, the Council considers that superannuation payments should not be paid by them, and you be asked to give a ruling to this effect.[128]

On receipt of a reply from the Minister, the detail of which is not included in the Minutes, the Finance Committee resolved to make no superannuation payments.[129] Mr Jones appealed this decision to the

---

[126] Skipton UDC, Council Minutes, 18 June 1940, Item 5, North Yorkshire Archives.
[127] Skipton UDC, Finance Committee Minutes, 13 May 1941, Item 3, 'Armed Forces Act 1939', and, Skipton UDC, Finance Committee Minutes, Item 4, 'Armed Forces Act 1939'.
[128] 'Staff Called-up', Skipton UDC, Finance Committee, 12 November 1941, item 6.
[129] 'R. C. H. Jones', Skipton UDC, Finance Committee, 10 December 1941, Item 4.

Minister. The Finance Committee on 13 May 1942, on being advised that the Minister had rejected the appeal, resolved:

> That Mr Jones be informed that he is not regarded as an employee of the Council since the day he left. He therefore must seek employment elsewhere at the termination of the war.[130]

The Council had in practice dismissed Jones as a result of him obeying the direction of the tribunal. They were also not content with limiting their actions to their own employees. Colonel F. L. Smith, Chairman of the Fire Brigade Committee, is reported in the *Yorkshire Observer* on 19 June 1940 as saying: 'Fires at premises of Conscientious Objectors will be left until the last.' He urged that each street in Skipton organise its own fire-fighting squads, advising conscientious objectors to make their own arrangements.'[131]

Trade Union Support For Conscientious Objectors

Councils in the North-East of England had followed a variety of routes to deprive conscientious objectors of employment. The *Evening Chronicle* blamed a lack of government direction on the issue.[132] Darlington, Middlesbrough, Easington and York had simply dismissed them. North Yorkshire had given teachers leave of absence without pay for the duration of the war and taken steps to ensure that no conscientious objectors could take the place of staff who had left. The latter course had also been followed by Hartlepools. The most unusual method employed was by Skipton who used the compliance with a tribunal decision as de facto resignation. The numbers affected were undoubtedly a small proportion of the total local authority workforce, and would have expected the support of their trade union, NALGO. This was the view of Mr Radford, a conscientious objector asked to resign by Littleborough UDC in Lancashire, who turned up for work as usual confident that 'the Association will look after my interests.'[133] The fate of Mr Radford is not known but

---

[130] 'R. C. H. Jones', Skipton UDC, Finance Committee, 13 May 1942, Item 3b.
[131] Mass Observation File Report 312, p. 127.
[132] 'State Lead Awaited.' *Evening Chronicle*, 20 July 1940, p. 6.
[133] 'Council Office "C.O." asked to Resign', '*Evening Chronicle*, 28 March 1940, p. 1.

less than two weeks later, NALGO decided that it could take no action regarding the dismissal of two men by Altrincham Council, declaring:

> If a man is called up his employer must reinstate him when
> he is demobilised. A man cannot be dismissed if he is liable
> for call-up at a future date. If a man is called up and is reg-
> istered as a conscientious objector there is no provision to
> prevent his dismissal. There were no legal grounds on
> which we could contest the dismissals.[134]

NALGO had previously made a decision to protect members against victimisation, but on 5 July 1940 announced that, 'any member who finds himself in difficulty because of his refusal to undertake some sort of service in defence of the realm will now rely on his own claims to such protection as the law of the land provides.'[135] Mass Observation also noted, 'NALGO has now ceased to protect its C.O. members from victimisation and locally even taking part in agitation against them'.[136] Council employees therefore had no recourse to the main local government union if dismissed for being conscientious objectors. They certainly did not in Fulham where the Branch Secretary wrote to the Council Staff Committee:

> That this branch disassociates itself from the attitude of that
> small section of its membership which claims conscientious
> objection to military service and shows its unwillingness to
> shoulder any responsibilities whatsoever. It considers that,
> apart from the material advantages enjoyed by those who
> remain at home, this attitude is incompatible with the sen-
> timents expressed in the resolution of the Council (to do all
> in its power to secure victory…), and is of the opinion that
> the retention of their services must necessarily undermine

---

[134] 'Legal Right to Dismiss Objector', *Evening Chronicle,* 9 April 1940, p. 7.
[135] 'Action Calls against C.O.s: Firmer Control Demand', *Evening Chronicle,* 5 March 1940, p. 1.
[136] Mass Observation File Report 312, p. 132.

the whole-hearted co-operation of the Council's officers and employees which is essential at the present time.[137]

Other local authority unions showed more constructive support to objectors, such as the NUGMW (National Union of General Municipal Workers) in the case of Sunderland Transport workers, and NUPE (National Union of Public Employees) who urged the Minister of Health to issue instructions to local authorities discouraging the dismissal of workers: 'it is inexplicable that any public body should embark on a policy of wholesale dismissals.'[138] The NUGMW went further in condemnation of reprisals against objectors:

> Cases have been brought to the notice of the Union of local authorities discharging objectors who have been exempted from military service on condition they remain in local government service. By such action it is pointed out, that they are going against the express wish of the Prime Minister that genuine C.O.'s should not be made martyrs.[139]

In reality, there was little that any union could do to prevent objectors being dismissed, and they were normally unsuccessful.[140] But there were instances of unions persuading their members to drop their protests, for example, disputes at Newmarket Co-op, Walsall Co-op and Rossendale Shoe and Slipper Company.

Summonses for alleged wrongful dismissal brought by three conscientious objectors against Huddersfield Industrial Society were dismissed. The Stipendiary decided that they failed to establish the commission of any offence. He found that each was dismissed for being a conscientious objector but no man was bound to employ another of whose opinions he disapproved and, providing proper notice was given, he might dismiss for such reason.[141]

---

[137] 'Conscientious Objectors: Fulham Council Decides', *Fulham Chronicle*, 28 June 1940.

[138] 'Dismissal of Workers', *Northern Daily Mail*, 5 October 1939, p. 1.

[139] 'Reprisals Against C.O.'s Condemned', *Daily Herald*, 14 April 1940.

[140] Mass Observation File Report 312, p. 128.

[141] 'Need Not Employ Objectors', *Sunderland Echo* 29 October 1940, p. 5.

The trade unions were in a difficult position. They existed to represent their members and in the case of conscientious objectors the majority of their members were often for taking action against a minority of their members. In addition, the tribunals included a trade union member and often the agitation resulted from a tribunal decision allowing an objector to remain in his current employment

In the North-East a potential area of such conflict was in coal mining, the largest source of employment. The Northumberland Miners' Association recognised the issue and passed a supportive resolution at its annual council meeting:

> That this meeting views with alarm the action of certain trade unionists in attempting to have members of the trade union movement dismissed from their employment who have been accepted by the tribunal as being sincere conscientious objectors to military service, and pledges itself to do everything possible to safeguard the interests of any such members.

It should be noted that a large number of abstentions were recorded.[142]

The Press and Local Authority Objectors

The press and public did not restrict their comment on public employees to local authorities. The *Northern Echo* reported that governors of Darlington Memorial Hospital, at their AGM, had rejected a motion that the hospital should not employ conscientious objectors, and invited readers to comment.[143] A porter at the hospital had received full exemption and volunteered for the FAU. One director, Percy Blott, said he had no time for a man who had developed a conscience since the war but a little sympathy for one who held these views before the war. Even

---

[142] 'Miners and C.O.s', *Sunderland Echo*, 18 May 1940, p. 3.
[143] 'Views wanted on C.O.s: Appeal to Darlington Hospital Contributors', *Northern Echo*, 8 June 1942, p. 3.

less empathy was expressed by J. W. Noble, whose opinion was that nine out of ten conscientious objectors' only conscience was that they did not want to be killed.

Some readers did respond. F. Foster was disgusted that the motion was turned down: 'This job was made possible by money given by townsmen and women to build this hospital as a memorial to those brave fathers and sons who sacrificed their beliefs and lives in the last war.'[144] Mr Noble also felt the need to clarify his reported comments about employing a conscientious objector at the hospital: 'It is also an insult to those whose names are in the memorial hall of the hospital who have made the ultimate sacrifice for liberty and against aggression.'[145]

Correspondence to newspapers quoted in this chapter relates only to public and local authorities. When considered along with the comments about conscientious objectors detailed in other chapters, it creates a strong impression of hostility to objectors which councillors were no doubt aware of. Editorial comment by newspapers, and disparaging references to 'conchies' and 'shirkers,' can only have added to the pressure on authorities to take decisive action against them. *The Yorkshire Evening Post* sought to explain the necessity for local authorities to debate the position of their conscientious objector employees:

> Under the direct threat of invasion, the protection of those who won't fight by those who will is more than ever an anomaly; they are assured not only the necessities of life but luxuries as are still possible, and in many cases continue in highly paid employment, on just one condition – that others will protect them. They may actually enjoy greater possibilities of advancement through the absence of the men who are doing the fighting. The position of the public servant is particularly anomalous, since he profits and is made more secure by every action of that Government of authority which he is unwilling to support in the field.[146]

---

[144] 'Employing C.O.s at Darlington Hospital', *Northern Echo*, 10 June 1942, p. 2.
[145] 'Employment of C.O.s at a War Memorial Hospital,' *Northern Echo*, 19 July 1942, p. 2.
[146] 'Editorial: Conscience at Work', *Yorkshire Evening Post*, 19 July 1940, p. 4.

The *Northern Daily Mail,* in calling for conscientious objectors to receive no more pay than men in the services, added: 'this war is not being fought to keep conscientious objectors comfortable in their precious ivory towers of intellectual or political make-believe.'[147]

Considering the dire situation facing the nation at the time most of these decisions were made, councillors had to make the difficult choice between appeasing the understandably strong anti-objector opinion expressed and following their own consciences as to the right thing to do. Where councillors voted to take no action, they would have been aware that it could potentially have a detrimental effect on their electoral chances. What is clear from the records of the debates, was that both sides of the argument had strong and sincerely held views. The debates appear to have been conducted in a civilised manner; more civilised than the manner in which it was discussed in the local press. The press very enthusiastically reported councils who decided to dismiss conscientious objectors. Very little comment was made when a council decided not to do so. This was evident with the Newcastle-based *Evening Chronicle* which, despite the intensity of the 1940 debate, had limited coverage of it, yet in 1942 was giving comparatively greater coverage to the renewed attempt to impose a ban. The Middlesbrough-based *North-East Gazette,* was a vociferous reporter of the decisions of Darlington and NYCC to dismiss their objectors but made very little comment on the decision of Middlesbrough to follow the same course of action. It also quoted examples from other parts of the country, such as Gillingham's decision to dismiss an objector who: 'has grossly misbehaved as a conscientious objector and a member of the PPU, and habitually expressing his views as such, so as to interfere with the smooth running of the Corporation's workshop.'[148] The Darlington based *Northern Echo* had no such difficulty in giving extensive coverage of the dismissal of objectors wherever it occurred.

The national press, which had a presence in the North East of England, was of course not silent on the question of conscientious objectors. The popular press was not averse to reporting the decisions of

---

[147] 'Editorial: Work and War', *Northern Daily Mail,* 30 April 1940, p. 2.
[148] 'Dismissed C.O. Seeks Damages', *North-East Gazette,* 31 March 1941, p. 5.

local authorities under such sensational headlines as, 'Sack Our Conchies Say Citizens.'[149] There was, however, a more measured view expressed in *The Spectator*:

> Local authorities who are dismissing on the ground of conscientious objection men who have been working satisfactorily for them for years are not acting in the interests of efficiency or following the wise lead given by the Government. Conscientious objectors of military age might well be asked to hand over to some good cause such as the Red Cross any excess of their earnings over what they would have drawn as pay and allowances in the Army, but to evict them from jobs that need doing is both uncharitable and short sighted. Everyone's work is wanted today.[150]

Unfortunately for conscientious objectors employed by local authorities, *The Spectator* had only a limited circulation in the region.

Conclusion

As Barker, Gardiner and others assert, many conscientious objectors employed by local authorities faced significant personal and employment consequences. The First World War may have been described as the 'Great War for Civilisation' yet it was in the Second World War that the conflicting ideologies of democracy and fascism were in direct opposition; the democracies seeing themselves as the defenders of civilisation against the barbarism of Nazi Germany in particular. A great division between the ideologies was how they tolerated opposition, including conscientious objection. The British government took the unprecedented decision to enshrine this tolerance in the National Service Act. Employers showed less tolerance and this included many local authorities.

The government had not helped local government with the issue. It had set up the tribunal system which it expected would fully deal with issue of conscientious objection, but had not laid down clear guidelines

---

[149] 'Sack Our "Conchies" Say Citizens', *Sunday Express*, 23 June 1940, p. 5.
[150] 'Conscientious Objector and the Land', *The Spectator*, 7 June 1940, p. 766-767.

for how objectors should be treated by employers. The best it could offer was a condemnation of victimisation, but without a legal process to prevent it, and a vague, unworkable, promise to examine the setting up of a central fund in which to pay the difference between an objector's and a soldier's pay. This left local authorities open to criticism in Parliament that they had defied the Act of Parliament and cruelly dismissed men simply because they were conscientious objectors. Mr Cecil Wilson MP stated that he did not know why they should be allowed to continue their defiance of Parliament.[151] Mr G. Strauss MP was so adamant that local authorities were acting contrary to government policy that he asked the Minister of Labour on both 22 May and 29 May 1941 if he would make a further statement reminding them of it. As before, the response was to refer to previous vague statements, although he did agree to take up with West Riding of Yorkshire County Council their alleged decision to ask heads of institutions to report the names of people believed to be conscientious objectors but who had not yet registered as such.[152]

The available statistics show the course taken by councils in the North-East of England was no different from the average for the England and Wales. There are however obvious limitations to these statistics, not least the large number of the smaller authorities, both locally and nationally, about whose policy nothing is known. Most significantly little is known about the position of Sunderland, the largest county borough after Newcastle. Whilst there is no reference to conscientious objectors in Council minutes, the Libraries, Museum and Art Galleries Committee decided *Peace News* should no longer be stocked in their reading rooms.[153] That its Mayor, Councillor Summerbell, was a leading pacifist in the region, may have tempered its approach to the issue.

There were, however, many major local authorities whose intolerance led to the dismissal of objectors, and they employed a variety of ways of doing so. Debates on conscientious objection centred on the tolerance of its peaceful objectors defining a democracy and making it different from the Nazi dictatorship that the country was fighting. The statement of Councillor Mowbray which opened this chapter epitomises

[151] 'National Service Bill', *Hansard,* HC Deb. 26 March 1941 vol. 370 cc645-71.
[152] 'Conscientious Objectors (Local Authorities Employees)', *Hansard,* HC Debs. vol. 371 cc1602 and c2002.
[153] 'Organ of Peace Union', *Sunderland Echo*, 29 May 1940, p. 3.

the argument that the fight was also for liberty of conscience. To those who expressed the opposite point of view it was liberty itself that was the issue, especially in the months leading up to the evacuation of Dunkirk in May 1940 and the period of uncertainty that followed.

Strong feelings about conscientious objectors employed by local authorities were not confined to the uncertain period of 1940 and 1941. The controversy was clearly ongoing in 1942 and 1943 as the analysis of Newcastle, West Hartlepool and NYCC shows, and in 1945 as shown by the comments of Lord Elton. Press coverage of the issue undoubtedly decreased from its peak in 1940 when the majority of the decisions had been made.

It was teachers who aroused the greatest animosity from their local authority employers. The presence of war objectors in the classroom was seen as counter to promoting patriotism, and a poor example to pupils whose brothers were likely serving in the forces. NYCC in particular demonstrated intolerance to teachers who were objectors throughout the war even if a teacher shortage meant children's education suffered.

The dismissed local authority employee was not to receive much support from his fellow workers or from his trade union. Despite early promises to defend the rights of their members the unions found themselves bound by the wishes of the majority of their members. The objector's final recourse was to the government who had given them the legal right to object. All the government gave them was a condemnation of intolerance with no actual practical support. They did after all have more pressing concerns.

In the animosity often surrounding conscientious objectors in local government there has to be recognition that the local authority officer himself, as today, was not universally popular among ratepayers. It is, therefore, appropriate to note the comments of a local government officer who considered he had to respond to criticism in the press that they were hiding behind their jobs protected by deferment of call-up:

> Please afford me the opportunity of expressing my strong disapproval of the critical and unkind statements...about local government clerks shirking their responsibilities by not joining the Forces. Your correspondents infer that substitutes to fill up our important positions can be picked up

off the streets so to speak. Provide them with a pen and ink and you have a clerk ready for the Shire hall, or other similar public offices, handling thousands of pounds, provided by the ratepayers. Nothing is further from the truth.

I am under the conviction that those correspondents who are airing their views against us never made any effort or sacrifice to qualify for the positions we hold, preferring to get through life with the least possible effort. Today, at 37 years of age, I am a married man with a wife and small family depending on me.

Does anyone suggest that I would be worthy of the name of husband and father if I gave up specialised work and a decent salary secured after years of studious effort just for the purpose of appeasing some of your jealous correspondents who are waiting to jump into my shoes and have a laugh at my expense.

Nothing doing, I assure you, so long as I am fully satisfied that my service in my present capacity is of vital interest to the community.[154]

His comments are unlikely to have advanced a better understanding of the local government officer, and this was likely to have been understood by the newspaper when they published it. The press played a leading role in attempting to influence action by Councils, but, as the cases of Newcastle and South Shields show, they were not always successful. The next chapter will examine broader patterns in the stance taken by newspapers.

---

[154] 'Readers' Views – County Council Staff', *Durham County Advertiser*, 30 January 1942, p. 4.

CENTRAL BOARD FOR CONSCIENTIOUS OBJECTORS

BULLETIN

MAY, 1943   No. 39   PRICE 3d.
EDITED BY DENIS HAYES

TOLSTOY SENT GREETINGS TO C.O.s

Oxford University Press
From the portrait by I. N. Kramskoy.

THIS message of greeting to conscientious objectors was written by Leo Tolstoy in 1909. It was addressed to Russian liberals: at that time there was much persecution of those who objected to serving in the army for religious reasons, and of those who stood for reform of the governmental system. The police were corrupt and often at heart sympathetic to the reforms; considerable "subversive" propaganda was carried on in the prisons and concentration camps, while rioting and murdering were frequent.

Tolstoy disapproved of such violence and stood for passive resistance, spiritual freedom and education; he made no secret of his views, and was in a strong position because of the general admiration of his integrity, force of character and literary genius. The authorities not only feared to lay hands on him; they approved of his anti-violence teaching.

The message was translated by Vladimir Chertkov, Tolstoy's son-in-law and literary executor, in 1917; Robert Tatlock, a Friends' worker in Moscow, was living with Chertkov during the

while shells were screaming over their house, Chertkov characteristically suggested that they should listen to something more important. He then produced the original in Tolstoy's handwriting.

We have been able to trace only one previous publication of this message in English, and by kind permission of Robert Tatlock and of John L. Nickalls, Librarian at Friends' House, we print it for the world-wide C.O. movement of 1943:

Greetings to Conscientious Objectors:

"GREETINGS to you, our brothers, who are suffering for our common cause, the cause of all mankind! Poor, bewildered men who understand not what they do, torment you. Millions and millions studiously shut their eyes on what is being done to you, so that they fail to see the simple, plain question which, whether they wish it or not, stands now so vividly before all men, especially before those who call themselves Christians.

"You are few, you are units among millions, but the real power is not on their side but on yours. This, in a vague manner, they feel, and so they attempt to exclude from their minds the question involved, to pretend indeed that no question exists. But you who give a direct reply to it, confirming your reply by suffering, render the issue so apparent that they can no longer prevent themselves from realising it.

"The question, clear and simple, is this: which of the two laws dost thou regard as binding for thyself,—thou, every man of our present time—the law of God, which is of thy conscience, or the law of man, which is of the State? Dost thou believe in the civil code or in the Gospel? Which command dost thou regard as most binding for thyself, the Command of God or of the military statutes? Some

Chapter Four

Treatment of Conscientious Objectors (Press, Public and Priests)

The attitudes displayed by the press, public and churches towards conscientious objectors are now examined in greater detail.

The War involved the whole population, both military and civilian, in sacrifice. In a democracy, the goodwill of the people is necessary to accept this sacrifice, and the inconvenience of compulsion. Fighting for one's country was the mark of a good citizen in the First World War. In the Second World War it was more. As well as military conscription from the outset, it also involved industrial, civil defence and fire-watching compulsion. Those who objected to the compulsion were not just seen as not pulling their weight, but to many it was offensive that they were not fighting for their country's survival. However, to others in a war of democracy versus fascism, conscientious objection was the embodiment of the freedoms that the country was fighting for. It is perhaps for this reason that the satirical postcards of objectors in the First World War, do not appear to be so evident in the Second World War – there was much more at stake.

Whatever the point of view held, it was often forcibly expressed. The press, and to a lesser extent the churches, provided a safety valve for the expression of such strong feelings, rather than their being manifested in more unpleasant ways.

Public tribunals meant conscientious objectors were easily identified. They were an easy target for the press and its readers, attracting, as is usual from contributors to the press, letters strongly condemning them or supporting them. Not all views were polarised as this chapter demonstrates. Similar conflicts of opinion were evident in the main churches. A great many of their members were in the armed forces, but at the same time most conscientious objection was on religious grounds. How they balanced support for the war, and with it the actions of many of their members, with ministering to conscientious objectors among their congregations is examined here, as are the conflicting views of the clergy towards war.

Press Treatment of Conscientious Objectors

The government was concerned with the morale of the population, particularly when the course of the war was not going in Britain's favour. The Ministry of Information believed that the factors determining morale could be divided into 'material' and 'mental'. The latter included two factors strongly featured in the debates surrounding conscientious objectors: 'belief that the war was a just cause; and, belief in equality of sacrifice.'[1] Newspapers were important instruments in influencing these factors and as such were subject to a voluntary scheme of censorship. Voluntary of course meant that newspaper editors, as were ordinary citizens, were subject to Defence Regulation 3 which prohibited them from 'obtaining, recording, communicating to any other person, or publishing any information that might be useful to the enemy.'[2] Apart from the *Daily Worker*, the paper of the CPGB, no major newspaper was banned for breaching the regulations, although the *Daily Mirror* came close. On 5 March 1942, the *Daily Mirror* published a cartoon on the government's decision to increase the price of petrol. The cartoon showed a torpedoed sailor with an oil-smeared face lying on a raft with the message was "Don't waste petrol. It costs lives." Winston Churchill believed that the cartoon suggested that the sailor's life had been put at stake to enhance the profits of the petrol companies and the Home Secretary considered closing down the paper. [3]

Therefore, the threat of censorship meant that newspapers were limited as to what they could report and how they could report it. They were also limited by the government controlling the release of information regarding military engagement. For most of the early years of the war, journalists were not present at the front. This usually meant the under-reporting of defeats and the over-stressing of small victories, but

---

[1] Robert Mackay, *Half the Battle: Civilian Morale in Britain during the Second World War* (Manchester: Manchester University Press, 2002), p. 141.
[2] Gardiner, *Wartime Britain 1939-1945*, p. 154.
[3] http://spartacus-educational.com/Jmirror.htm.

it also meant, with the quiet encouragement of the Ministry of Information, the castigation of those seen as not doing their bit for the war
effort.[4] This was extremely important for local newspapers, as they identified people within their readers' localities, including conscientious objectors. It is not surprising that the local newspapers gave the majority
of their coverage of objectors up to the end of the Blitz in1941. Once
the tide of the war changed, there was much more good news to report
to fill the space, which was also limited by paper rationing. As the need
to artificially maintain morale diminished, so did the coverage given to
conscientious objectors. The call-up of many journalists meant the press
could not cover all the courts and tribunals. This kind of coverage did
not, however, disappear.

Local newspapers were more abundant during the Second World
War than they are today, representing just under half of all the daily
newspaper sales. In Britain in 1937 there were 27 morning titles, 83
evening and 7 Sunday, one of which was the Newcastle based *Sunday
Sun*.[5] Those titles still in existence today also had far higher circulation
figures than now: The *Newcastle Evening Chronicle* had a circulation of
190,000 in 1945, down to 52,486 in 2011; the *Sunderland Echo* down
from 57,000 to 32,711; and, the *Evening Gazette* (Teesside) down from
57,000 to 40,546. [6] The local press was therefore a major informer of
opinion at a time when they, along with newsreels and state radio were
the only media available to the majority. Its role was to inform the population and to provide a platform for readers to express their views. Individual newspapers also reflected the political views of their proprietor
through the editorial comment and style of reporting. The rise in regional newspapers had its roots in the radical press of the nineteenth
century but by the Second World War the majority were in the owner-
ship of five leading conservative publishing chains. There was no re-

---

[4] John Tulloch, 'The Return of the 'Conchie': Newspaper Representations of Conscientious Objectors
and Pacifists in World War II,' in Stephen Gibson and Simon Mollon, eds., *Representations of Peace and
Conflict* (Basingstoke: Palgrave Macmillan, 2012), p. 46.
[5] James Curran, and Jean Seaton, *Power Without Responsibility: The Press and Broadcasting in Britain*
(London: Routledge, 1997), p. 291.
[6] The Audit Bureau of Circulations, http://www.abc.org.uk/,

gional newspaper equivalent to the left-wing *Daily Mirror* or *Daily Herald* in the North-East of England (although even the *Daily Mirror* recognised that, as a large number of its readers were serving in the forces, it had to balance its promotion of civil liberties in its leader columns with jeering sarcasm at objectors in its letters page).[7] The *Northern Echo* which had started as a liberal counter to conservative newspapers, was owned for a time by the Rowntree (Quaker) controlled North of England Newspaper Company until that company was taken over by the conservative Westminster Press.[8]

The way the press treated conscientious objectors was to publicise the polarised views of their readers. It was not limited to this, but was more nuanced. In times of war a further dimension was added. The press, more commonly during the period of greatest national danger, gave them disparaging names in their column titles such as 'dodgers,' 'shirkers' and 'conchies;' words also used within articles. The term 'conchie' was a 'contemptuous representation of the conscientious objector, invented in 1916, reinvented to meet the needs of 1940'.[9]

They also used headlines and column titles to create a negative image of objectors' character: 'I Am Too Sensitive' (*Durham County Advertiser*, 29 March 1940); 'Judge on "Poisonous Christians"' (*North-East Gazette*, 15 July 1940); 'Horrible Pacifists Teaching Boys' (*North-East Gazette*, 16 August 1940); 'Objector "Biggest Example of a Coward"' (*Northern Echo*, 15 December 1939); 'Better Off Dead: Middlesbrough C.O.'s View of War Injured' (*Northern Echo*, 21 October 1941), etc.

A letter from the Ministry of Information to local newspaper editors, leaked to *Peace News,* encouraged them to give less space to the reporting of objectors' arguments at tribunals, as if any encouragement was needed.[10] This also ensured that articles gave prominence to the more sensational statements of objectors, making them appear as either unreasonable or strange. There was, of course, the hint of sexual inadequacy. The *Evening Chronicle* and the *Northern Daily Mail* quoted a member of the French Military Mission saying there was no such thing

---

[7] Tulloch, 'The Return of the 'Conchie,' p. 63.
[8] https://en.wikipedia.org/wiki/The_Northern_Echo.
[9] Tulloch, 'The Return of the 'Conchie,' pp. 45-46.
[10] *Peace News*, 22 April 1940, p. 5.

as a conscientious objector in France: 'The French military system is based on conscription of the whole of the manhood of the nation, and young men who cannot pass the physical test do not carry favour with their girls.'[11] France was also used by the *Ripon Gazette* to criticise British objectors:

> The French are a practical and democratic people. They treat their conscientious objectors as cranks. If the misguided fellows persist in their error, they are treated as ordinary criminals. But, in France there are remarkably few conscientious objectors. Few young men will agree to be branded as cowards. I am certain that the legalised existence in Great Britain of a class of conscientious objectors is the source of continuous wonderment to our allies across the Channel. Some Frenchmen ask me about that. My advice to them is to leave the question alone for a time. The nation has only begun to find its stride. As the war develops and its aspect becomes more terrible the conscientious cranks will disappear and the conscientious criminals will be dealt with as they deserve.[12]

The same headlines were often used in more than one newspaper. It would seem reasonable to assume that the aim was to create a negative impression of objectors in the minds of readers. The almost total absence of such lurid headlines after 1942, when victory was looking more assured, supports this assumption.

The statistically low number of objectors in the North-East of England also aided the local and regional press in marginalising them as a minority within the community. It also aided the Ministry of Information whose Home Intelligence Reports in May 1940 were expressing concern that conscientious objectors might become the 'object of antagonism which may develop in an ugly way. The public should be told

---

[11] 'France Has No Conscientious Objectors,' *Evening Chronicle*, 7 February 1940, p. 1, and, 'Why There Are No Conchies in France', *Northern Daily Mail*, 7 February 1940, p. 3.
[12] 'A Conchie Talks To Me', *Ripon Gazette*, 15 February 1940, p. 2.

that C.O.s do not make good soldiers and are therefore not wanted in the Army. Their small and decreasing number should be emphasised.'[13]

The Ministry were therefore willing to see objectors negatively targeted by the press, but there were limits. The local press obliged with headlines: 'Only Four in a Thousand Are C.O.s';[14] 'Only One C.O. at Shields,'[15] and many similar examples. It was also emphasised in editorials carrying titles such as 'No Shirkers':

> Proudly we record the dwindling number of C.O.s. of the North-East coast registration. Only one in every 250 sought exemption from combatant duties, and in Middlesbrough the number was smaller still. The PPU pickets at the Labour Exchange had a thin time. Hitler has blown their feeble sophistries to smithereens and united the whole nation in the inflexible determination to destroy his power for evil.[16]

Newspapers delivered an anti-objector message through the use of editorials and feature articles. The message was usually direct. Nothing was more direct than the article by B. C. McDonald in the *Sunderland Echo*:[17]

> So long as a man remains a citizen of the community of a nation organised for war he is so dependent upon others, so enmeshed in the machine that it is impossible for him to avoid being associated in the general effort. This association necessarily destroys the sincerity of a pacifist. Moreover, all food entering this country does so because of the British Navy, which cannot be maintained without killing. Thus, the pacifist cannot, in sincerity, even eat the food obtained

---

[13] Paul Addison and Jeremy A. Crang, *Listening to Britain: Home Intelligence Reports on Britain's Finest Hour – May to September 1940* (London: Vintage Books, 2010), 19-20 May.

[14] *Northern Echo*, 11 March 1940, p. 5.

[15] *Shields Gazette*, 8 April 1940, p. 6.

[16] 'Editorial: No Shirkers,' *North-East Gazette*, 11 March 1940, p. 4.

[17] 'Is the Pacifist Sincere?', *Sunderland Echo*, 27 May 1940, p. 2.

for him by a means to which he is totally opposed. The conclusion is inescapable.

It is equally unfair to those serving with the Forces that any man should be able to cut completely adrift from his liabilities to the State, and quite possibly retain a good job in the comparative luxury and comfort of home...However lofty the principles of the pacifist, he cannot enjoy freedom maintained by others by means to which he says he is utterly opposed.

Pacifism in an organised form presents a more sinister aspect. It is a subversive propaganda inimical to the interests of the State.

We are told variously by men who will not kill because of the Sixth Commandment that they would not aid a wounded soldier, would not aid a civilian injured in an air-raid, would use an air-raid shelter but would not help make one. This is surely as base a morality as could ever be conceived. Such persons are anti-social, anti-human, and, in fact, are parasites with a consciousness more animal than human, if they do mean what they say, which is more than doubtful.

Let us keep our eyes open to the truth, however unpleasant it may appear; moral cowardice is a far greater failing than physical fear.

A refusal to face up to the difficulties in life would abrogate its usefulness. Above all the refusal to repel evil at whatever cost is a negation of all morality and contrary to the very motive of the human spirit.

The above article has been extensively quoted because, whilst encapsulating many of the criticisms levelled against conscientious objectors and pacifists in various quarters, it was by far the most comprehensive criticism found in any of the local newspapers examined. The article was preceded in the same newspaper by an article by C. Miller in which he attacked those 'whose consciences are so delicately constituted that they must endure endless misery that that delicacy is not violated,' concluding that for the individual 'his nation's body is threatened by a disease called Nazism, but, unlike his own body's living defence forces, he refuses to fight.'[18]

Other newspapers also criticised objectors in their editorials. The *Northern Daily Mail* was critical of our 'somewhat curious regulations' which allowed 60,000 objectors, equating to four army divisions, and asserted that the war had been invited by 'a deluded pacifism.'[19] In response to the conscientious objectors' right to freedom of thought the *Evening Chronicle* expressed the view that: 'In War, individualism must be in part subordinated to mass thought, or else the collective purpose disintegrates.'[20] The *Alnwick Gazette* also wondered if: 'Perhaps the C.O.s have a totally different standard of ethics to plain mortals.'[21]

---

[18] 'The Conscience', *Sunderland Echo*, 1 January 1940, p. 4.

[19] 'Britain's Man Power,' *Northern Daily Mail*, 9 December 1942, p. 2.

[20] 'Problem of C.O.s,' *Evening Chronicle*, 13 August 1940, p. 4.

[21] 'The Chimney Corner: No More War,' *Alnwick County Gazette and Guardian*, 9 August 1940, p. 4.

Examples of Headlines in the Local Press

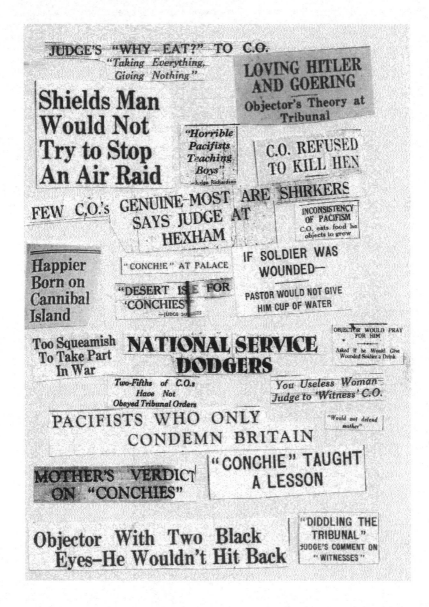

One thread running through the press treatment of objectors was their selfishness. The *Yorkshire Evening Post*, considered that this could be explained by the fact that many objectors were either the only child or only son in a family. Commenting on Judge Stewart's observation that this applied to 40% of applicants to the Leeds Tribunal, their Editorial asserted:

> Those who argue for give and take (sometimes the rough and tumble) of family life have perhaps contented themselves with saying they are not surprised; at any rate the facts support those who contend that the only child is bound to be more self-centred than the member of a large family. The only child is in no way certain to be an odd man out, but a child with brothers and sisters is used to sharing in enterprises, not merely in the home but outside it (because of the extended circumstances of companionship), it learns something of mutual responsibility, and it learns also where a good many of its ideas may be wrong.
>
> ...The life of an only child must turn a good deal upon itself with the result sometimes seen in the Objectors' court in appeals that are less the consequence of conscience than of an inadequate and sequestered point of view.[22]

Regarding selfishness, the *Northern Daily Mail* reported the comments of the Exeter Recorder to an actor who had refused to submit to a medical examination:

> Try to think a little less of yourself. Try to put your conscience and your self-conceit into their true proportions, and think a little more of the sufferings of those people who are fighting and risking their lives every moment of the day to look after all of us, including you.[23]

---

[22] 'Editorial: Only Sons and Pacifism,' *Yorkshire Evening Post*, 15 January 1940, p. 6.
[23] 'Actor's Self Conceit,' *Northern Daily Mail*, 4 October 1941, p. 4.

One article, published in the *Ripon Gazette* and the *Hexham Courant*, was uniquely condescending to objectors. It related to an alleged conversation between the author and a conscientious objector. The conversation is reproduced in full in Appendix D where its meaning and effect can be fully portrayed, however, its main features are detailed below.[24]

The incident took place in the dentist's waiting room where the writer engaged in conversation with what he describes as 'a handsome young man,' a description used more than once to set up a subtle stereotypical image of a conscientious objector as being vain, if not effeminate. The conversation began with the writer establishing his right to be critical by reminding the reader that, unlike the objector, he had served in the previous war: 'This endless waiting for the dentist reminds me of occasions when I waited to go over the top.' With what is described as a 'disgusted air' the man replies: 'Oh, I see, you are making comparisons with war conditions, I did not understand you at first, because my mind does not work that way. I am a conscientious objector, you see.' The final sentence was delivered with 'a condescending smile.' The writer then describes in detail the objector's responses to the writer's questions on his beliefs. Here the writer presents himself as using his intellectual superiority, falsely feigning ignorance of the issues, to defeat the arguments of the conscientious objector who eventually walks out of the room a defeated man.

The aim of the writer was quite clearly to ridicule the conscientious objector, who he says displayed an 'apostolic fervour', and whose views would not stand up to scrutiny. He implies that the objector is also not wholly truthful about his tribunal experiences when he states: 'these war-mongers speak so much utter nonsense that it is childishly easy to defeat them in debate.' The writer of course puts the typical tribunal questions concerning a German soldier raping his wife, and would he like the Germans to win, to which the objector is presented as not having a reasoned answer. He also in his questioning hints that to be an

---

[24] 'A Conchie Talks to Me,' *Ripon Gazette*, 15 February 1940, p. 2., and, 'Five Questions To a Conscientious Objector,' *Hexham Courant*, 17 February 1940, p. 4.

objector is also to be a communist sympathiser by getting him to admit that he would not like to see the Russians beaten, and asking him, 'What has Russia specially to do with your conscientious objection to war in any form?'[25] Finally, the writer sums up his views on conscientious objectors, presenting them as people to be pitied and not feared:

> To me it was a real revelation of the addled condition of the mind of a fellow like that. I felt no anger, only a great pity. Those fine gentlemen, who speak fine words about their anti-war attitude based on high moral principles, they lose their balance when you suddenly confront them with a stark fact.

It is easy to criticise the attitudes displayed in this, and other articles quoted, as being unbalanced. They have, however, to be taken in the context of the time when uncertainty was felt as to how the war would end. The press at the time and the government propaganda was very much concerned at any potential Fifth Column activity that would undermine the war effort. This concern is illustrated by some of the bizarre rumours circulating. The Chief Constable of Hartlepool and a Professor of French at Newcastle were rumoured to be German spies which may explain how Lord Haw Haw could have known that Darlington Town Hall clock was two minutes slow, which it was.[26]

They were therefore encouraged by the progressive decline in the proportion of those claiming conscientious objection which, 'provides the most conclusive proof that the country pays little heed to stop-the-war cranks and defeatist propaganda.'[27] They could feel equally encouraged by being able to report cases, such as in Sheffield where men had ceased to be objectors, as a result of meeting Moral Re-Armament, an organisation that could 'vanquish those fifth columnists in each of us.'[28]

The press also reminded conscientious objectors of how lucky they were in comparison with the previous war. The *Yorkshire Evening*

---

[25] Russia at this time was not at war with Germany and was militarily engaged in Finland.
[26] Addison and Crang, *Listening to Britain,* 27 May to 1 June and 6 June.
[27] 'Editorial: Treason and Plot,' *Hexham Courant,* 4 May 1940, p. 4.
[28] 'Conscientious Objector's Confession,' *Durham County Advertiser,* 14 June 1940, p. 4.

Post commented that in providing for conscientious objection; 'British practice, even in time of war, carries liberty to the extreme limit of consideration alike for the unhelpful and the hostile.'[29] L. A. G. Strong, writing in the *Sunderland Echo* after the war, pointed out that, 'We do not harry our cranks. They are allowed to make a considerable nuisance of themselves before the law reluctantly steps in,' and, that there had been very little of the public molestation, ridicule, ignominy, and the charge of cowardice common in 1914-1918.[30] It is doubtful whether the objectors who suffered multiple prison sentences would agree with this analysis, particularly regarding some attitudes portrayed by his, and other, newspapers.

Once granted conditional exemption by the tribunal objectors were not free from press attention. The *Evening Chronicle* reported: 'feeling is widespread that conchies are not playing the game and are encouraged in this by a lack of proper checks by the authorities.'[31] They quoted three objectors who had not found work eight months after their registration. Even when they later reported the low numbers of conscientious objectors in the region, and an official statement that only half a dozen had failed to take up work directed, they sought the assurance of the Ministry of Labour that they kept 'a continual check on these men.'[32]

One group of conscientious objectors who escaped the displeasure of the local press were the Quakers. There was widespread acceptance of their genuineness and bravery in serving at the front line. The North-East also had two of the major Quaker centres in Darlington and York, where leading Quakers were major employers and social philanthropists. The *Alnwick Gazette* published a full-page article on the FAU praising its work on both the Home Front and under fire: 'Some have been killed on the scene of battle, others have been taken prisoners of war, but even in the restricted amenities of a German Oflag they are bringing peace of mind and body to their fellow captives.'[33]

---

[29] 'Editorial: Our Foes Within,' *Yorkshire Evening Post*, 21 February 1940, p. 8.
[30] 'Freedom of Conscience,' *Sunderland Echo*, 28 December 1945, p. 2.
[31] 'Two-Fifths of C.O.s have not Obeyed Tribunal Orders,' *Evening Chronicle*, 13 August 1940, p. 5.
[32] 'Few C.O. Dodgers in the North-East,' *Evening Chronicle*, 27 February 1941, p. 6.
[33] 'Quaker Ambulance Unit's Devoted Service,' *Alnwick County Gazette and Guardian*, 21 November 1941, p. 8.

The local press was prepared to take the moral high ground when it came to the giving out of white feathers to conscientious objectors, although their concern was more for those who may receive them who were not objectors. The *Northern Daily Mail* ran an editorial against the practice following two instances involving non-objectors reported in West Hartlepool and the suicide of a person in Oxford who had received white feathers.[34] The suicide incident was also reported in the *Sunderland Echo,* and the practice also condemned in a *Ripon Gazette* editorial.[35] The *North-East Gazette* presented a fuller condemnation:

> Even assuming that the unwitting recipients of her insulting attentions were the shirkers this skirted crusader assumes them to be, by what right does she assume the role of ambulating recruiter? It is a matter of indifference to her whether or not the individual is a soldier on leave, a possible hero in mufti. It is of no consequence that her victim may be snatching some all too brief leisure form long hours in the nation's service. "Here is a young man", she argues, "let's label him." So, the badge of the shirker is only presented by an individual whose own contribution to the national service is probably nil.[36]

Despite this apparent defence of the conscientious objector the editor could not refrain from using the term 'shirker.'

The press in the North-East of England were hence unsympathetic to the conscientious objector. This they shared with the majority of readers who wrote to them. In many respects, they were following the example set by a mainly unsympathetic national press. A more sympathetic opinion was available in minority papers such as *The New Leader* and *Peace News.* These publications did, however, encounter difficulties when news of Nazi atrocities began to reach Britain. *Peace News* left itself

---

[34] 'Editorial: White Feathers,' *Northern Daily Mail,* 28 February 1942, p. 2; and, 'White Feathers,' *Northern Daily Mail,* 9 June 1943, p. 6.

[35] '"White Feathers" Inquest,' *Sunderland Echo,* 9 June 1943, p. 8.; and, 'Editorial: "White Feather" Foolery,' *Ripon Gazette,* 9 July 1942, p. 4.

[36] 'Editorial: White Feathers,' *North-East Gazette,* 21 October 1941, p. 2.

open to criticism, firstly with an article by Robert H. Thouless who questioned whether such atrocities were relevant to whether the Nazis were beaten or not.[37] They followed this with an article in January 1943 which suggested that there may be a degree of exaggeration in the stories and questioned the reasons for their release:

> We are not for one moment suggesting that the story of these mass-pogroms is a wartime invention. They may be exaggerated but if only one-quarter of the charges are true, it is more than enough to damn the Nazi instigators and their instruments, who are mainly non-Germans: Latvians and Lithuanians. Why now?
> - To prevent us giving way at Christmas to thoughts and hopes of peace.
> - To whip up a hatred at a moment when a turn in military fortune has awakened an expectation of an early victory that will probably prove elusive.[38]

They then criticised all propaganda as anti-German with only ugly news, which they countered with a story of a U-Boat Captain who had shown kindness to the passengers of a sunken ship.[39]

The accuracy of such information was difficult to determine at the time, however, by Autumn 1942, 'a clear picture of the Nazi extermination campaign could be constructed.'[40] The government, as Tony Kushner argues, was reluctant to publicly address the 'Jewish dimension' to Nazi atrocities and therefore did not speak out as strongly as it might have done.[41]

---

[37] 'The Truth About Atrocities,' *Peace News*,24 February 1942, pp. 1 and 4.
[38] 'Will We Help the Jews?' *Peace News*, 1 January 1943, p. 2.
[39] 'Those Germans! Not All Are Ugly,' *Peace News*, 8 January 1943, p. 1.
[40] Tom Lawson, *The Church of England and the Holocaust: Christianity, Memory and Nazism* (Woodbridge: Boydell and Brewer, 2006), p. 82.
[41] Tony Kushner, *The Holocaust and the Liberal Imagination: A Social and Cultural History* (Oxford: Blackwell, 1994) pp. 168-201.

However, it would be wrong to stigmatise pacifists as pro-Hitler. Being anti-fascist does not equate to being pro-war. As Maurice Rowntree had stated, pacifists clearly thought of fascism and Hitler as bad but were not accepting that the only way to beat them was to kill people. The problem for pacifists was how else could fascism be beaten. This book gives examples of how pacifists contributed to the war effort, e.g. FAU and acceptance of work as directed by the Ministry of Labour. The scale of the holocaust was such that it required action on an international scale, although some pacifists were involved in the rescue of some Jewish people. There was also criticism after the war that the Allies themselves had done little until the war was over to alleviate the suffering. Also, as Cynthia Eller states, the Holocaust was unknown at the time that most conscientious objectors made their decision.[42] Eller's interviewees were also adamant that a later justification for the war being to save the Jews was 'fanciful'.[43]

Letters to the local press

Both sides of the debate featured in letters to the local newspapers. The majority of letters published were anti-objector and usually vociferous in their condemnation, reflecting the maxim that a view must be strongly held to prompt the writing of a letter to the press.

Many expressing anti-objector views were keen to offer suggestions as to what should be done with them. 'A Proud Mother' was one of many to propose financial penalties:

Had I my way these cowardly Conchies would not be allowed any consideration. I wouldn't allow them to draw the dole or benefit in any way in a country they are afraid to fight for. Why should decent brave men die for these rats?'[44]

---

[42] Cynthia Eller, 'Oral History as Moral Discourse: Conscientious Objectors and the Second World War' *Oral History Review*, 18/1 (Spring 1990), p. 47.

[43] Ibid., p. 63.

[44] 'Nothing for C.O.s,' *Evening Chronicle*, 11 April 1940, p. 4.

'Soldiers Mother' expressed the widely-held view: 'if they were made to work for a soldier's pay there would not nearly be so many of them.'[45] It was a commonlystated that they were just shirkers and very few were genuine objectors. 'Soldier's Mother' stated: 'Most are not genuine. They have just found a way to avoid military service.'[46] 'Anti C.O.' of Durham summed up the feelings of many:

> We read that there are so far 26,000 C.Os. These men should be ashamed to call themselves Englishmen. To quote Lady Astor we are all C.Os. There are few men who enjoy killing fellow men, but fortunately many realise what would happen should we lose this war...
>
> I am prepared to admit that there is such a thing as a true C.O., but in the above 26,000 I can say quite safely say no more than 2,000. The others are pure shirkers, prepared to live in comfort while men lose their lives to bring them food.[47]

'Backer of Freedom' referred to objectors having no compunction eating food paid for in men's lives suggesting:

> If they persisted in this attitude, they should all be rounded up and interned. In the meantime, they should all be boycotted, and no one with their dear ones in the fighting services should work with them. They should be deprived of all civil rights, and certainly none should be employed by any municipal or government body. They have no right to anything that brave men are fighting for...[48]

Some suggested that objectors should be treated even more harshly. 'Ubique' referring to a man who told him he was an objector

[45] 'Mother's Verdict on "Conchies",' *Evening Chronicle*, 2 March 1940, p. 4.
[46] 'Nothing for C.O.s,' *Evening Chronicle*, 11 April 1940, p. 4.
[47] 'Ignore C.O.s,' *Evening Chronicle*, 14 April 1940, p. 4.
[48] 'Conscientious Objectors,' *Sunderland Echo*, 4 March 1940, p. 5.

on religious grounds, and would not help a soldier: 'I would order him to be shot.'[49] 'A. E. T.' criticised the sending of Jehovah's Witnesses to prison on the grounds that: 'Freedom has to be hard fought for, and their place is in the front line to stop a German bullet killing a man, not put in cold storage until hostilities cease.'[50] J. T. Leonard was of the opinion that: 'We should make conscientious objectors stretcher bearers at the front line ....they could test if love would be better for the Germans than a gun.[51] Similarly 'Ebenezer' suggested: 'I think the best thing to do is to accede to their public declaration of their innate love for our enemy, and drop them by parachute for an afternoon cup of tea among their friends in Germany. That would soon settle the problem of their conscientious objection.'[52]

The above are just some of the extreme views expressed. Clearly few of their solutions were likely to be implemented. The aim of these comments was most likely the humiliation of objectors. There was no greater humiliation than to say, 'I believe they are cowards,' as stated by 'A Mother.'[53] To Tom Jack: 'There is no distinction between cowardice and the expression "conscientious objector".'[54] Many, such as W.W. objected to 'the broad back of our Lord being made a bomb-proof shelter by many who don't care about anything other than their precious skins,' and concluded that 'we have no room for the man whose conscience is so poisoned and sickly that it does not bid him to rally to the call of the Motherland.'[55]

What would lead to such extreme views being expressed? In the majority of cases quoted the view has been preceded by one of the following factors: a reported statement by objectors that they would not help a wounded soldier; a refusal by objectors to work in hospitals; or, a willingness by objectors to eat food that men had died bringing in to the country. The main point of antagonism was therefore those who took

---

[49] 'Conscientious Objectors Should Lose Civil Rights,' *Sunderland Echo*, 8 April 1940, p. 5.

[50] 'C.O.s – Why Send Them to Prison,' *Sunderland Echo*, 18 June 1942, p. 2.

[51] 'C.O. Badges,' *Evening Chronicle*, 17 May 1940, p. 4.

[52] 'Judge and the C.O.s,' *Durham County Advertiser*, 2 October 1942, p. 4.

[53] 'A Mother Who Would Also Fight for Her Country – Scathing Comment on C.O.', *Durham County Advertiser*, 5 April 1940, p. 6.

[54] 'Conscientious Objectors Should Join Defensive Services,' *Sunderland Echo*, 19 December 1939, p. 5.

[55] 'Readers' Views on Conscientious Objectors,' *Hexham Courant*, 18 May 1940, p. 8.

the absolutist stance of refusing to do anything which could in any way contribute to the war effort. To many the government intention that those exempted should do work of national importance was not regarded with hostility. One correspondent hostile to objectors was willing to concede that some were genuine and prepared to take part in non-military duties at great risk, quoting Quakers as a good example.[56] Others were also accused of dodging military service in other ways. Those who secured work in reserved occupations also drew public ire. 'Green Howard Sister' was particularly critical:

> I detest the sneaking rats who have secured reserve jobs to evade military service. There were many I know who never did work……. Why should a man who has worked all his life be made to join up in preference to those would-be idlers. They only took those jobs to evade service and are laughing at the rest.[57]

'Scotchman' referred to them as 'Quitters,' worse than conscientious objectors, whilst another correspondent criticised air-raid wardens, asking, 'how many are there, eligible for military service, who have enrolled for the express purpose of evading the call to the colours?'[58]

However, conscientious objectors were the object of most criticism, and the criticism levelled focussed on inequality of sacrifice. To many such as 'Victoire' the inequality in wages between those in the armed forces and those whose objection allowed them to remain in jobs paying more was an anathema: 'Why not cut down the wages of conscientious objectors until it is the equivalent to the soldiers allowance, and see how the objectors would face that action.'[59] Such people were 'not objectors on pay day,' in the view of '1914-1918.'[60] The more drastic

[56] 'Letter from W. Faulkner: Conscientious Objectors,' *Durham County Advertiser*, 9 October 1942, p. 4.
[57] '"Rats" Who Evade Military Service,' *North-East Gazette*, 1 April 1941, p. 5.
[58] '"Voice of the North: "Quitters" are worse than C.O.s,' *North-East Gazette*, 7 August 1940, p. 2., and, 'Straight From The Shoulder: The Dodgers,' *North-East Gazette*, 28 September 1939, p. 6.
[59] 'Letter to the Editor,' *Durham County Advertiser*, 7 June 1940, p. 4.
[60] 'ARP Misfits,' *Yorkshire Evening Post*, 17 May 1940, p. 5.

action of refusing ration coupons to objectors was advocated by Edward McLoughlin of Harrogate: 'People in a leaking boat at sea would be justified in throwing out any who refused to bale.'[61] To rectify the unequal sacrifice a correspondent suggested in 1945:

> I would like to suggest training C.O.s to serve in the occupation of Germany then maybe the demobilisation will get a move on. It's about time we sorted out some of those men one sees swaggering about the town with permanent waved hair ready to run into the nearest shop doorway when a few drops of rain appear. Perhaps a year or two spent with men like those of our gallant 14th Army would give them more to think about.[62]

Despite adverse comments in the local press, there were also a small number of letters of support from people who, to some extent, felt able to use the press to try to combat the negative views towards objectors. Given this negativity, it is perhaps surprising that many letters from objectors themselves were published. One such letter from G. W. C. Nunn of Northallerton emphasised that the war was supposedly being fought for the freedom to hold one's own political, economic, religious and moral views. He also sought to counter criticism by explaining in a measured way the difficulties he faced as a conscientious objector:

> The vast majority of C.O.s are in an exceedingly difficult position, because we desire perhaps even more strongly than most people, to put an end to Hitlerism, and yet cannot conscientiously support or assist in war, even if that war is directed against evil things. No one who has first-hand contact with C.O.s can justifiably suggest that we are unpatriotic fifth-columnists or traitors. And no one who understands the word "conscience" can fail to appreciate the

[61] 'Conscientious Objectors,' *Yorkshire Evening Post*, 17 November 1942, p. 4.
[62] 'Demobilisation – Get a Move On!' *Yorkshire Evening Post*, 30 July 1945, p. 2.

difficulty of our position. We believe that aggression, murder, pillage and wholesale destruction are wrong, and for that very reason we cannot undertake to prevent these terrible things by adopting similar methods…

…C.O.s have a good idea of what is in front of them when they register. The prospect is far less attractive, so far as the saving of skins goes, than joining the RAF. They know that the risks they take includes losing their "friends" and becoming social outcasts, losing their jobs and being unable to get others, sometimes losing their homes, losing their freedom inevitably, and possibly losing their lives. The proportion of C.O.s prepared to make this final supreme sacrifice for their ideals, like Christians of old, is much higher than generally supposed…[63]

Another objector, W. J. Holbrough of Darlington, reacted strongly to accusations of cowardice made by 'Registered 24', suggesting: 'if all the people of the earth possessed one quarter of the moral courage of a sincere conscientious objector on ethical and political grounds, merchantmen would be able to sail the seas for all time in perfect safety, and war between nations would become impossible.' He also expressed the view that objectors would become more vulnerable than those actively engaged at the front, a view unlikely to receive much support.[64]

Isaac W. Braithwaite of Richmond, a political objector, responded to criticism with a strong defence of his position:

Mr J. W. Noble says that 9 out of 10 C.O.s don't want to be killed. Do 9 out of 10 soldiers want to be killed? Hats off to the C.O.s who were in British gaols during the last war, fighting for freedom of thought, as much as to those pals we left behind in Flanders. Some of us were comrades of the men whose names are on the war memorials. We

---

[63] 'Yorkshire Conscientious Objector Answers Some Critics,' *Northern Echo*, 17 June 1940, p. 4.
[64] 'Conscientious Prepared to go to the Front,' *Northern Echo*, 9 March 1940, p. 4.

came back to 5 or more years on the dole. We were too worn and battered to find a place in the labour market. We protested in hunger marches, we got gaol and the policeman's baton. It's from us that some of the C.O.s are coming now.[65]

He received further criticism for these comments but also the support of Olive Baker of Picton, who understood how his experiences of ingratitude and hardship had helped formulate his opinion, and believed that to deny the right of a person to act according to their conscience was to act no differently to the Nazis.[66] Mr Braithwaite commented further the following week:

When did I learn that C.O.s are made by the teachings of ex-servicemen? When I volunteered in 1914 a Boer War veteran told me I was a fool, that it was just a war for money. Three years of modern butchery in France made me realise that he had made me a conscientious objector to capitalism....[67]

Correspondents other than objectors were prepared to defend their right to a conscience and condemn accusations of cowardice. 'Boscawen' of Darlington used the FAU in Finland as an example of bravery by conscientious objectors to vilify those who would 'round off their crass judgements by suggesting that shooting or hanging is the only way to deal with such miscreants.'[68] J. Tweddle of Sunderland saw objectors as fighters against social injustice and the causes of war, and as an asset to Britain and not 'shirkers' or 'blacklegs.'[69] However, the most comprehensive defence came from Muriel Poulter of Durham, who, quoting Bertrand Russell, stated:

---

[65] 'An ex-Service Man and the Objector,' *Northern Echo*, 15 June 1942, p. 2.
[66] 'Ex-Servicemen and C.O.s', *Northern Echo*, 19 June 1942, p. 2.
[67] 'He Met a Boer War Veteran,' *Northern Echo*, 19 June 1942, p. 2.
[68] 'The Friends and Finland,' *Northern Echo*, 11 January 1940, p. 4.
[69] 'Conscientious Objectors are Sincere,' *Sunderland Echo*, 31 October 1939, p. 5.

The reason why the state ought to respect the claims of conscience is not that conscience does not err, but because the determination to live according to conscience is a thing of infinite value. The pacifist can respect those who sincerely believe it is right to fight and the British government, as it has shown by the provisions in the National Service Act, respects the pacifist's desire to follow the dictates of his conscience. In view of this, and the fact that intolerance, as seen in Nazi Germany, is one of the things this country is fighting to overthrow, is it too much to ask that even the daughter of a soldier should be tolerant towards the sincere conscientious objector.

The conscientious objector, I am sure in no way wishes to contract out of his responsibilities to his fellow countrymen. He feels however that he can only be truly loyal to them if he is first loyal to the truth as he sees it.

For this reason, I hope I shall never condemn those who refuse thus to defend me. [70]

Comments to Mass Observation regarding Conscientious Objectors

The anti-objector stance taken by local newspapers and the extreme comments by correspondents were intended to influence public opinion. The attitudes of some employers, fellow workers and council tenants towards objectors may have been influenced by this stance, although some employers resisted the moral pressure being placed on them. Apart from the white feather incidents, there is no evidence in the local press of public antipathy resulting in direct action. There was certainly nothing recorded similar to that which took place in the village of Dalston in Cumberland.

---

[70] 'Conscientious Objectors,' *Durham County Advertiser*, 27 October 1939, p. 2.

In Dalston, a group of conscientious objectors were billeted in the Village Hall. Previously soldiers had been billeted there and a canteen opened for them by a Mrs Jackson. After the arrival of the conscientious objectors she shut the canteen saying:

> I refuse to serve them. I told the vicar so and he is very angry with me and said I was no Christian. Many lads have gone from the village to the war and I could never look them in the face again if I ran a canteen for the C.O.s. The C.O.s came to the village in luxury buses, but the soldiers, whom they succeeded, had to walk to Carlisle. I have closed the canteen until the boys come back again.

The vicar said the position of conscientious objectors was recognised by the government. He also said they were not cowards but that there were various shades of objection and: 'There were men for whom he personally had no use, but there were also men who were convinced it was wrong to take life, and who were ready to undergo hostility and unpopularity.' Again, the rhetoric concerning how a democracy treats its peaceful objectors was evident as cries of dissent were recorded when the vicar described the attitude of some to the conscientious objectors as being akin to Hitlerism. He said he was going to set up another canteen for them but it was a bitter pill that the help he was going to get was from members of the Methodist Church.[71] The Dalston incident raises the question of tolerance, one which concerned Mass Observation as a measure of public morale. Using a sample of 120, they compared the change in attitudes towards objectors between April and September 1940, i.e. the period covering Dunkirk and the Battle of Britain. The results are shown below:[72]

---

[71] 'Canteen Shut When "Conchies" Arrived,' *North-East Gazette*, 26 November 1940, p. 6.
[72] Mass Observation File Report 405, September 1940 – Conscientious Objectors.

Tolerance of Conscientious Objectors – Mass Observation 1940

	April	Sept.
Tolerant	38%	16%
Antagonistic	46%	65%
No Opinion	16%	19%

September

%	Male	Female	Middle Class	Working Class	30+	30-
Tolerant	25	8	32	12	11	32
Antagonistic	68	51	62	66	79	44
No Opinion	7	41	6	22	10	24

The figures highlight four main factors: The significant shift in attitude from tolerance to antagonism over the period; men were more tolerant of objectors than women; the middle class were more tolerant of objectors than the working class; and, the under 30's were more tolerant than the over 30s. Unfortunately, Mass Observation did not repeat the exercise but commented in 1943 that antagonism did not compare with 'the practically universal disgust they aroused in the last war.'[73]

The increased level of antagonism is reflected in the extreme opinions of those writing to the press and the attitude of certain employers, particularly those in the public sector. Was the increasing intolerance reflected in the responses made by Directive Respondents to Mass Observation from the North-East of England? Three directives were issued in October 1942, January 1943 and June 1944 where, in the latter two, they asked respondents if their attitudes towards conscientious objectors had changed. In the first directive they were asked if, from their own experience, people were getting more or less tolerant of minorities which included pacifists. The results, albeit from a small sample, are varied.

---

[73] Mass Observation Bulletin: Issue dated 1 September 1943, p. 8.

One of those whose tolerance decreased as the war progressed was D. Todd, a woman from Northallerton, who in June 1944 wrote:

> Pre-war I was inclined to be a conscientious objector myself because it seems to me that there can be nothing worse than war. I am not quite sure that this is so now because I did not envisage the wholesale slaughter of innocents as the Nazis have done to the Jews… I still think there are two kinds of conscientious objector, the 'brave' and the 'cowards'. The 'brave' are those who are not afraid either of physical danger or of being penalised for their opinions. These are usually either intelligent or strong biased people. The second class are those who used conscientious objection to get them out of danger. The braver members of the second class usually join up all right but are soon invalided out with what used to be known as shell-shock.
>
> The war has made me think that the members of the first class are in error, not because they think it is wrong to go to war, but in thinking that any residual action of this can make it better or less likely to happen. Whether we like it or not we are cogs in a machine and not working will not stop the war but will help the enemy. 'He who is not with us is against us.' Therefore, these people are fighting willynilly. These comments do not apply to the less extreme people who are quite willing to drive ambulances and do civil defence work etc.[74]

A. J. Hall, a Harrogate housewife born in 1900, also had in June 1944, 'less general respect for COs now, but can appreciate them when they show great courage during air-raids etc.' In April 1947 during the period of National Service she stated: 'I respect them but feel they are wrong and making a lot of fuss over their private consciences.'[75] William

---

[74] Directive Respondent 3426, Directive Report, June 1944, *Mass Observation Online*, Adam Matthew Digital, accessed at Durham University Library.
[75] Directive Respondent 3644, Directive Report, June 1944, *Mass Observation Online*.

Hodgson, a laboratory worker from West Hartlepool, also expressed his increasing intolerance in January 1943:

> At the start of the war I had a good deal of sympathy with C.O.s. I prayed in public for consideration for them (This led to me being pestered for months with literature from one. Perhaps that accounts for my decreasing sympathy). But seriously, I am losing patience with them. The political objector takes too narrow a view of the war. It may have been engineered by devils in armament firms, but the war is on, and things can't be improved by allowing the German militarists to dominate the world. As for the religious objector, he is immature... I don't believe in the persecution of C.O.s.[76]

Mrs E. Dawson, born in 1887, of Springwell, found the subject exasperating. In January 1943, she was 'all agin' it,' and in June 1944 she responded: 'No! At least most of the Service men are C.O.s – they hate war and all connected with war. I blame no man for this, but why single out a few and let them off? I could weep as the silly refrain goes on and on.'[77] Similarly exasperated was Enid Atkinson, born in 1899, of Newcastle who wrote in June 1944:

> They irritate one the conscientious objectors because in most part they, a) encourage Fascism, b) see themselves off so lightly... They enabled the peace movement in this country by confusing the issue, they then left us in the lurch while we did the fighting, and are now trying to return in order to have a say in the peace settlement. Bah![78]

---

[76] Directive Respondent 2656, Directive Report, January 1943, *Mass Observation Online.*
[77] Directive Respondent 1016, Directive Reports January 1943 and June 1944, *Mass Observation Online.*
[78] Directive Respondent 2457, Directive Report, June 1944, *Mass Observation Online.*

Whilst these respondents may have had little tolerance towards conscientious objectors, and expressed some exasperation, they nevertheless refrained from the more extreme views expressed by correspondents to the local newspapers. The respondent who came closest was A. W. Dickinson, a Newcastle newsagent and sub-postmaster. In January 1943, he commented: 'I can understand their attitude but cannot agree with it. I feel they claim the protection of their country's forces without appreciable return. They should certainly be forced to work at menial work.' His attitude hardened by June 1944:

> I have to stretch my imagination to find excuses for them as I have in the case of men who love dogs or music. I think I should be inclined to give them dangerous work if I had control of them. They are always unsociable, often contemptuous of we ordinary people, and sometimes rationalise a very real weakness of the nerves.[79]

There were of course some who maintained their level of tolerance. F. Bosomworth, born in 1909, a female teacher and Labour Party member, from Thornaby confirmed in June 1944: 'My attitude has not changed. I think they have a right to their objection if that is how they feel. Of course a tribunal is necessary to decide upon the applicant's sincerity.'[80] J. Moss, a grocer from Ripon, born 1909, commented that he still quite respected them.[81] Similarly, Miss E. Walker, born 1911, of Tynemouth stated: 'I have always sympathised with the genuine conscientious objectors who are willing to serve.....and my attitude has not changed;'[82]and, in January 1943, D. L. Carew-Shaw, a woman from Howden-le-Wear, also expressed a continuity of feeling: 'As I sympathised before the war with their attitude I continue to do so. The ones I

---

[79] Directive Respondent 1248, Directive Report, June 1944, *Mass Observation Online*.
[80] Directive Respondent 2975, Directive Report, June 1944, *Mass Observation Online*.
[81] Directive Respondent 1105, Directive Report, June 1944, *Mass Observation Online*.
[82] Directive Respondent 3429, Directive Report, June 1944, *Mass Observation Online*.

know (Quakers) are sincere.'[83] But perhaps the most measured consideration was from Patricia M Durrant, born 1912, of Newcastle, working at St Mary's College, Durham:

> I have become more tolerant of C.O.s since the war. In pre-war days, when I felt conscious of the German danger to Europe, they used to exasperate me beyond all belief. Now, without in any way admitting the correctness of their attitude to war, I have obtained some understanding of their point of view. I, too, feel that war is destructive of all that is best in life, regardless of the causes for which it is being fought. Unlike the C.O.s, however, I feel that the alternative is too terrible to be faced. For me, war is the lesser of two evils. I think that the actual experience of living through a war has led me to examine my beliefs in the matter more closely, a process which would almost inevitably lead to greater toleration.'[84]

Whilst no hard and fast rule can be determined from such a small sample, nevertheless those showing the greatest toleration tended to be the younger respondents, giving some support to the conclusions of the Mass Observation File Report. No similar conclusion can be drawn with regard to social class. It does, however, show that opinions were varied, a situation summed up by A. Dalrymple Smith, a female office worker of Sunderland, in January 1943:

> It's a very difficult subject. Most men are conscientious objectors and yet fight for the sake of what they think is right so it is hardly fair to let others off. Where there was great mental strain or physical fear, where the man would suffer undue mental strain I'd feel he should do something other

---

[83] Directive Respondent 3367, Directive Report, January 1943, *Mass Observation Online.*
[84] Directive Respondent 2989, Directive Report, January 1943, *Mass Observation Online.*

than actual fighting, but he'd have to sacrifice his home life and liberty and earn the same as soldiers.[85]

One of the Directive Respondents who expressed a view on conscientious objectors was an unknown serving soldier. His opinion, expressed in June 1944, is worth noting:

I have sympathised with, and partly shared, the viewpoint of the conscientious objector and after two years in the Army have still more sympathy and respect for him. I speak of course of the true, sincere, honest C.O. and not of the fastidious butterflies or the wishy-washy molly-coddlers or the holy willies, for all of whom no one can have anything but contempt. The, 'I would not defend my sister if she was being raped' type deserve having their own virginity rudely shattered, and only the tortures of Tantalus are sufficient for the, 'I wouldn't give a starving soldier a crust' shower, but for the man who stands up bravely in the face of universal contempt and considerable physical discomfort, and says, 'I think war is a disgusting waste of splendid young life and effort to absolutely no purpose', I have nothing but respect. The majority of them are enjoying His Majesty's pleasure of course.[86]

On balance the contributions of Mass Observation respondents from the North-East were more equally distributed between pro and anti-objector than contributors to the local press. Of greater significance is the absence of any inclination by those hostile to objectors towards direct action against them or of any reported incidents. This does not mean that such incidents did not occur. Examples from Mass Observation diarists from other parts of Britain indicate that a propensity for extreme intolerance was likely to manifest itself. L. E. England, a soldier, recorded in October 1940 that he had, 'just heard of a benevolent old

---

[85] Directive Respondent 2985, Directive Report, January 1943, *Mass Observation Online.*
[86] Directive Respondent 3631, Directive Report, June 1944, *Mass Observation Online.*

gentleman who went up to a girl selling *Peace News* and spat – one of the few signs of absurd patriotism so far this war.'[87] Two similar incidents occurring in the same week were recorded by A. G. Errey, a music student of Bexhill-on-Sea, in May 1940, the second of which illustrates that not all were intolerant:

> I watched to see if there would be another incident over *Peace News*. There was. A very much lip-sticked young woman tore up the poster (there were two other people, discussing pacifism with the vendor) and then tore up the papers. The usual crowd gathered and all the shops within view emptied themselves of assistants and there were groups of people here and there making abusive remarks – but not a policeman!
>
> After a few minutes the vendor and one of the two who were talking to her and who was also a pacifist slipped away to a café for a coffee – where they found themselves sitting next to their assailant! The crowd gradually dispersed…Incidentally, it has since come out that one result of last week's episode was to inspire a non-pacifist bystander to send 2 guineas to the PPU headquarters – a very profitable incident indeed.[88]

The limited oral testimonies obtained showed different responses towards conscientious objectors. Wendy Acres stated that her grandfather, Ben Bishop, received abuse because his sons were conscientious objectors. People crossed the street to avoid speaking to him, which upset him.[89] Conversely, Paul and Louis Ronchetti did not suffer any abuse from friends and neighbours. However, when they were released from prison they were unable, as conscientious objectors, to get jobs. That

---

[87] Diarist 5061, *Mass Observation Online*.
[88] Diarist 5062, *Mass Observation Online*.
[89] Telephone interview with Wendy Acres, 28 October 2013.

they went straight to the community farm would partly account for the lack of hostility.[90]

Religious Bodies

If conscientious objectors could not rely on the press to exhibit tolerance towards them then religious objectors could perhaps hope their Church would be supportive. Before considering how the Christian Churches responded to conscientious objection, the attitude of the one Jewish objector found in the North-East is examined. He was, Theo Lazarsohn of Newcastle who objected on moral grounds. In view of the extent of their persecution, it was no surprise that the Chief Rabbi issued a statement declaring that there was no basis in Judaism for an objection in conscience to war, a statement which Carl Heath, writing in *The Friend*, concluded, 'would rule out all Jewish C.O.s and make it hard for any before the tribunal.'[91] Mr Lazarsohn who said, 'he had great sympathy for his race who had suffered persecution but this did not overcome his moral objection,' was, however, conditionally registered.[92]

At a time of national crisis, the role of the Churches in maintaining morale was important, even though church attendances had been in steady decline from the nineteenth-century. This was particularly so with regard to the Church of England, however, a Mass Observation survey at the end of the war found that over two-thirds of the sample still had a belief in the existence of God.[93] Conscious of criticism that the Church of England had been too jingoistic in the First World War, the retired Bishop of Durham, Hensley Henson, noted: 'The conventional tub-thumping is out of the question. We have got past that phase.'[94] The official position of the main Christian denominations, Anglican, Roman Catholic and Methodist, was supportive of the war and all provided chaplains to the forces. The *Church Times* was unequivocal:

---

[90] Telephone interview with Paul Ronchetti, 1 November 2013.
[91] 'The Jewish Conscience and War,' *The Friend*, 14 June 1940, p. 365.
[92] 'Conscientious Objectors' Tribunal,' *Durham County Advertiser*, 20.10.39, p. 8.
[93] Calder, *The People's War*, p. 478.
[94] Alan Wilkinson, *Dissent or Conform?: War, Peace and the English Churches 1900-1945* (London: SCM Press, 1986), pp. 234-235.

The logical pacifist who is determined to have no part in the business ought to pay no taxes, direct or indirect; he cannot buy a packet of cigarettes without paying for some bullets with the extra price of his tobacco; he is part of the social order and the world economy and can no more disconnect himself from it than jump off his own shadow.[95]

The Archbishop of Canterbury, Cosmo Lang, in a joint wartime message with the Moderator of the Free Church of Scotland and the Evangelical Free Churches stated: 'At all costs the policy declared by the German Fuhrer must be overcome. It is based on force. It must be met by counter-force.... May God help us to be patriots and not to forget we are Christians.'[96] Lang had also welcomed the provisions for conscientious objection.[97] The Archbishop of York, William Temple, broadcast: 'No positive good can be done by force, but evil can be checked and held back by force.'[98] Temple, later to be Archbishop of Canterbury 1942-1944, was, however, adamant in ensuring the protection of the rights of conscientious objectors, of whom he said: 'I have deep respect for those who take the complete pacifist view, and I believe God called some to act on it, giving them a special conviction to bear witness to the unity of all God's family and the sovereignty of love.'[99] His defence of the right to objection led to him criticising the BBC for banning pacifist preachers. He demanded that there should be 'a real respect for one another's consciences between those Christians who are pacifists and those who are not,' and urged that no man should be excluded from broadcasting on the grounds that he is a pacifist. He failed to get the full support of Stuart Morris of the PPU for his actions when he added: 'providing that he undertakes not to use the occasion to advocate the pacifist position.'[100] His efforts on behalf of conscientious objectors, and Stanley

---

[95] 'Leader', *Church Times*, 27 October 1939, p. 2.

[96] 'Two Voices from the Church,' *Peace News*, 22 September 1939, p. 5.; Wilkinson, *Dissent or Conform*, p. 234.

[97] Wilkinson, *Dissent or Conform*, p. 234.

[98] 'What Defending Democracy Means,' *The Friend*, 1 September 1939, p. 733.

[99] 'The Archbishop on Pacifism,' *The Friend*, 8 September 1939, p. 764.

[100] 'Conscripting Christianity,' *Peace News*, 7 February 1941, p. 1.

Hilton in particular, were, however, acknowledged by *Peace News* on his death in 1944.[101] Some bishops were positively opposed to war and the methods of war. The Bishop of Birmingham contradicted his leader in his diocesan magazine:

> Do not acquiesce in a self-righteous patriotism which assumes that in the past our national policy has been wholly good in motive or effect…Repudiate the idea that Hitlerism can be conquered by force. Evil political systems can only be destroyed by moral victories. It is not Christian, or even religious, to say that force must be met with force.[102]

Others, such as George Bell, the Bishop of Chichester, were outspoken critics of saturation bombing: 'a policy predicated on the destruction of tens of thousands of enemy civilian lives could never be reconciled with the ethics of Christianity.'[103] Not all the clergy shared this view. The Rev. C. W. Whipp, in the parish magazine of St. Augustine's, Leicester in September 1940, wrote:

> There should be no RAF pilot returning home because he cannot find a military target for his bombs. The order should be 'Wipe them out' and to this end I would concentrate all our science towards discovering a far more terrific explosive.[104]

No evidence was found of clergy in the North-East of England sharing the views of the Rev. Whipp, and neither is there any evidence that he would not have ministered to conscientious objectors.

The majority of Christian objectors would, in view of the official policy of the main churches, expect to receive the support of their church against intolerance. Most had their own peace groups.[105] The reality was

---

[101] 'Dr Temple Defended C.O.s Rights,' *Peace News*, 1 December 1944, p. 1.
[102] 'Two Voices from the Church,' *Peace News*, 22 September 1939, p. 5.
[103] Michael Hughes, *Conscience and Conflict: Methodism, Peace and War in the Twentieth Century* (Peterborough: Epworth, 2008), p. 116.
[104] Stuart Hylton, *Reporting the Blitz* (Stroud: The History Press, 2012) p. 186.
[105] *Mass Observation Report,* July 1940, pp.130-131.

different, with support on an individual level often being at odds with the public utterances of particular clerics. The Bishop of Grantham, in reminding pacifists that they shared responsibility for England being at war, was unlikely to promote tolerance:

> It may yet be proved that the greatest tragedy of the present war is that the Nazi tyranny was allowed to grow until it reached unparalleled proportions, precisely because so many citizens of Christian civilisation were prevented by these scruples from resisting the monster while there was still time.[106]

Whilst many individual churchmen did provide support there were others whose actions could be interpreted as contributing to the intolerance. This somewhat contradicts Callum Brown's assertion that clerical attitudes in the Second World War were 'more sombre, calm, resolute and much less gung-ho and naïve.'[107] Be it from the pulpit or through the letters page of the *Durham County Advertiser* the Anglican Rev. F. H. Pickering of St Nicholas's Church, Durham, was forthright in his views. Before war was declared he made his support for the coming military campaign clear:

> We have got to be realists and face facts. The individual pacifist may have conscientious objections to bearing arms and killing men. We can honour and respect him if he is sincere, but he can still offer to do some redemptive work for his nation if he is worthy of it. Whatever may be right for the individual Christian, it is altogether another and bigger problem when statesmen are advising the best methods of security for 400 million of people."

---

[106] 'The Bishop's Letter,' *Peace News*, 16 February 1940, p. 5.
[107] Callum G. Brown, *Religion and Society in Twentieth-Century Britain* (Harlow: Pearson, 2006), p. 163.

Common sense dictates in a world where demonic spirits make war in a night, without warning, and rob defenceless people of their rights and liberties, that Britain and her colonies must be united with all the strongest nations of the world to prevent any further acts of aggression and to consolidate the forces of peace. We have tried the ways of disarmament, but others have accepted it to further their aggressive designs and lawless ambitions. We have called a halt to this international lawlessness and chaos, and so hourly we are growing stronger in armaments, wealth and men. It is the new power politics of appeasement. [108]

Once the military campaign was underway, and not going well, the Rev. Pickering was preaching in his sermon: 'Young men! Beware of Hitler's agents masquerading under the guise of peace and truth. Beware unless you find yourselves inveigled into the traitors' camp.' While respecting the sincere objector who refused to shed blood, the Vicar declared that when this refusal was associated with a refusal to do anything to help his country in its hour of need, sympathy hardened into distrust because he suspected him of being an agent of Hitler:

> I think it is about time that something was done to stop the practice of sending private letters to young men in this city who are about to be called up, trying to dissuade them from military service by pointing a way to easy escape on conscientious grounds. These letters have as their object to create doubt and distrust in the minds of our young men at the rightness of our cause, and to congeal the blood of their patriotism and their service. [109]

The letter referred to was claimed by a 20 year old from Durham to have been sent to himself and three of his friends. It was allegedly

---

[108] 'Vicar's Appeal to Pacifists,' *Durham County Advertiser,* 9 June 1939, p. 2.
[109] 'Young Men Beware! Vicar Exposes Hitler's Agents,' *Durham County Advertiser*, 3 May 1940, p. 7.

produced by the PPU under the heading 'An Open Letter to Men of Conscription Age and Their Parents,' and stated:

> Before you decide in what way you will endeavour to influence your lads, think of what soldiers are required to do. Their first duty is not to lay down their lives for their country, or anything else. It is to make themselves efficient in the work of killing other lads, who like themselves, would be dragged from their homes by the hand of authority and set to learn the task of killing your sons. Make up your minds to stand firm on your right to live and act like civilised human beings. Do not let the old men of Westminster steal your lives away under the illusion that it is noble so to do......[110]

He would also not have approved of one similar sent to the *Durham County Advertiser* from three churchmen, including a fellow Anglican, offering assistance to objectors:

> The National Service Act makes provision for dealing with those who have a conscientious objection to military service. It may be that some of those who intend to appeal on these grounds would like an opportunity of discussing their position with the object of clarifying their own minds before lodging their appeal. Any of the undersigned would be willing to meet them for this purpose....[111]

One signatory, Rev. H. Gibson, Methodist, criticised the Rev. Pickering for his confusing a desire for peace with support for Hitler. Pickering responded in the manner typical of many letters sent to the local press:

---

[110] 'Durham Men Get "Don't Fight" Letters,' *Northern Echo*, 30 April 1940, p. 5.
[111] 'Conscientious Objectors,' *Durham County Advertiser*, 13 October 1939, p. 5.

..... there are many enemies at home, who, whilst surreptitiously thwarting the powers that be, are being very well fed and clothed by them. And I am amazed that these enemies have no scruples about eating the food that comes to their table through the blood and service of the armed forces they oppose. ...the only' honourable course for such a man is to resign his citizenship and give his allegiance to another realm whose administration is more in accord with his own scruples.[112]

These comments caused W.T.C. of Coronation to enquire: 'We all know that this is a life and death struggle but before Mr. Pickering condemns anyone else is he aware that many are asking why so many young clergymen and Ministers of other denominations who are of military age are exempt from service.'[113]

Despite his outspoken comments the Rev. Pickering was prepared to testify as to the sincerity of Kenneth Leslie Taylor at the Newcastle Tribunal. He was, however, not in favour of his 'cultural views,' commenting: 'He is going through a period of idealism. In a few years, he will look back and call himself very silly.'[114] Taylor was conditionally registered.

The Rev. Pickering, although uniquely vociferous in his public comments, was not the only representative of a religious organisation to show an intolerance of objectors. The Newcastle Presbytery had members, such as bank manager George Richardson, who were dissatisfied that the Church general assembly had not laid down a definite policy on conscientious objection, declaring instead that they should respect each other's opinions. Mr Richardson, claiming to represent many, was of the view that: 'We are fighting this war for our very existence and for religion itself, and many of our office-bearers have sacrificed their lives in a just

---

[112] 'Letter to the Editor,' *Durham County Advertiser*, 17 May 1940, p. 4.
[113] 'Letter: Conscientious objectors and the Church,' *Northern Echo*, 1 May 1940, p. 4.
[114] 'Conscientious Objectors' Tribunal,' *Durham County Advertiser*, 1 August 1941, p. 3.

and righteous cause.'[115] The Newcastle Presbytery, reportedly in secret, agreed not to accept students who were conscientious objectors.[116]

The Presbyterian Church reflected the dilemma facing many of the Church leaders. Their Churches had many committed Christian pacifists yet at the same time many of their members serving in the armed forces. The Rev. J. A. Patten, speaking at the annual assembly of Evangelical Free Churches, made his views clear as to how he viewed the dilemma:

> I respect every genuine pacifist for the stand he takes, but I do not exhaust my respect or admiration for him. I keep the better part of it for the boys in our homes and churches who, without murmuring, without a trace of self-pity, have taken up the stern test in H M Forces. The percentage of C.O.'s was small and the percentage of genuine ones was smaller.[117]

The Methodist Church seemed to have found a way through the dilemma when its President pointed out that whilst not being committed to pacifism, it was committed to its 1937 policy to do all in its power for men who were in the services and stand by those it regarded as genuine conscientious objectors:

> The Methodist Church recognises that, in the present circumstances, both decisions may express true loyalty to personal spiritual conviction, and an earnest endeavour to do the will of God and serve the highest interests of mankind. In view of this recognition, the Methodist Church will uphold liberty of conscience and offer unceasing ministries to all her sons and daughters, in whichever direction loyalty to inward conviction may carry them.[118]

[115] '"C.O.s" and the Pulpit,' *Evening Chronicle*, 4 June 1941, p. 4.
[116] 'Presbytery C.O. Ban Criticised,' *Evening Chronicle*, 2 July 1941, p. 8.
[117] 'Pacifists Not Real Church Type,' *Evening Chronicle* 17 April 1940, p. 2.
[118] 'Methodist C.O.,' *Peace News*, 25 October 1940, p. 4.

A way was certainly needed if the earlier discussions of the Sunderland and Durham Methodist Synod were typical. The Rev. Stanley Wilding of Tow Law, declaring himself not a pacifist, unsuccessfully moved a resolution condemning the dismissal of exempted conscientious objectors from their jobs. The resolution carried was one from Rev. Frank Spencer of Sunderland, expressing pride in the Methodist men of Durham whose conscience had led them to fight to defend their country.[119] He was perhaps pre-empting the 1941 Methodist conference in Leeds which declared the war to be 'a sacred cause.'[120] The dilemma was also likely to be played out with discrimination at the grass roots as related by S. H. Jarvis in *Peace News*:

> There are two distinct strata in the Methodist Church. There is official Methodism, bustling, business-like and patriotic; and, on the other hand, there is local Methodism, lay and clergy alike, which is homely and kindly and intensively pacifist.
>
> We are the rank and file of Methodism. We do not appear at conferences, we are poorly represented in its councils, we are deemed misguided by its great ones.
>
> One of our members and his wife are avowed pacifists. At their work they had to deal with a Methodist board of governors who victimised them with a savagery that few secular authorities have equalled, and left them jobless and penniless in the street. At the same time the local Methodist clergy ministered to them in their need and showed the utmost kindness in their distress.[121]

For the majority of the Churches, the stance taken was to support their members whether they be soldiers or conscientious objectors, often collaborating to give support to objectors. A Newcastle clergyman, be-

---

[119] 'Men Who Will Not Fight,' *Northern Echo*, 9 May 1940, p. 5.
[120] 'A Methodist Statement on the War,' *Peace News*, 15 August 1941, p. 4.
[121] 'Methodism and War,' *Peace News*, 29 August 1941, p.2.

moaning the lack of such an organisation in Newcastle in 1939, reiter-
ated that all clergymen were willing to give sympathetic advice to genuine conscientious objectors.[122] He was correct, as there are many examples of ministers of differing denominations testifying to the genuineness
of applicants before the Newcastle Tribunal, often declaring that they
did not share the applicant's view. One such case was that of A. E. M.
Harbottle of Ponteland; another was the previous example involving
Rev. Pickering.[123] The key word again is 'genuine.' If support for objectors by clergymen was going to be effective in reducing intolerance, it
had to be seen to be for genuine objectors within a general support for
the war effort. The previously mentioned intervention by the Bishop of
Whitby concerning the dismissal of local authority objectors is such an
example. Whether this support was successful is doubtful, and it was
always going to be difficult when they themselves were exempted from
military service, a point made by 'Parent' writing to the *Shields Gazette*:
'The clergy, like the French priests, have an obligation and should be in
the fighting forces.'[124] They also ran the risk of alienating their own supporters as another correspondent to the newspaper summed up:

> The list of persons who are willing and eager to encourage
> conscientious objectors are not likely to receive any bou-
> quets from the general public. Any young man with "any
> guts" will take up arms at once in defence of his home and
> country. When we find our educated church leaders back-
> ing up and promising assistance to conscientious objectors,
> is it worth attending any church conducted by such par-
> sons?[125]

---

[122] 'Ministers Will Advise Conscientious Objectors,' *Evening Chronicle*, 4 October 1939, p. 5.
[123] 'Judge Told Churches Respect Fighter and Pacifist Views,' *Evening Chronicle*, 11 October 1939, p. 8.
[124] 'Are Conscientious Objectors Genuine,' *Shields Gazette*, 29 January 1940, p. 4.
[125] 'Letter: Disappointed at the Clergy,' *Shields Gazette*, 10 February 1940, p. 4.

The cause was also not likely to be helped when a Christian Pacifist correspondent, whilst declaring his pro-British and anti-Nazi opinion, conceded that: 'it is possible that there are people who use the Pacifist movement as a cloak for their own fear and timidity but they are greatly in the minority.'[126]

The various Churches were therefore unable to exert a great deal of influence over intolerance towards conscientious objectors, and in some cases their actions or words could be seen to have contributed towards it. Always aware of the presence of servicemen and objectors in their congregations they steered a careful middle path, ensuring the word 'genuine' was stressed.

Conclusion

Previous chapters have described some institutions and individuals displaying intolerance towards conscientious objectors. This chapter has shown how this intolerance was fuelled by the local press and, to a certain degree, by members of the clergy. This was most prominent in the early years of the war when Britain's plight appeared grim and less so as the nation's prospects improved. Was it this improvement in war prospects that led to the reduction in this promotion of intolerance or the reduced percentage of those registering as objectors? Perhaps the nation just got used to objectors being a fixture in society doing, in the main, more useful tasks than they would ever have been able to do in the armed forces. Perhaps, as news of Nazi atrocities became more prevalent, there was a growing feeling that the acceptance of conscientious objection was one of the factors that made Britain superior to Nazi Germany. Most likely it was a combination of all these factors.

Nevertheless, there was a clear intolerance demonstrated by the local press towards conscientious objectors through their sensational headlines, their presentation of objectors as odd, and their, often vitriolic, features and editorial comments. They also provided through their letters pages a vehicle for the expression of the more extreme degrees of

---

[126] 'Pacifists Not Cowards,' *Shields Gazette*, 14 October 1941, p. 3.

intolerance. They were, however, also aware that the right to conscientious objection was an example of the freedoms for which we were fighting, and it was on the defence of these freedoms that support for the war was predicated. Therefore, they did not go as far as arousing hatred and in fact their intolerance was partially balanced by allowing the publication of letters from, or in favour of, objectors, and later reporting the good work done by the Friends Ambulance Unit and others. The later positive stories about conscientious objectors, particularly where they lost their lives, is referred to by Tulloch as demonstrating that by their sacrifice, 'the best "conchie" was a dead "hero".'[127]

That newspapers, both national and local, contributed to an increasing level of intolerance shown by the Mass Observation sample survey is not in doubt. That they led to the population becoming considerably more intolerant is doubtful, as the more moderate and balanced views was expressed by contributors to Mass Observation demonstrates. The lack of reported incidents of violence towards objectors in the local press is further evidence that that attitude of the general population to them did not upset the equilibrium of society.

This chapter has also shown the difficulties faced by objectors seeking the solace of their Churches, and the careful path the Churches had to follow of supporting the war effort and those of their members who objected to it. In some instances, the public utterances of the clergy, particularly the Rev. Pickering, can be seen as encouraging rather than discouraging intolerance. Yet, despite the personal beliefs of clergymen, the support of them in verifying the sincerity of objectors to the tribunal was very much evident. Perhaps fighting a war to preserve freedom made it easy for churches, and churchmen, to support both the war and the conscientious objector.

---

[127] Tulloch, 'The Return of the 'conchie,' p. 62.

THE NO MORE WAR MOVEMENT

ALL ABOUT PACIFISM AND ARMAMENTS

Something for :—

CHRISTIANS.
TRADE UNIONISTS.
SOCIALISTS.
LIBERALS.
CONSERVATIVES.
CO-OPERATORS.
PARENTS.
TEACHERS.
WOMEN and
MILITARISTS.

2d.   2d.

Published by the No More War Movement, 11 Doughty Street, London, W.C.1, from whom additional copies can be obtained.

Chapter Five

Treatment of Conscientious Objectors
(Prison, Land and Medical Experiments)

This chapter examines the treatment experienced by North-East conscientious objectors in three apparently distinct areas: in prison; on the land; and, in medical experiments. Experiences in these spheres were not always as different as would be expected. This chapter questions the general assumption made in the secondary sources that being sent to prison was the treatment likely to have the greatest impact on the objectors concerned. In particular, it contradicts Barker's assertion that the most distressing part about serving time in prison for a sensitive person was neither the physical conditions nor the attitude of prison officers or other prisoners but the social stigma that it carried with it.[1] The chapter also examines how treatment in the region compared to that in other parts of the country. Durham Prison did not fare well in this comparison.

Life in Prison

For many conscientious objectors in the North-East of England, the ultimate expression of their objection was a willingness to go to prison. This was matched by a willingness on the part of the state to send them there, despite the Home Secretary, Herbert Morrison, stating that conscientious objection was not a criminal offence and no-one could be imprisoned on account of it. As there was nothing to prevent imprisonment for actions resulting from objection, this statement was described in the *New Leader* as 'likely to be received with cynical amusement.'[2] Of the 820 on the Database of Conscientious Objectors, 146 (18%)

---

[1] Barker, *Conscience, Government and War*, p. 94.
[2] '477 C.O.s in Prison,' *The New Leader*, 25 October 1941, p. 8.

suffered this fate and were imprisoned for something that was not in effect a criminal offence.

Twenty-four of those identified as having spent time in prison had been in the Armed Forces when they were sentenced, and these are discussed in Chapter 7. For the remaining 122 civilians, the reasons for their incarceration are analysed below:

Reasons For Incarceration

Refusing to Submit to a Medical	93
Disobeying Work Instruction	23
Refusing to Fire Watch	9
Refusing to register for National Service	7
Refusing to join Home Guard	2
Unknown	5
Looting	1

(Note – some individuals were sentenced for more than one reason and on more than one occasion)

The majority of sentences were imposed for refusing to submit to a medical examination. A medical examination was a requirement for those removed from the register and liable for military service. It was also required for those assigned non-combatant duties in the armed forces. The other sentences reflected the extension of conscription to industry, fire watching and the Home Guard. It is no surprise, given the previous analysis, that the majority of religious objectors imprisoned were Jehovah's Witnesses, and, the majority of political objectors imprisoned were members of Newcastle War Resisters.

Length of sentences varied before and after 1941. Originally, the only penalty available for refusing a medical examination was a maximum fine of £5 or one month's imprisonment on default.[3] This created a loophole, not for conscientious objectors, but for others who could take advantage of the small penalties to avoid service in the Armed Forces. The Minister of Labour, in presenting the 1941 National Service

---

[3] Barker, *Conscience, Government and War*, p. 93.

Bill, referred to an allegation that a prominent Fascist had refused a medical examination and effectively 'got off scot free.' To remedy the situation, the law was changed to:

(a)   on conviction on indictment, to imprisonment for a term not exceeding two years, or to a fine not exceeding one hundred pounds, or to both such imprisonment and such fine;

(b)   on summary conviction, to imprisonment for a term not exceeding twelve months, or to a fine not exceeding fifty pounds, or to both such imprisonment and such fine.[4]

The same penalties applied to conscientious objectors who wilfully failed to comply with the conditions of their registration, i.e. that they must take up specified work. These were the maximum penalties that could be imposed. At least 40 cases of 12 month's duration were handed down in the North-East. Christopher Shrimplin, a North Shields Jehovah's Witness who had been unconditionally removed from the register by both the Newcastle and the Appellate Tribunals received a sentence of 18 months, although actually served only 12. Emphasising the non-criminal nature of his offence of not submitting to a medical, the Recorder at his hearing commented: 'There is no doubt you are a man of good character, but it is a good thing that there are very few Englishmen who think to act as you do.'[5] Hayes describes Shrimplin being visited in Durham Prison by the CBCO Advisory Bureau Secretary for North Shields, the Rev. R. G. Bell. Shrimplin informed Rev. Bell: 'I don't need your help. I've prayed to God who'll give me all the help I need.' Bell replied, 'Shrimplin, I'm the answer to your prayer.' Apparently, the pair got on famously afterwards.[6]

The CBCO was formed in the summer of 1939 to serve as an organisation *for* conscientious objectors, but not an organisation *of* conscientious objectors. Its role was a co-ordinating body linking with ex-

[4] National Service Bill, Hansard, *HC Deb 26 March 1941 vol. 370 cc594-644*.
[5] 'Shields C.O. Gets 18 Months in Prison,' *Shields Gazette*, 6 January 1942, p. 4.
[6] Hayes, *Challenge of Conscience*, p. 162-163.

isting bodies to provide a specialised service to their conscientious objector members. One function was to provide advice and guidance to those
facing a tribunal through one of its several hundred local advisory committees and advisors. As Brockway stated, an objection could lead to
prison so the purpose of the CBCO was not to create an objection but
to clarify it. The Board also established a maintenance fund for families
of men and women in prison but in most cases this help was declined.
They also established an employment agency for objectors who found it
difficult to get work on their discharge from prison.[7]

The CBCO produced a number of information pamphlets for objectors, one of which was *Civil and Military Prison Routine*.[8] With separate sections for civil and military prisons, it provided a guide as to what
an objector receiving a prison sentence could expect. It did, however,
include the caveat: 'In reading this pamphlet you should remember that
conditions vary from one prison or barracks to another.'[9] This was indeed true. It was also not without humour when it referred to the prisoner receiving a monographed toothbrush which, 'you will probably be
allowed to keep when you leave with instructions to bring it back if you
return!'[10] As many did return, there were likely a number of tooth-
brushes making the return journey. The pamphlet did point out that
some allowance was made by the prison regime for conscientious objection:

> There are some prison industries in which you may find
> yourself asked to do work to which you conscientiously ob-
> ject, for example, projectile bags may take the place of mail
> bags, or, though a vegetarian, you may be asked to work
> with the butchers in the kitchen. Such an objection can be
> made to the Governor and will be sustained in most cases.[11]

As a guide, it was undoubtedly useful but unlikely to fully prepare
someone for the experience.

---

[7] Forward by Fenner Brockway in: Hayes, *Challenge of Conscience*, p. vii-xiv.
[8] Central Board for Conscientious Objectors, *Civil and Military Prison Routine*, September 1941.
[9] Ibid., p. 2.
[10] Ibid., p. 4.
[11] Ibid., p. 7.

Brockway had himself been imprisoned as a conscientious objector during the First World War. During this war nine conscientious objectors had died in prison and an estimated 60 had died later as a result
of their prison experiences. [12] There is no evidence of this in the Second
World War, but objectors in prison were not safe from enemy bombing.
The *New Leader* reported the death of two conscientious objectors due
to enemy action.[13] Sybil Morrison refers to the decision of Holloway
Prison to unlock women's cells during air raids, but not those of men.
She also refers to an objector being killed when a bomb hit a wing of
Walton Prison in Liverpool.[14] In an interview for the Imperial War Mu-
seum, Alexander Bryan of York referred to the danger: 'Air-raids made
me scared as you were locked up in your cell and there was a feeling
anything could happen.'[15]

Prison conditions had improved since the First World War but
were still not good. Some modest improvements had taken place largely
due to prison reformers highlighting more enlightened practices in other
countries. One was Brockway, who, along with fellow conscientious objector and prisoner, Stephen Hobhouse, one of a family of well-known
social reformers, produced a report criticising the failure to introduce
many reforms recommended as far back as the 1895 Gladstone Committee.[16] They highlighted the boredom, brutality, degradation, humiliation, and injustice of the prison system, drawing particular attention
to the destructive features of the strictly imposed silent system that virtually suppressed human discourse.[17] The reforms introduced included
some reduction in the time spent in solitary confinement and fewer restrictions on non-violent prisoners, but overall conditions remained
harsh.

Given the conditions for prisoners in Durham Prison discussed
later, it was comforting that objectors were able to receive sympathetic

---

[12] Anthony Taylor, *The Prison System and its Effects: Wherefrom, Whereto, and Why?* (New York: Nova Science Publications, 2014), p. 28.
[13] 'C.O. Kicked and Punched,' *The New Leader*, 4 October 1941, p. 1.
[14] Sybil Morrison, *I Renounce War: The Story of the Peace Pledge Union* (London: Sheppard Press, 1962), pp. 52-53.
[15] Interview with Alexander Bryan, Imperial War Museum, Catalogue No. 4746, Recorded 5/9/80,
[16] A. Fenner Brockway and Stephen Hobhouse, eds., *English Prisons Today: Being the Report of the Prison System* Committee (London: Longmans Green and Co., 1922).
[17] Taylor, *The Prison System and its Effects*, p. 29.

visitors such as the Rev. Bell. It is also good considering the number who received multiple sentences. Of the previously mentioned 122 who received prison sentences, 15 were found to have served two sentences, 6 served three sentences, and the previously mentioned Robert Morley, four sentences. One who served three sentences was Donald Hersom (or Henson as he is referred to in some newspapers)) of Morpeth. Fined for refusing to carry out fire-watching, on refusing to pay Hersom was sent to prison for 28 days. He previously served a similar sentence for non-payment of a fine imposed for not following the directions of the National Service Officer. In his unsuccessful defence Hersom quoted the principle of English law of not being tried twice for the same offence:

> I would like to say that by refusing to perform fire guard duties, and rather go to prison, I am doing so on ethical grounds. Whether I am a conscientious objector or not, I have decided to follow the course conscientiously. I would like to suggest to you that I have already paid the penalty for this offence. I think it is a principle of law that a man should not suffer twice for the same offence. This is the second prosecution for the same offence, and I suggest a nominal penalty should be imposed.[18]

Although the two offences were similar in nature they were technically different, therefore there was nothing to prevent the imposition of additional sentences of increasing length. The CBCO lobbied for civilian objectors to be put on the same legal footing as those in the Armed Forces. Brockway published an open letter to the Minister of Labour and National Service. At the time of writing the letter, as Brockway pointed out, there were 477 young men in prison for refusing to undergo a medical examination and 100 of those were serving the maximum sentence of twelve months:

> …. Mr Winston Churchill said that anything in the nature of the persecution of C.O.s would be odious to the British people. To prevent such persecution a C.O. who refused orders in the Army and was sentenced to three months or

---

[18] 'Fire Guard Order Disobeyed,' *Morpeth Gazette*, 28 April 1944, p. 4.

more imprisonment by a Court Martial was given the right to appear before an Appellate Tribunal a second time. In the great majority of cases such C.O.s have been discharged from the Army on the recommendation of the Tribunal.

When this provision was made it was not foreseen that a considerable number of C.O.s would begin their refusal before being taken into the Army. They declined to go for medical examination, and for this offence they are sentenced to imprisonment up to one year.

These men have been impelled to take this course although they knew that such action would withhold from them the right to come before the Appellate Tribunal again, and that at the end of their sentence they would be liable to still further imprisonment.

I put it to you that this clear proof of sincerity justifies the proposal which the CBCO is now making that, in order to avoid the persecution which Mr Churchill condemned, these men should now be given the same opportunity to come before the Appellate Tribunal as men who are sentenced by Court Martial....[19]

The lobbying was successful and limits on prison sentences were included in the 1941 National Service Act:

If any person undergoing a sentence of imprisonment for a term of three months or more imposed on him for an offence by a court.... claims that the offence was committed by reason of his conscientiously objecting to performing a duty imposed by this Act, he may apply in the prescribed manner to have his case considered by the appellate tribunal and that tribunal shall, if it finds that the offence for which he was sentenced was committed by reason of such conscientious objection as aforesaid have power to recommend to the Minister that he be discharged from the

[19] 'Open Letter to Ernest Bevin,' *The New Leader*, 8 November 1941, p. 7.

service of Civil Defence as soon as may be after serving the sentence imposed upon him.[20]

Civilian objectors were now on the same footing as those in the Armed Forces (see Chapter 7). But, as Barker points out, this new law did not prevent the possibility of men being rejected by the Appellate Tribunal and summoned again for a medical examination. The record of prisoners in Durham Prison referenced nine, including three civilians, referred to the Appellate Tribunal. However, on 7 August 1942 the prosecutor in the case of Stanley Orford of Manchester announced that in future objectors sent to prison for three months or more for refusing to submit to a medical examination would not be prosecuted again for the same offence. Instead they would be directed to civilian work.[21] The absolutists were of course going to refuse direction and this usually meant a sentence for refusing a medical was followed by a sentence for failing to follow a work direction. The three members of the Morley family, Alfred Hemmings of Houghton-le-Spring, and Thomas Goulden of Consett are examples.

The expected further sentences did not generally materialise. The Ministry of Labour unofficially refrained from further prosecutions if they considered the work objectors were doing was of some value to the state. This condition was satisfied by the majority.[22] The minority not satisfying the conditions were mainly Jehovah's Witnesses, who accounted for four North-East objectors who received three sentences. The one who received four sentences was the Newcastle War Resister, Robert Morley. Nationally 28 out of 34 third time prosecutions by August 1944 were of Jehovah's Witnesses. Appeals to the Minister of Labour, including from the Archbishop of Canterbury, against what was perceived to be persecution, were unsuccessful on the grounds that their recalcitrance was due to their unwillingness to do any useful work.[23]

Despite the reduction in the potential number of repeated prison sentences the number of objectors in prison remained a cause for concern for the Duke of Bedford, as were the conditions of their incarceration. Speaking in the House of Lords he complained that:

---

[20] 'Debate on the National Service Act', *Hansard,* HC Deb. 02 April 1941 vol. 370 cc1122-33.
[21] Hayes, *Challenge of Conscience*, p. 167.
[22] Ibid., p. 169.
[23] Ibid., p. 173.

The position is made worse by the extremely bad conditions that now prevail in many of our prisons. In some cases, the cells are dirty and badly heated and may even be verminous. Many young conscientious objectors are sent to Borstal, where they have to associate with house-breakers, black-marketeers and persons convicted of assault. Sometimes they are bullied by their associates, and cases have been known where persons in charge have, out of spite, given them less than the normal food ration.[24]

Prison conditions varied considerably according to Barker, who cites Wormwood Scrubs as a particularly bad example: 'even the most uncomplaining of conscientious objectors reported that the physical conditions were appalling, especially the sanitary arrangements, the quality of food and the lack of it.' The *Prison Routine* pamphlet had warned objectors of primitive sanitary conditions and poor quality food: 'if you do not like your dinner you have no alternative.'[25] Barker reported conditions improving enough for Wormwood Scrubs to be placed fourth on the Quaker visitors 'order of pleasantries' list.[26] Durham Prison, the central prison for North-East objectors, did not appear on the list, leading to the assumption that pleasantries were hard to find.

In January 1945, Mr C. A. Sage in his capacity of visiting magistrate, painted a positive picture of life in Durham Prison:

The prison continues to be efficiently, firmly, justly and sympathetically administered. The food is wholesome and sufficient, and a special diet is provided where necessary. Many prisoners on admission are in a poor state of health, but it is remarkable how rapidly they improve with regular hours, work, exercise, cleanliness and sufficient food.[27]

[24] 'No Extension of Rights to Exemption,' *Manchester Guardian*, 3 March 1943, p. 6.
[25] Central Board for Conscientious Objectors, *Civil and Military Prison Routine*, September 1941, p. 8.
[26] Barker, *Conscience, Government and War*, p. 95.
[27] 'Tribute to Durham Prison' *Northern Daily Mail*, 20 January 1945, p. 2.

Such a description would not have been possible three years earlier. Prisoner Kitty Alexander, in her revealing portrait of prison life in early 1942, painted a somewhat different picture.[28] She described the food as 'absolutely appalling,' and lost half a stone in weight while in prison. She could not eat for the first few days and other prisoners asked for any left-over food because they were underfed. Her bed was a straw mattress on the floor and there was no heating whatsoever. As there was only one blanket she kept most of her clothes on. Exercise was limited to 20 minutes each day, officially in silence. No visitors were allowed for those whose sentence was only one month, although they were allowed to write a letter once a week.

Her days were occupied by working on the sewing machines, repairing the clothing of the men who had deliberately torn the sleeves off their shirts. Prisoners got books once a week but there was no choice so she swapped with other prisoners who liked love stories, as she 'wanted something more intelligent.' She described some prison officers as pleasant and some as horrible, but was more impressed with the other prisoners who looked after her like a mother. 'They showed me how to clean the cell ready for inspection and brought me hot water every morning. They were very kind indeed.' All prisoners mixed together except those with venereal disease, who she was told to keep away from.

She described the head lice inspection, known as 'Dickie Day.' Prisoners stood in a long queue to be examined by the nurse: 'You felt absolutely crawling by the time you got there even though you were clean.' This surprised her as the facilities were inadequate for washing properly: 'You got a bath when you went in, were stripped and given prison clothes and shoes which did not fit.'

The conditions described by Kitty were, therefore, far removed from the picture painted by Mr Sage. Bad prison conditions concerned Parliament and there were some improvements, mainly relating to the relaxation in the amount of time spent locked in cells and being allowed to read more books, a concession described by Barker as an opportunity to become acquainted with books and authors which otherwise they

---

[28] Interview with Kitty Alice Hall (nee Alexander), C900/11093, British Library Sound Archive, recorded 11 March 1999. This and further quotes are directly from the interview tapes.

would not have encountered.[29] There is evidence from Paul Ronchetti that conditions had improved by the time he and his brother, Louis, were imprisoned in 1945.[30] Paul recalled having had a relatively easy time in prison and being taken on outside work parties. Louis had also told his son that prison food was fine and comparable with rations outside prison.[31]

Another objector sent to Durham Prison was Alan Brian Davie of Glasgow, sentenced to three months in early 1941. Part of his sentence was spent in Durham but most of it in Wakefield, where, in contrast to Kitty's description of Durham, he described conditions as reasonably good with boredom the main problem. 'There was a library, where you could borrow one book at a time as well as a Bible and Buchan's Progress in each cell.'[32]

Kitty Alexander's description of the women prisoners is a poignant and revealing insight into a part of British society at the time:

> Prison life was more difficult for a woman than a man, particularly for anyone who had any sort of home life, but most of them did not have a home life. Many were in for drunk and disorderly or for attacking their husbands who probably deserved it, yet they were all kind and pleasant. One young girl, very pretty, was a prostitute who said she could have got married but didn't know who to. Her mother was in prison at the same time for keeping a disorderly house, so you couldn't expect more for the girl. So attractive, what a waste, could have been a film star. I had led a sheltered life and had never been in contact with people like this.
>
> I wrote letters for the prisoners who could not read or write. They were to people who could also not read or write so they would get someone to read them for them.[33]

---

[29] Barker, *Conscience, Government and War*, p. 96.

[30] Telephone interview with Paul Ronchetti, conducted 1 November 2013.

[31] Interview with Steve Ronchetti, conducted 30 October 2013.

[32] Interview with Alan Brian Davie, Imperial War Museum, Catalogue No. 8994, Conducted 16 September 1985.

[33] Interview with Kitty Alice Hall (nee Alexander), British Library Sound Archive.

Kitty Alexander was the only objector who left a detailed description of prison conditions in Durham but other objectors from the region recorded their experiences in other prisons.

Alexander Bryan, influenced by his father's description of the horrors of the First World War, decided not to register for military service. This he realised would likely lead to prison, and in March 1941 received 28 days in Strangeways for refusing to pay the fine imposed for not registering. Here he referred to being given a grey and ill-fitting prison uniform and a pair of shoes two sizes too small. The other conditions he described were similar to those described by Kitty Alexander:

> The other prisoners were curious about new prisoners, especially me as I was the only conscientious objector in Strangeways at the time. I began work in the mail bag shop where I occasionally sewed mail bags and was then promoted to landing cleaner in the junior wing where my cell was. Some jobs were barred from me because of my offence. We had one half-hour exercise per day where warders kept people apart to ensure silence. The same things happened every day at the same times. I had two library books during the month I was in. I was able to send out one letter. No visits were allowed for a 28-day sentence.[34]

In September 1941 Bryan refused to carry out compulsory fire-watching, his objection being to the compulsory element. In March 1942, he received his summons to submit to a medical examination. This time he was better prepared, and made ready for the tribunal which he could go to once he had received a one-year sentence. He received that sentence and appeared before the tribunal while in prison. He was sent in error to Wandsworth Prison as the court treated him as a second offender. Alexander Bryan explains that it had been officially agreed that no matter how many times an objector received a prison sentence for refusing military service he would be treated as a first offender. But, he was subsequently transferred to Wormwood Scrubs.[35] He recalled a

---

[34] Interview with Alexander Bryan, Imperial war Museum, Catalogue No. 4746, Recorded 5 September 1980.

[35] Peter Brock, ed., *'These Strange Criminals': An Anthology of Prison Memoires by Conscientious Objectors from the Great War to the Cold War* (Toronto: University of Toronto Press, 2004), p. 187.

hanging at Wandsworth having a terrible effect on the prison population.[36] Steve Ronchetti also recalled his father describing Durham Prison
going into lock-down when a hanging took place.[37]

Alexander found conditions in Wormwood Scrubs more relaxed
as there were a considerable number of conscientious objectors. He was
perhaps fortunate to have been sent to Wormwood Scrubs after February 1942 when the conditions had improved. By June 1942, Wormwood Scrubs had achieved its ranking of fourth on the "pleasantries list".
He had a Quaker visitor and was allowed a visit after the first month
from two friends. There was no rule of silence and the officers quite
friendly. He had two library books a week and was granted the complete
works of Shakespeare. Those who wished could have a Quaker meeting.
He was not a Quaker, at this time, but joined in September 1942, after
the Tribunal in June granted him exemption on condition of him doing
relief work. These concessions, along with their classification as first of-
fenders, show that in some prisons conscientious objectors, from 1942
onwards, received special treatment in comparison with those who had
committed criminal offences. However, despite the better conditions,
they would still have upset his parents so he requested they not visit.
Also, the long periods alone in a cell he considered a waste of valuable
time.[38]

How prison sentences affected North-East conscientious objectors is difficult to gauge as their testimonies are rare. The available evidence suggests they were not isolated, or stigmatised in the eyes of their
families as Rachel Barker states. In many cases, such as the Morleys and
Sadlers, they came from families of objectors, either siblings or parents,
who were unlikely to stigmatise them. Another was George Brown of
New Seaham, whose father had served a prison sentence in the First
World War for being a conscientious objector.[39] Alexander Bryan recorded his family being fully supportive of him; his brother and sister
becoming objectors. He also felt no humiliation as he had chosen to go
there voluntarily.[40] The evidence from the tribunal appearances also

[36] Interview with Alexander Bryan, Imperial war Museum.
[37] Interview with Steve Ronchetti, 30 October 2013.
[38] Interview with Alexander Bryan, Imperial war Museum.
[39] 'Convinced he did the wrong thing,' *Sunderland Echo*, 1 December 1939, p. 4.
[40] Interview with Alexander Bryan, Imperial War Museum.

shows many supported at the tribunals by family members, some declaring that whilst they did not support their views they confirmed their sincerity. The mother of Walter Rutherford went even further in telling the Appellate Tribunal that she would be proud to see her son in prison and would rather be tried for the murder of her son than to see him take life given by God.[41] Many, such as the Newcastle War Resisters, also had the comfort of like-minded comrades who either shared their experience or provided them with strong moral support. Alexander Bryan felt the comradeship of the large number of fellow objectors in Wormwood Scrubs.[42]

It is, however, likely that there were some objectors who did not experience the full support of their loved ones. George Springett records in his Mass Observation Diary on 20 March 1941:

> letter arrived: …I'm very sorry to say so, but my parents made it very obvious to me last night that they resented your presence in our house…The reason for their objection to you is that you are a 'Conchie'! I'm afraid it will be impossible for me to see you here for knowing my parents' attitude if you did call. I beg you not to …I am afraid that is the position and there is nothing I can do about it…[43]

The Mass Observation archive also includes a letter to an objector, not from the North-East, from his 20-year-old girlfriend who clearly does not support his stance. The following are extracts:

> Quite frankly Jags I think you talk a lot of tripe. You might be a C.O. but it won't do you a bit of good. I know it isn't the least bit of good talking to you or even trying to change your opinions about War but the fact still remains that you, as an individual, cannot do one bit of good trying to stick to what you consider to be very high ideals about fighting etc.…

---

[41] 'Proud to see son in Prison,' *Northern Echo*, 6 May 1941, p. 3.
[42] Interview with Alexander Bryan, Imperial War Museum.
[43] Sandra Kos Wing, ed., *Our Longest Days*, p. 72.

Go to War my lad and be a man. Suffer the Lord.
Serve with a smile and don't go to kill but to defend and
with that thought in your mind coupled with the thought
that God is with you, and then whether you die or live you
will have done your bit to help your country and nation in
a War, which will be added to the other wars. These Wars
have to be fought – probably all through this century but
into the next. Through the sacrifices of you and others,
Wars will be over for all time, so for once in your life stop
thinking of yourself and concentrate on those unborn sons
of the next century.[44]

What course their relationship took is not known.

Jehovah's Witnesses, the largest group of those imprisoned, also
had the comfort of fellow prisoners who shared their beliefs, but not
necessarily of all fellow objectors. Alexander Bryan recalled meeting a
number of Jehovah's Witnesses on the exercise yard where they expounded their religious views, and how he tried to avoid them as they
were not interested in his views.[45] Stanley Iveson, another objector in
Walton Prison, was also less than complimentary when he referred to
them as grumblers, arrogant and aloof.[46] Jehovah's Witnesses were therefore as isolated in prison as they were outside.

Did objectors feel stigmatised on their release from prison? Did
being in prison carry a greater stigma than simply being a conscientious
objector did? These questions are difficult to answer. Paul Ronchetti did
not recall prison carrying a stigma. He and his brother had not committed a criminal offence or, in their eyes, have a criminal record.[47] Kitty
Alexander was also not disadvantaged by prison: 'After prison I worked
for an architect who accepted me on my merits and ignored the loss of
my green card.'[48] Similarly, Alexander Bryan, who gave up his degree

[44] Letter from a girl to a pacifist, July 1940, Press cuttings, *Mass Observation Online*.
[45] Interview with Alexander Bryan, Imperial war Museum.
[46] Interview with Stanley Iveson, Imperial War Museum, Catalogue No. 4686, Recorded 1980.
[47] Telephone interview with Paul Ronchetti, conducted 1 November 2013.
[48] Interview with Kitty Alice Hall (nee Alexander), British Library Sound Archive.

studies to register as a conscientious objector, was awarded a war degree in 1946 which he found was accepted by employers.[49]

There is little doubt that the prison experience was an unpleasant one. It would appear that being in Durham Prison, even though its conditions improved as the war progressed, was more unpleasant than being in many other prisons. It could be dangerous if your prison was located in an area subject to enemy bombing. There is little evidence to support the view of Rachel Barker that the most distressing part of being a civilian in prison was the stigma on being released. There was certainly some stigma attached to being a conscientious objector, as their treatment described so far indicates, but it appears this was not accentuated by being in prison. It is therefore concluded that the most distressing part of being in prison was the conditions experienced. Yet many were prepared to repeat the experience rather than act against their conscience. There were also many who served only one sentence, some perhaps finding that it was enough.

Life on the Land

Not all conscientious objectors took the absolutist route to prison. Many conditionally registered were prepared to obey the tribunal directions. The most common directions given to objectors were to either remain in their current occupation, if it was considered contributing to the war effort, or work in hospitals or on the land, either in forestry, horticulture or agriculture.

The onus to find work as directed was placed on the objectors themselves, and for those directed to work on the land this was not easy. The matter was discussed by the National Union of Agricultural Workers where executive member, Mr Holmes explained that as a union they did not want any repressive legislation. They wanted to maintain freedom of thought and opinion and he hoped agricultural workers would not take any action against men who had real moral objection to taking human life.[50] Most members were not so charitable. There was reportedly a strong feeling among workers that they should not be called upon to work with people exempted from military service to the detriment of

---

[49] Interview with Alexander Bryan, Imperial war Museum.
[50] 'Equal Pay for Both Sexes,' *Yorkshire Evening Post*, 4 May 1940, p. 5.

young land workers. The National Farmers Union (NFU) also had concerns. They were concerned that most objectors were untrained and had to be paid a wage fixed by the agricultural wages board, thus making it difficult to place them in farm jobs. This difficulty was summed up by Fred Marshall, Secretary of the Durham NFU:

> The feeling amongst Durham farmers is strongly against the employment of these men.... Members protested vigorously against the calling up of farmers' sons and farm workers, all skilled men, while other men – they called them shirkers- are suggested to replace them. It was appreciated that the labour position in agriculture was acute, but if it is to be suggested that C.O.s are the only substitutes for skilled farm labour, then they should not receive any higher pay than men who have joined the armed forces.[51]

The call-up of the sons of tenant farmers occupying key positions was raised in parliament by the MP for Sedgefield, J. R. Leslie. It is, however, uncertain from an economic point of view whether it was the loss of the skilled worker or the level of wages that had to be paid to their replacements which was the main concern.[52]

When the Stokesley branch of the NFU raised its objection to the employment of conscientious objectors it was correctly pointed out that, 'farmers were not compelled to take this class of worker.'[53] This lack of compulsion created difficulties for some objectors in the early years of the war but they did not receive any sympathy for their predicament in the *Sunderland Echo*. Reporting a likely comb-out of conscientious objectors granted exemption on condition they took up work on the land:

> Artful dodging is known to have been practised by some of the C.O.s who have never seen a farm since the day they said, 'Thank you' to the Tribunal which released them.

[51] 'Little Trouble in North over C.O. Jobs,' *Evening Chronicle*, 3 April 1940, p. 1.
[52] 'Conscientious Objectors – Sedgefield M.P. Protests,' *Durham County Advertiser*, 22 March 1940, p. 8.
[53] *Teesdale Mercury*, 13 March 1940, p. 7.

In other cases, some sort of effort has been made to secure a job. But, not unnaturally, a percentage of farmers, whose sons have been called-up and willingly gone, refuse to engage these men, who, in any case, are not of a type suitable for farm work. Difficulty in finding a job does not, however, absolve the objector.[54]

The newspaper did little to help their search for work: 'Still others have formed themselves into little 'farming communities' where, say 12 or a score of them are doing, badly, work that would not take the time of more than 2 or 3 skilled agricultural labourers.' It was not going to convince farmer J. Armstrong of Middlestone Moor who, on hearing that he may be compelled to take members of the Women's Land Army and conscientious objectors, said:

I sincerely hope that we shall never have to come down to the level of having conscientious objectors palmed upon this industry. I do not know whether farm workers will work side by side with them, but if we have to take them they should receive Army rates of pay.[55]

Some farm workers residing in an agricultural hostel near Alnwick were so worried that they might be thought of as conscientious objectors that they asked the warden to write to the local paper to contradict this to avoid friction.[56]

The difficulties in employing objectors directly on farms were addressed by a Ministry of Agriculture announcement: 'All conscientious objectors are to be organised and given a quick course on farm training, and it is possible that they will be sent to work in gangs wherever required.'[57] *The Spectator* was supportive:

It is stated that as part of the new agricultural drive just announced that conscientious objectors to military service are

---

[54] 'Comb Out of Objectors,' *Sunderland Echo*, 27 February 1941, p. 4.
[55] 'Children to assist harvesting potatoes in Durham County,' *Sunderland Echo*, 17 March 1941, p. 3.
[56] 'Not C.O.s', *Alnwick County Gazette and Guardian*, 28 November 1941, p. 4.
[57] '"Conchies" to be trained for the land,' *Evening Chronicle*, 3 June 1940, p. 5.

to be mobilised, apparently compulsorily, to work on farms. That is obviously a sensible step, and it will be regrettable on economic as well as other grounds if the success of the experiment is prejudiced by the hostility to such objectors which is being manifested in certain quarters.[58]

The newspaper feared that hostility might compromise objectors making a useful contribution to the national effort, particularly in the vital area of food production, which was the rationale behind tribunals granting conditional exemption. It was also the desire of many objectors, despite their conscience not allowing them to fight, to contribute to the national effort.

Government action may have eased some of the difficulties of objectors in fulfilling the requirements of their registration, but it raised concerns regarding the rate of pay, particularly when in 1940 the Agricultural Wages Board lowered the minimum rates payable to inexperienced workers.[59] This may have addressed some of the concerns of the farmers but offered little comfort to objectors. One such objector was 'Agricolae' of Houghton-le-Spring, who may have been a worker from the agricultural hostel there, writing to the *Northern Echo*:

.... he suggests that C.O.s should be sent to work on the land, but many pacifist land workers are victimised... While other persons employed by Durham War Agricultural Committee receive a commencing wage of £2, 6s with which to provide clothing, board and lodgings, a C.O. receives only £1, 18s. To make matters worse the C.O.s are housed in a hostel with other people.[60]

Such claims of victimisation would not have impressed the West Yorkshire N.F.U. meeting in May 1942. Mr Webster of Selby said: 'whilst land girls and ordinary land workers started work at 7.30, and

---

[58] 'Conscientious Objectors and the Land,' *The Spectator*, 7th June 1940, p766-767.
[59] Kramer, *Conscientious Objectors*, p. 77.
[60] 'Hear All Sides: Treatment of Pacifist Land Workers,' *Northern Echo*, 28 July 1941, p. 2.

put in the proper number of hours, conscience objectors came in between 8 and 9 and some were not doing 40 hours a week.' Mr Wright
of Goole said they were a 'lot of louts' and the committee should send a
real sergeant-major with them – 'with a bayonet' said another.' They
passed a resolution requiring objectors to work the same hours as ordinary agricultural workers.[61] Such criticism was not confined to farmers.
A Mass Observation diarist referred to comments from a friend:

> He is thoroughly disgusted at the outrageous behaviour of
> the majority of them (C.O.s). Some have been in jail and
> bragged that they refused to do physical jerks because it was
> 'military training'. The Communist ones are still 'Objec-
> tors' because we aren't doing enough for our Russian allies.
> If I could, I should give them a free passage to Russia by the
> next convoy and let them give Russia the help that is
> needed. The farmers are at their wits end to know how to
> deal with these C.Os. who can't be sacked no matter how
> they shirk.[62]

Many objectors found themselves working in gangs on large
country estates. Sheila Ross was a Land Girl working at Thropton Hostel
near Rothbury, often required to do forestry work on the Cragside Es-
tate. Male conscientious objectors were working at Cragside, which ironically was the home of the armaments manufactures, the Armstrongs,
and when the 'women were struggling with a task,' would often help.
She said they were very pleasant and, whilst never talking to them about
being objectors, commented that she thought they were very brave to
believe so strongly.[63] Work on large forestry estates was organised by one
of the six Christian Pacifist Forestry Land Units, established by July
1940. Three of these were in Durham, Yorkshire and Northumberland.
The men employed were fulfilling the directions of the tribunals, although some, yet to appear before the tribunal, had lost their jobs due to
hostility from employers or fellow employees.[64]

---

[61] 'C.O.s on the Land,' *Yorkshire Evening Post*, 9 May 1942, p. 1.
[62] Diarist 5423, Bradford Housewife, 7 August 1942, *Mass Observation Online*.
[63] Telephone interview with Sheila Ross, conducted 23 October 2013.
[64] Report of Henry Carter in *The Christian Pacifist*, July 1940, *Mass Observation online*.

One conscientious objector working in the forests of Northumberland was the poet James Kirkup. The nature of the work and its remoteness required that the objectors were placed in camps. The Ministry of Labour had established training camps to re-train long-term unemployed miners and shipyard workers, where skills such as land drainage and road building were taught. For those employed in forestry it was necessary to establish hutted camps remote from towns and villages, as any neighbouring village was likely to be occupied by refugees or evacuees. One such hutted camp, known as Lewiefield (later as Kielder) was built near the railway on Forestry Commission land. In the Second World War the camp also accommodated conscientious objectors sent by the Ministry of Labour who were given work in forestry. James summed up his life in the camp:

In that isolated part of Northumberland, on the North Tyne, miles away from anywhere, living by candlelight and lamplight in the midst of desolation, we might have been in Siberia, and all the war news had a quality of remoteness and unreality. During the long, tedious hours we spent on the fells each day, sometimes we would wonder where the German bombs had fallen the night before, or if the planes we had heard thrumming northwards over our camp had again struck Glasgow or Belfast. Occasionally a Nazi plane would jettison its cargo of bombs on the moors before crashing, and I once found a dying German airman who had parachuted into a deserted glen. I was able to talk to him in German before he died in my arms. That was the nearest we ever came to war…

We had all been sent from the distressed areas of North-East England ('depressed' areas we called them) on some government scheme. We had come in the hope of finding a new life and a decent wage in the forests. I was the only conscientious objector; afforestation was part of my wartime service.

We had been here for two years. Many of the men who had come from the pit towns and villages could not endure the solitude and wilderness, and had gone back to the dole queue, the unpaid rent and, now, the bombings. In those two years, the work had been laborious and un-changing, the money small and eaten away by illness. We had expected to find standing timber to fell and log at good prices. Instead we had been given these acres of shires of bog and moor and steep-sided, stony glens to drain and sod-plant with young trees.

Day after day passed in work that was heavy and heartbreakingly monotonous in the vast sweep of silence and rain lashed desolation......[65]

Despite this bleak existence, he never lost his creativity. On the contrary he began to write prose, writing many stories about his daily life in the camp. He also carried with him the poems of Wilfred Owen which he found inspirational and relevant to the Second World War. The last verse of 'Insensibility' confirmed his view of the war, 'in which both sides were led by dullards – men whose stupidity is the quality I most associate with war, for war is madness, murder, mass destruction, and all unnecessary.'[66] However, he gave up the work and returned home, only to be called to the Labour Exchange to answer anonymous accusations that he was not carrying out the instructions of the tribunal. He was escorted to a labour camp in East Witton, near Leyburn, which had a number of objectors among its residents:[67]

The first thing I had to do was stuff my mattress cover with dry hay and bracken and pack it into my bunk. The bunks were arranged in tiers round the hut, with a wood-burning stove in the centre. There were no baths and the washing facilities were primitive. The lavatory was even more so – a deep pit with a wooden bar laid across it on which one had to squat. I was reminded of the place in later years when I read Solzhenitsyn's description of a gulag.[68]

---

[65] Kirkup, *I, Of All People*, pp. 60-61.
[66] Ibid., pp. 72-73.
[67] Ibid., p. 87.
[68] Ibid., p. 88.

He went absent from the camp but the Labour Exchange caught up with him and sent him to a hostel run by the War Agricultural Executive in Thirsk:

> We were working mostly on the big gentlemen's farms around Thirsk, ditching and draining and breaking open potato clamps in weather so icy the ground was like cement. At one farm where there was a problem with the drains from the gentleman-farmer's big house, we had to dig up the drains until we found the cause of the blockage: the farmer had been throwing his condoms down the flush toilet, and they had formed a dense mass at a bend in the pipes. We had to clean that up.[69]

These conditions were comparable to the worst aspects of prison conditions. How much better off were these objectors being granted conditional registration? The occupations of the majority of conscientious objectors had not given them the physical attributes or experience to equip them for hard labour on the land and farmers were fully aware of this. Mass Observation quoted the Deputy Manager of Shepherd's Bush Employment Exchange: 'Where I think they fail is that many of them are physically unfit. They needn't go to all this trouble – they'd be turned down by a medical board.'[70] They also record in their file report summary that conventionally minded people say their physical condition is poor.[71] One objector, Edward Blishen, would not have disagreed with the statement applying to him, but showed, like many, he could adapt:

> I was unfitted for the work, quite a weedy, intellectual type, but at the end of five and a half years I could lift. I could load a five-ton lorry of wheat in about five minutes, and I

---

[69] Ibid., p. 93.
[70] Mass Observation File Report No. 312, p. 149.
[71] Ibid., p. a).

could carry a two and a quarter hundred-weight sack on my back.[72]

The difficulties faced by many working on the land were recognised by War Resisters International, whose Treasurer wrote to many newspapers:

George Lansbury was a man widely respected and loved by many besides those who shared his politics and his pacifism…War Resisters' International, of which he was the splendid chairman and leader, are collecting funds for a memorial to him. This is to take the form of a farm where conscientious objectors are to be trained for work on the land and where it is hoped to form a permanent community when the longed-for days of peace return.[73]

Coincidentally, James Kirkup, after another period on the run from the Ministry of Labour, was offered a job at the completed Lansbury Gate Farm in Essex, which he described as, 'a happy, hard-working community.'[74] Unfortunately, as the farm animals aggravated his asthma, his stay was short-lived. He finished the war working for a farming gang near South Shields.

The unpleasant conditions experienced on officially organised work gangs led to some conscientious objectors forming communities. They bought empty farms cheaply and worked them together, 'combining ideas of self-sufficiency and a practical microcosm of an idealised peaceful, sharing world with removal as far as possible from the total warfare state.'[75] An example was the farm which Louis and Paul Ronchetti went to on their release from prison. No such farms specifically for conscientious objectors have been located in the North-East of

[72] Felicity Goodhall, *We Will Not Go To War: Conscientious Objection during the World Wars* (Stroud: The History Press, 2010) p. 157.
[73] 'Hear All Sides: Farm for C.O.s as Memorial to George Lansbury,' *Northern Echo*, 12 December 1940, p. 4.
[74] Kirkup, *I, Of All People*, p. 96.
[75] 'Conscientious objection: An Introduction,' Peace Pledge Union, http://www.ppu.org.uk/coproject/guide.html.

England, however, Jim Elder purchased a derelict farm in Upper Tees-dale in 1934, which, 'during the early years of the Second World War became a safe haven for those, who for political or religious reasons, found themselves on the margins of the war effort.'[76] One visitor was the anti-war communist Steve Lawther. Steve was one of four brothers active in, or supportive of, the Communist Party, during the 1920s and 1930s in Chopwell which became popularly known as 'Little Moscow.' One of his brothers was Will Lawther, the Durham miners' leader, with who he had opposing views on the war, often played out in public.[77]

Elder was forced to sell his farm in 1943 for economic reasons, a fate not unusual for community farms. The Mass Observation archive contains a letter from a Birmingham conscientious objector illustrating how one such community came about; how it operated; and, its failure:

> .... a certain friend of pacifists became interested in the idea of community. He bought a large house standing in 10 acres of ground and several C.O.s and wives, who had lost their jobs took up residence there. Another friend lent the furniture. The women looked after the house whilst the men started cultivating the land and produced their own vegetables. They also kept fowl and goats for milk.
>
> Each C.O. paid £1 per week for his keep until his funds were exhausted. A few C.O.s had obtained jobs out-side and they paid 25/- p. w. into the funds.
>
> This community was hoping to be self-supporting af-ter a year or 18 months. Of course, after initial periods var-ying in each case, the C.O. could no longer afford to pay his keep, and the land would not produce enough profit until a year later so a number of pacifist friends lent or con-tributed towards the community.
>
> The whole community was dedicated to a pacifist and Christian way of living, living a simple life and working in agriculture.

---

[76] 'Idealist who started a kibbutz in Teesdale,' Memories Issue 105, *Northern Echo*, 24 November 2012.
[77] Ibid.

Unfortunately, we did not all have a share in the responsibility and running of the community and on the matter of principle the majority of us disagreed with the leaders and left the community.[78]

The objector was not, however, discouraged by his experience and stated his intention to:

...find a suitable small farm or house with land attached which I can rent. I have the nucleus of a new community who are ready to live together on a co-operative basis.

We would be on an agricultural basis, i.e. for C.O.s working outside the centre, they would pay in their wages up to 48/- per week to the centre and those working on the land would work a 52 hour week receiving from the centre, 48/- per week which would of course be paid back to the community. After all expenses, food etc. had been paid for, a certain proportion of the week's income would be put into the funds and the rest equally divided for pocket money. In time, as the land was cultivated the members losing their jobs outside would start work on the community land. Fowl, pigs and bees would also be kept.

There would be the time for and discussion of present day affairs.[79]

Whether he achieved his idyll is unknown but some were successful in providing an alternative to the state run agricultural gangs.

The Database of Conscientious Objectors shows at least 70 objectors recommended to work on the land, many of whom would have suffered the conditions experienced by James Kirkup. Some, unlike James, would have adapted. For those who did not adapt the conditions would have been unbearable, and could have lasted for up to five and a half years. There was also an element of danger as illustrated by a conscientious objector killed by a bull when at work.[80]

---

[78] 'Letter from a Dismissed C.O.,' Press Cuttings, *Mass Observation Online.*
[79] Ibid.
[80] 'Scottish C.O. Gored by Bull,' *Evening Chronicle*, 25 September 1941, p. 1.

Despite the conditions experienced on the land, *Peace News* remained positive.[81] They blamed the County War Agricultural Committees, who employed most of the conscientious objectors, for failing to appreciate the mental qualities of objectors in giving them the menial labouring tasks, and often providing unsuitable accommodation. Nevertheless:

> The hardships suffered have in the majority of cases served only to increase their determination and indomitability of spirit. Characters have stood out for their cheerfulness in times of trouble, for their truly pacifist living, and for their sympathetic understanding; and these, by their example, have inspired others to better living and a nobler testimony to their cause.
>
> It is the prerogative of the pacifist to find a constructive response to every situation, and yet we must be grateful to those in authority that in the midst of so much destruction the pacifists have been given such a fine opportunity for really constructive work on the land.

They, unsurprisingly, complimented the work done by objectors, claiming the government were adopting a hush-hush policy towards their work; 'the second secret service of the war.' The reason given was: 'it is not good for public morale that they are being seen as being saved from starvation by those who professed the folly of the war and have made their stance against it.' Not all objectors saw things this way. Arthur Page, a teacher from farming stock working on the land, thought it ridiculous to say that officials treated them as merely farm labourers and supressed their mental qualities, and they in fact treated them with courtesy and friendliness.[82]

The conditions experienced by those working in agricultural gangs contrasted sharply with conditions experienced by those who followed another direction of the tribunals, that is, to do hospital work. No evidence has been found of conditions in the North-East, but the Mass

---

[81] 'C.O.s in Agriculture,' *Peace News*, 28 March 1941, p. 3, and 4 April 1941, p. 3.
[82] 'C.O.s in Agriculture,' *Peace News*, 27 July 1941, p. 3.

Observation archives include a description of a camp for conscientious objectors attached to a sanatorium in Wales, the type of which objectors from all parts of the country would have experienced:

> The hut is built of brick covered in white rough cast and roofed with smooth grey-green roofing composition. (It) is about 150 feet long and commands views across the wide Welsh valley....
>
> The passage is flanked by lavatories, bathrooms, linen cupboards etc. There are two small rooms, a kitchen and a laundry which have been turned respectively into a quiet room and a radio room...The rest of the hut, which is one big room divided from the passage into cubicles...Each cubicle is lit and ventilated by either a large steel framed window covered by anti-splinter netting or a French window underneath a fanlight which opens.
>
> The walls and ceiling are a green colour and the floors are of a dark brown composition, except in the bathroom and lavatories which are tiled. The building is electrically lit and centrally heated. We use the first cubicle on the left as the common room. It is furnished with a few armchairs, a small table, a mat, a bookcase and one or two pictures of Cezanne reproductions and postcards of other artists...
>
> Those of us who live here take turns each week to work on the house, i.e. we make the beds and keep the place clean. This job, which comes round about every 3 months, is much looked forward to as a welcome break from ward routine and is by comparison a sinecure.[83]

No direct evidence was found of how objectors were treated in hospitals in the North-East. Some indication was gleaned from an interview with Bob Faldon, an objector to National Service in 1953, allocated to a hospital in Ponteland. He referred only to some mild ribbing about his religion, though not his objection, but recalled an incident where a fellow objector had sugar placed in the petrol tank of his motorbike, for what reason he did not elaborate. His overall impression of his National

---

[83] Mass Observation Directive Respondent 3350, January 1943.

Service was that it was an experience he would not have liked to miss. On its conclusion, he went on to be a successful businessman.[84]

As many had the choice of working on the land or in some capacity in a hospital, some must have later regretted choosing the land.

Medical Experiments

Some conscientious objectors took part in medical experiments. (Similar experiments were also carried out on C.O. volunteers in the U.S.A. where 122 took part in research into virus pneumonia and influenza)[85] The participants were volunteers and no conscientious objector was sent there by the tribunals. The aim of the experiments was to relieve discomforts suffered by men in the armed forces and the civilian population, and could therefore be described as humanitarian.

There were about 47 objectors, including three women, who volunteered to act as human guinea-pigs under the leadership of Dr Kenneth Mellanby at the Sorby Institute in Sheffield. One was an unnamed objector from Barnard Castle.[86] The only recorded conscientious objector from the town was Clarence L. Watson, whose objection was to anything compulsory, and this was a process for volunteers.[87] The newspaper reported that the objector had recently received a Medal of Honour.

The experiments included 12 objectors undertaking a long diet of virtually nothing but national bread, to find out the digestibility of wholemeal flour compared to white, an experiment so successful that wholemeal flour became compulsory. Another dietary experiment was for the same men to live on lifeboat rations for three months to discover the physical reactions to being ship-wrecked.[88] Others, mainly volunteers from the FAU, took part in tests on the effectiveness of anti-malarial drugs, taking high doses and allowing themselves to be bitten by mosquitoes.[89]

[84] Interview with Robert Faldon, conducted at his home in Gateshead, 8 November 2013.
[85] 'Guinea Pig Conchies Help Army Scientists, *The Globe and Mail (Toronto, Canada)*, 26 June 1944, p. 15.
[86] 'Britain's Volunteer "Guinea Pigs",' *Teesdale Mercury*, 2 June 1943, p. 7.
[87] 'Conscientious Objector, opposition to anything Compulsory,' *Teesdale Mercury*, 29 May 1940, p. 8.
[88] 'Bread Experiment,' *Sunderland Echo*, 2 May 1942, p.3.
[89] Kenneth Mellanby, *Human Guinea Pigs* (London: Victor Gollanz Ltd., 1946) p. 81.

The main experiment involved the men being infected by scabies and the course of the infection followed on their persons, an experiment which led to a new cure.[90] Bernard Hicken described the process:

We had scabies mites introduced into our bodies and then allowed to multiply and that was unpleasant, not too bad in the daytime but when you got into bed at night and became warm then the mites became active and you spent all the night itching.[91]

The discomfort involved led to the Minister for Health, Ernest Brown, having to respond to a question in Parliament: 'They have suffered discomfort rather than danger, but I am advised that they have not been free from the risk of incurring prolonged disability.'[92] There is no evidence to suggest that they suffered any long-term effects from this experiment or from one to introduce body lice to the head and head lice to the body to see if they migrated to the right place. But the same could not be said of being subjected to a diet without Vitamin A, as Bernard Hicken testified:

After eighteen months of this diet I suppose nature caught up with me and I had to be taken into hospital and given massive doses of Vitamin A and I was six months in hospital with a pleural effusion......When I came out of hospital I was like an old man...[93]

A 2003 article in the *Sheffield Telegraph* stated that four volunteers contracted major illnesses over the period of the research up to 1948: TB; impetigo and migraine; irregular heartbeat; and, collapse of capillaries in the knee.[94] The objector who contracted TB was the husband of Una Stimson:

---

[90] 'Pacifists' Aid in Scabies Investigation,' *Evening Chronicle*, 19 September 1941, p. 4.
[91] Kramer, *Conscientious Objectors*, p. 96.
[92] 'Suffered Discomfort,' *Sunderland Echo*, 14 May 1942, p. 4.
[93] Goodhall, *We Will Not Go To War*, p. 165.
[94] 'Commentary: Guinea-pigs' Private War,' *Sheffield Telegraph*, 29 August 2003, p. 12.

He went to the hospital and they found that he had a TB abscess on his chest due to the experiments he'd taken part in. I don't think they expected him to pull through.

There was this empty bungalow available at the seaside and my mother told us to go there to help him get better. This [abscess] on his chest had to be bandaged because it was suppurating all the time but an osteopath in Sheffield said if he took the bandages off and lay in the sun, the sun would help him get better......[95]

The *Sheffield Telegraph* article differs from a statement made by John Pemberton, a clinician to the Vitamin A and D depravation teams: 'None of the volunteers died or had any permanent disability as the result of the experiments.'[96] If Pemberton is correct then the effects described from the other sources may not have been permanent.

Why would men volunteer for such an unpleasant experience? It certainly was not for the money as they were only paid a private's wage. For Bernard Hicken it arose from a feeling of guilt that he was living at home as a civilian while others were dying abroad, and whilst working on the land was a useful contribution it was not as positive as being a medical guinea pig. It also had an element of risk.[97] Mellanby himself believed: 'many pacifists appeared to think that the duties they were performing, or to which they had been directed, were very unimportant.'[98] He also reinforced their selflessness:

Had they not volunteered they would have been in other work which was allowed by their tribunals' ruling, and would have at any rate received considerably more pay and probably (especially if they had accepted work in Civil Defence) less work.[99]

[95] Article I.D. A5568735, BBC Peoples' War, www.bbc.co.uk/history/ww2peopleswar/.
[96] Pemberton, John, 'Medical experiments carried out in Sheffield on conscientious objectors to military service during the 1939-45 war,' *International Journal of Epidemiology*, No 35, 2006, pp. 556-558.
[97] Goodall, *We Will Not Go To War*, p. 162.
[98] Mellanby, *Human Guinea Pigs*, p. 17.
[99] Ibid., p. 31.

Their selflessness was not his only motive for seeking conscientious objectors as volunteers, there was a practical dimension: 'they were the only section of the population not likely to be called up or compelled to leave the experiment due to military or industrial necessity.' [100]

The majority of volunteers were sourced by the Pacifist Service Units. These were formed in Liverpool and Manchester 1940 to enable conscientious objectors anxious to provide a service to other people to do so. They worked, for example, in hospitals and assisted the emergency services during air raids.[101] Mellanby considered he would get a good response to his appeal for volunteers provided the research could be shown to be of value in alleviating suffering, and that it was not solely directed to improving military efficiency.[102] The experiments did of course have a value to the military. Having got his volunteers, Mellanby was impressed:

> I myself am not a pacifist, but for three years I have lived and worked with these volunteers and I think it is possible for me to give a fairly detached view of them and the contribution they have made to research and medicine. It will appear that the volunteers, except for their views on war, were a fairly normal selection with perhaps more virtues and rather less vices than the average members of the population, but for the most part they were neither saints or "cissies." …they co-operated in the experimental work with complete trustworthiness and loyalty.[103]

Admiration for the work they had done for his research made him responsive to newspaper enquiries. Pointing out that newspapers usually wanted to say something derogatory about objectors, it seemed to him to be only fair that when they wanted to give a certain amount of credit;

---

[100] Ibid., p. 94.
[101] See: Pat Starkey, *Families and Social Workers: The Work of Family Service Units, 1940-1985* (Liverpool: Liverpool University Press, 2000).
[102] Mellanby, *Human Guinea Pigs,* p. 17.
[103] Ibid., p. 7.

'they should be allowed to do so, particularly where the credit was entirely deserved.'[104] Such credit was accorded to Richard Wodeman, who objected to having his conscience judged by a tribunal, which resulted in a three-month prison sentence. Dr Mellanby refers to spirited protests at the sentence from newspapers, for example:

> Richard Wodeman, for a soldier's pay, does the job of a human guinea pig. He has been inoculated with dangerous germs. He denies himself food and water as part of an experiment to aid shipwrecked sailors. He is a hero with a conscience which commands respect.
>
> Unfortunately, the military authorities do not share the public's respect for conscience. Because Wodeman objects to military service he has been sentenced to three months' imprisonment in defiance of his record and of the government's clear pledge that such men will not be the victims of stupid officialdom. This sentence should be quashed.[105]

This somewhat overstating of the public's respect for conscience did have an effect. Public disquiet, and pressure in Parliament on the Minister of Labour, resulted in Wodeman, despite again refusing to attend a tribunal, being released.

As well as the beneficial results derived from the experiments, there were also benefits to the objectors. The public saw them as being willing, despite their conscientious objection, to put themselves at risk. The volunteers were also allowed to live together as a community of like-minded people, separated from the prejudice encountered from some of the public.

Conclusion

This chapter has compared and contrasted the experiences of conscientious objectors in three different spheres and how these experiences had

---

[104] Ibid., p. 90.
[105] 'Conscience,' *Reynolds News*, quoted in Mellanby, *Human Guinea Pigs*, pp. 60-61.

impacted on them. A significant proportion of identified objectors in the North-East of England were to find themselves suffering terms of imprisonment. The majority of sentences were served in Durham Prison, where conditions were as unpleasant, if not worse, than any other centre of civilian incarceration. That so many were prepared to endure these conditions on several occasions of increasing lengths of time, is a strong indication of the sincerity of their objection. This also casts further doubt on Barker's assertion that they felt stigmatised by the experience. As Chapter 7 demonstrates incarceration in the North-East for soldiers who were conscientious objectors could be even worse.

For those who elected to accept conditional registration by the tribunal, or make a positive contribution, the treatment received varied. Some of those on the land suffered conditions every bit as unpleasant as those in prison with life in some of the camps akin to being officially incarcerated. Working on the land was not the most attractive of the conditions which could be imposed by the tribunal. Complying with the conditions of registration did not therefore always bring with it benefits over those who remained defiant. It did, however, provide, for those who desired it, a feeling that they were doing something useful to society, and for the government there was the satisfaction of a positive contribution to the nation's effort.

Finally, for those who volunteered for medical experiments the opportunity to live in a sympathetic community was combined with an almost unique opportunity to present themselves as objectors in a positive light. It also allowed them to avoid the military and industrial compulsion which would have tested those whose objection was absolute, and which would have led to them serving time in prison. Their experiences could not, however, be described as pleasant.

Durham Prison, 1930s

Chapter Six

Women Conscientious Objectors

In 1941, the author and pacifist Vera Brittain documented the experiences of people living through the Battle of Britain in London in *England's Hour*. In this she lamented the misuse of modern inventions which had blighted the lives of all those people:[1]

> We ourselves invented the instruments which make modern warfare so diabolical – the chemical industry begun in the Victorian age; the aeroplane which could have been used for the unification of the world and the saving of life, but instead has been converted into the cruellest vehicle of destruction ever conceived by perverted genius; the tank which has turned the roads of Europe into pathways of blood. We did not invent but could have done much to further the development of broadcasting, which might have increased knowledge and brought distant peoples into friendly contact, but instead has become the insidious servant of competitive propaganda, warping human integrity by the falsification or suppression of truth. Three out of four of these inventions could already have united mankind and enlarged human life. Instead, through lack of moral power and the bankruptcy of statesmanship, they have been turned to the erasing of a civilisation.[1]

Born in Newcastle, Staffordshire in 1893, and therefore over the age for call-up, Vera Brittain was neither a conscientious objector nor from the North-East of England. She was, however, quite prominent because of her writings and made regular contributions to *Peace News*. Most notably, in response to the Under-Secretary for Air's comment that the suffering of German civilians was their own fault, she disparaged the idea that 'that children of three and under, of which large numbers must

---

[1] Vera Brittain, *England's Hour* (New York: Continuum, 2005), pp. 225-226.

have been killed by our bombs, are responsible for a war which began before they were born'[2] She also combined her pacifism with feminism:

> The bankrupt civilisation now engaged in destroying itself is admittedly the creation of men. Realistic humility on their part might perhaps suggest that without the equal and unimpeded collaboration there will be no remedy. A pacifist movement which denied the potentialities and significance of that full contribution would rest upon as irrational and self-destructive a basis as Nazism itself.[3]

This full contribution included Vera being a member of the Women's International League for Peace and Freedom (WILPF), becoming its Vice-President in the 1930s.[4] WILPF was formed out of the 1915 conference at The Hague involving delegates from countries on both sides in the First World War. One of its aims was, 'the abolition of the war system, the elimination of the root causes of war and conflict.'[5] British representation at the conference included Dr Ethel Williams from Newcastle, a renowned suffragette and pacifist. Ethel Williams was the first woman General Practitioner in the country as well as, reportedly, the first woman in the North-East to drive a motor car.[6] She remained a prominent member of WILPF until the late 1940s, attending a number of congresses, including the 1921 Vienna congress where Olga Misar of Austria said, 'the real end to war would come when the masses of the people refused any form of war service.'[7] Whilst this was atypical of most in the mainstream peace movement, many women in the North-East did just that.

---

[2] 'Bombing Civilians,' *Peace News*, 19 March 1943, p. 3.

[3] Vera Brittain, 'Women and Pacifism,' *Peace News*, 15 August 1941, p.3.

[4] Patrick Deane, *History in Our Hands: A Critical Anthology of Writings on Literature, Culture, and Politics from the 1930s* (London: Leicester University Press, 1998), pp. 63–4.

[5] Women's International League for Peace and Freedom, UK at http://www.ukwilpf.org.uk/.

[6] David Neville, *To Make Their Mark: The Women's Suffrage Movement in the North-East of England, 1900-1914* (Newcastle upon Tyne: Centre for Northern Studies, University of Northumbria, 1997); and, Nigel Todd, 'Ethel Williams: Medical and Suffrage Pioneer,' *North-East Labour History*, Bulletin 30, 1996.

[7] Anne Marie Pois, 'Practical and Absolute Pacifism in the Early Years of the U.S. Women's International League for Peace and Freedom,' in Peter Brock and Thomas Paul Socknet, *Challenge to Mars: Essays on Pacifism from 1918 to 1945* (Toronto: University of Toronto Press, 1999), p. 210.

WILPF became especially active during the 1930s, paying particular attention to disarmament. Melissa Hensley argues that this was
largely due to the channelling of feminist activity after the achievement
of female suffrage.[8] Women also held prominent positions within peace
organisations such as the PPU but their increasing importance in the
pacifist movement is only one reason why a separate chapter is devoted
to women conscientious objectors, and, to those in the North-East in
particular. Firstly, as the arrangements for the registration of women for
national service and conscientious objection differed from those for men
a separate analysis is required. Secondly, the North-East of England was
home to a number of firsts in women's objection: the first to be unconditionally registered; the first to be prosecuted for refusing to fire-watch;
the first to be prosecuted for failing to register for National Service; and,
the first to be sent to prison. Finally, some have left valuable oral testimonies detailing the reasons for their objection and their experiences,
most notably Kitty Alexander.

The National Service (No. 2) Act 1941 extended the call-up for
National Service to single, childless women, initially those born in 1920
and 1921, later extended in November 1942 to women born in 1922,
and to age 31 by the end of the war. The first actual registration date
was decided on as 10 January 1942. For women, the call-up applied to
industry, civil defence and the armed forces where, with the exception
of special agents, they were not required to bear arms. Even the Axis
powers had not resorted to this degree of compulsion. Undoubtedly one
of the major reasons why it applied to single women was, according to
Hayes, the expectation of men serving abroad that their wives would be
adequately looked after whilst they put their lives at risk.[9] The arguments
put forward by men against conscription have been extensively covered,
but Constance Braithwaite, writing in *Peace News*, argued that women
had an even stronger case against it:

---

[8] Melissa Anne Hensley, 'Feminine Virtue and Feminist Fervor: The Impact of the Women's International League for Peace and Freedom in the 1930s', *Journal of Women and Social Work*, Vol. 21, No. 2
(2006) pp. 146-157.
[9] Hayes, *Challenge of Conscience*, p. 16.

Most women have a particular concern for the rearing, preserving and enriching of individual life. It is therefore particularly outrageous to compel women to participate in the prosecution of war, that is, in the wholesale and indiscriminate slaughter of individual life. Industrial conscription involves not only this but also the encouragement of many women to neglect their own children.

It is tragic that one of the results of political equality in this country is that women should participate equally in the most stupid of men's convictions – war. Violence is not women's method: they have often suffered from its use and rarely profited from it.

Convention has in the past recognised that women should not be required to fight, partly due to concern for the preservation of the race. But it is also due to the fact that men have expected a higher moral standard from women than they have expected from themselves.[10]

Anxious to avoid overloading the tribunals the government learnt from the experiences of dealing with male conscientious objectors. Whilst ultimately affording women the same rights to a tribunal hearing, they minimised women's tribunal appearances by introducing procedures designed to place women objectors into work of national importance acceptable to them. The Ministry of Labour, whilst seeking to be as accommodating as possible, were adamant that 'there are such things as the Women's Land Army and domestic service in hospitals to which no conscientious objection can in any circumstances be recognised.'[11] Both these options were rejected by objectors in the North-East of England. The Ministry also advised women that where their job had been deferred for call-up their conscientious objection was also deferred, or remained provisional, as long as they remained in their current employment. This deferral also disguises the true numbers of women objectors as many were never able to present their case to a tribunal. Hazel

---

[10] 'A Woman's View of Conscription,' *Peace News*, 25 April 1941, p. 3.
[11] 'Memorandum from Mr Wiles to Mr Goddard', 18 February 1942, Ministry of Labour and National Service, LAB 6/183, National Archives, Kew, London.

Nicholson asserts this did not allow many women to be expressly identified as conscientious objectors. The actual figure is not known but in February 1943 Ernest Bevin reported that 2,500 women had registered as conscientious objectors, at least double the number shown in the official statistics.[12]

For those women who did elect to go before a tribunal, the Act specified that wherever possible the tribunal should have a female member on it. If they thought that women were not going to cause them difficulties, then an *Evening Chronicle* article would suggest otherwise. It reported that Ministry of Labour centres throughout the country were tracking down 'hundreds of girls who thought they had dodged the call-up by not registering,' This had proved to be much harder than for men, as some may not have been in employment.[13]

Whether to register or not was to women pacifists not a question of dodging the call-up, but a dilemma. Grace Turner, who worked for the CBCO, was unhappy with the absence of an automatic referral to a tribunal but decided to register as she did not object to registering details of her occupation, only to her services being used for the war effort. She wrote to Ernest Bevin stating her objection and received a reply from the Ministry of Labour stating she was unlikely to be offered work 'likely to conflict with your conscientious scruples.'[14] On the other hand, Winifred Rawlins decided not to register as she objected to conscription being used to degrade women:

> I am aware that if I were to register and state my pacifist principles I should probably be given the opportunity to do some work which, in itself, I could take no objection. It is the fact of conscription with which I am concerned, not whether I can avoid work
>
> The greatest evil in the conscription of women lies in the fact that thousands of women who have not reached the point of any kind of resistance, many of them inarticulate working women of immature age, are by means of it drawn

---

[12] Hazel Nicholson, 'A Disputed Identity: Women Conscientious Objectors in Second World War Britain,' p. 417.

[13] 'Ministry Rounds Up Girl Dodgers', *Evening Chronicle*, 20 February 1942, p. 4.

[14] 'Why I have registered,' *Peace News*, 18 July 1941, p. 3.

into work which outrages all the deepest and womanly instincts in them, work which they would shrink from were it not placed before them as an unavoidable duty to the State.[15]

Women in the North-East of England took both routes, registering and not registering, to record their objection.

Women were also brought into the fire-watching regime. Compulsory fire-watching was first applied to women on 19 September 1942 and local authorities had to hold registrations of women aged between 20 and 45, to enrol them for duty in their neighbourhood if not doing fire-watching duty at work.[16] The first woman in Britain to be prosecuted for failing to register was Elsie Hunt of Scarborough. Elsie was fined £5 on 6 November 1942. On 11 November 1942, Hilda Marshall, a clerk in the Treasurer's Department of Leeds City Council, was sent to prison for 3 months, the magistrate, in response to her claim of conscientious objection, stating: 'I think you are a humbug!'[17] In total there were 80 prosecutions of women objectors for refusing to fire-watch, a modest number which Hayes asserts was due to the reasonableness of employers and a reluctance of local authorities to prosecute women.[18] Included in the 80, fined 20 shillings in September 1943, was Nancy Sadler of Newcastle (see Chapter 1 re Newcastle War Resisters).[19]

Women objectors were also treated differently in the regularly produced statistics of numbers of conscientious objectors, an indication that the true numbers of women objectors was publicly suppressed, 'to make them appear inconsequential.'[20] Ministry of Labour Officials were advised that if they wanted specific information about the women who had been specially interviewed then, 'this can be obtained from the records which it is suggested Local Offices should keep.'[21] The official statistics show a total of 1,056 women appearing before the tribunals up to the end of 1944, but this does not represent the true number of those

---

[15] 'Why I Shall Not Register,' *Peace News*, 11 July 1941, p. 3.
[16] Hayes, *Challenge of Conscience*, p. 307.
[17] Ibid., p. 307.
[18] Ibid., p. 308.
[19] 'Failure to Register,' *Morpeth Herald*, 10 September 1943, p. 4.
[20] Nicholson, 'Women Conscientious Objectors,' p. 410.
[21] 'Memorandum from W. Scott to L. Hardman', 11 February 1942, Ministry of Labour and National Service, LAB 6/183, National Archives, Kew, London.

with a conscientious objection. Hazel Nicholson estimates this as at least three times the number. [22] It is, however, useful to compare the tribunal decisions for men and women for the period, bearing in mind that women objectors who had been placed in work of national importance would most likely have been given and accepted conditional registration or non-combatant duties.

Tribunal Decisions 1939-1944 (G.B.)

	Men %	Women %
Unconditionally Registered as COs	5.9	8.8
Conditionally Registered as COs	48.6	73.0
CO - Liable Non-Combatant Duties	24.9	2.8
Removed from the Register	20.6	15.4

It would appear from the data that women received a more sympathetic hearing from the tribunals but the statistic on non-combatant duties is deceptive as there was no Non-Combatant Corps for women. With few exceptions, women called up to the forces were not involved in direct combatant roles, therefore the tribunals, it appeared, were more likely to conditionally register them instead of making them liable for non-combatant duties. There were still, however, a greater proportion being unconditionally registered and fewer removed from the register.

The available statistics for the North-East of England present a different picture. Of the 36 women on the Database of Conscientious Objectors, 24 are known to have been before the tribunal: 3 (13%) were unconditionally registered; 11 (46%) were conditionally registered; and, 9 (38%) were removed from the register unconditionally. The corresponding figures for the tribunal, men and women, for 1939-1948 were 9.9%, 37.6% and 27.4% with 25.1% being registered as liable for non-combatant duties. It would therefore appear, from albeit a small sample, that approximately half of women expected to be liable for non-combatant duties were removed from the register without condition and not

---

[22] 'Orders Made by Tribunals on Application for Registration in Register of Conscientious Objectors', LAB6/405, C588193, National Archives, Kew; Nicholson, 'Women Conscientious Objectors,' p. 409.

conditionally registered, contrary to the national position. This may in part explain Judge Richardson's comment to the Hexham Rotary Club, that the young women were more poisonous than the young men. It is, however, more likely to be case of who the women were that is reflected in both the figures and the comment of Judge Richardson.

Jehovah's Witness Objectors

The reason for objection is definitely known in twenty-three cases, of which seventeen (74%) were religious objectors. Twelve of the religious objectors were known to be Jehovah's Witnesses, seen by the tribunals generally as not holding a sincere objection on religious grounds. Judge Richardson's reported comments on Dorothy Reeve's and others' views are detailed in Chapter 2. As Judge Richardson had declared his strong dislike of Jehovah's Witnesses, these women were unlikely to be recognised by the Newcastle Tribunal as conscientious objectors, and only two were. However, the fact that two were recognised is indicative of the tribunal treating persons on a case by case basis. They were also more likely than most other religious objectors to appear before the tribunal, as their refusal to do anything to assist the war effort, even indirectly, negated their placement in work of national importance. They became such an irritation to the government that they took the step of banning the importation of *Watchtower* and *Consolation*, the organisation's magazines, although they did not go as far as Australia in banning the organisation outright.[23] Some local authorities outside the North-East took a hard-line approach to the organisation. Nottingham and Manchester banned weekend meetings of Jehovah's Witnesses under Defence Regulation 39E which empowered the Home Secretary to ban any meeting, 'as to which he is satisfied that the holding thereof would be likely to cause serious public disorder or to promote disaffection.'[24]

Jehovah's Witnesses ultimately did not get much sympathy from the courts either. It was fairly common for a number of Jehovah's Witnesses to share the same address, usually originating from various other locations. For example, Dorothy Charlton and Kathleen Jupp shared a property with another, male, Witness in Haydon Bridge. Dorothy

---

[23] 'Ban on Jehovah's Publications', *Evening Chronicle*, 10 March 1943, p. 5.
[24] 'Banned Meetings of Witnesses', *Evening Chronicle*, 17 September 1942, p. 8.

Charlton had been a supervisor and clerk at Dukehouse Camp from April 1943 until January 1944 when she terminated her employment. On refusing an instruction to return she was fined £5, saying that she had been a Jehovah's Witness for 16 years and her first duty was to give her whole time to God.[25] The chairman, J. M. Heslop, in jailing her for two months for failing to pay the fine remarked: 'It is a case of rank defiance of the law and we are bound to deal with it.'[26]

Kathleen Jupp received a fine for failing to attend an interview at a children's sanatorium. Whilst she refused to pay the fine it would appear that her parents paid at least part of it and there is no further record of her going to prison, only that her case was adjourned for her to reconsider her position.[27] It appears that she did take up employment in an evacuation camp, prior to appearing before a tribunal. These factors probably saved her from the inevitable prison sentence. The comments of the National Service Officer, Mr Welburn, to the Magistrates Court, are an indication of the efforts made in these cases to place women in suitable work, thus alleviating the need for such court appearances:

> In order to make the position as easy as possible for her orders were not issued for her to take up munitions work or work of that kind directly connected with the war, and it was suggested that work at the Children's Sanatorium might be suitable, and she was given direction to attend for an interview with the matron, but she refused to do so. I have tried to reason with her that this work of looking after ailing children was work which had nothing to do with the war, and had to be carried on whether there was a war or not. I suggested to her that there was nothing in the work to conflict with her religious beliefs[28]

When Miss Jupp was eventually allowed to appear before the tribunal, she was not unexpectedly removed from the register. In response to her admission that she left the Land Army to become a Jehovah's

[25] 'Witness Fined Won't Pay', *Hexham Courant*, 22 April 1944, p. 1.
[26] 'Woman "Witness" Gaoled for Refusing to Pay Fine', *Hexham Courant*, 17 June 1944, p. 1.
[27] 'Fine Payment Would Admit Guilt', *Hexham Courant*, 12 June 1943, p. 1.
[28] '"Witness" Read Bible in Court', *Hexham Courant*, 5 September 1942, p. 1.

Witness, Sir Frank Nicolson commented: 'You are an outstanding example, the only person in the country, probably, who has left the land because of a conscientious objection.'[29]

Another two Jehovah's Witnesses who spent time in prison were Joan Dodsworth of Red Row and Martha Reeves of Guisborough. Joan Dodsworth was sentenced to one month in prison for failing to obey a direction of the Ministry of Labour.[30] She had registered under the Registration for Employment Order, 1941 and was notified that employment was available for her as a housemaid at Bensham Hospital, Gateshead. Whilst the work to which she was directed was domestic in nature, there are some medical practices which are contrary to the beliefs of Jehovah's Witnesses, however, there is no evidence that this was claimed by Joan. She did not avail herself of the employment and was therefore directed by the National Service Officer (NSO) to do so.[31] She unsuccessfully appealed and was issued with a direction requiring her to take up the work which she also failed to do.[32] When interviewed by the Ministry she said she had no objection to performing the duties of a housemaid, but objected to giving up her full-time Christian work of preaching and distributing literature in the district.[33] It was pointed out to her that the Jehovah's Witnesses were not a recognised religious denomination therefore, although she may be a minister of that denomination, she was not entitled to exemption as were those of conventional denominations. Mr Wade, prosecuting, said that she had been offered other types of non-combatant work, but she had consistently refused to take up any of the work:

> We are engaged in total warfare. When people refuse to take up their duties without proper excuse, these duties have to be done by others, who possibly could be doing more skilled work. Much of this would result in a considerable slackening of our war effort.[34]

---

[29] 'Easy Refuge for Shirkers': Girl C.O. left land work', *Evening Chronicle*, 18 March 1943, p. 8.
[30] 'Jehovah's Witness at Amble Court,' *Morpeth Herald*, 17 April 1942, p. 2.
[31] Ibid.
[32] Ibid.
[33] Ibid.
[34] Ibid.

In sentencing, the Chairman reinforced this message and added: 'May I remind you what would happen if you took up this attitude in Germany? You would not be standing in court. This is a free country, but there are limits, and this is a time of total warfare.'[35] She was also advised that when she came out of prison she would not be absolved from carrying out the orders of the Ministry of Labour, although, as is detailed below, this was unlikely to be enforced.

Martha Reeves was sentenced to three months for failing to comply with the direction of the National Services Officer to work as a domestic at Holgate Hospital, Middlesbrough. She had joined the organisation in September 1941, just prior to the extension of conscription to women, and had repeatedly declined to take any part in the war effort: 'I have consecrated my life to Almighty God, and I feel it is my duty to carry out these things and to preach the methods of the kingdom.'[36]

Two kitchen maids, Dorothy Fisher and Edith Hillary, both Jehovah's Witnesses living in Kirtley Terrace, Bishop Auckland, were also given a fine with the alternative being 14 days in prison for refusing to obey a work direction. It is not known which option they chose.[37]

Not all Jehovah's Witnesses were treated harshly by the tribunal and the courts. R. D. W. H. Pearce was granted unconditional registration as a conscientious objector in May 1942.[38] It may have been significant that she was a teacher, an occupation depleted by the demands of the call-up and the actions of certain local authorities. Muriel Hayley was granted conditional registration by the tribunal and does not appear in the sources again, which suggests that she complied.[39] Doreen Heddon, however, was also conditionally registered, but received two fines from the court for failing to fulfil the conditions of the registration.[40] This was the course of action taken by many male Witnesses when unconditional exemption was not granted.

---

[35] Ibid.
[36] 'Would Not Do Hospital Work: Sent to Gaol,' *North-Eastern Gazette*, 23 June 1942, p. 3.
[37] News from the Courts – "Witnesses Warned", *Durham County Advertiser*, 8 May 1942, p. 4.
[38] Judge's "Why Eat?" to C.O., *Evening Chronicle*, 12 May 1942, p. 4.
[39] Ibid.
[40] C.O. Refused to Work in City Hospital, *Evening Chronicle*, 18 November 1942, p. 5.

Constance Bolam

A striking feature of women's objection in the North-East of England is the high proportion of those on the database who spent time in prison. Approximately 500 women nationally served time in prison, compared to 5,000 men who served time in prison and 1,000 men subjected to military detention.[41] Of the twelve imprisoned objectors only four are recorded in the sources as appearing before the tribunal; their sentences resulted from their failure to follow the tribunal direction. Five of the remaining eight refused to obey work directions, one refused fire-watching direction and one refused to register (the reason for the final one remains unknown). It is of note that at least four of the women who spent time in prison, and two who did not, would appear to have been associated with Newcastle War Resisters. One was Constance E. Bolam, a housemaid from Kenton, who became, in January 1942, the first woman conscientious objector in Britain to be jailed, described as 'a striking event' by Hayes.[42] Other members of Newcastle War Resisters were Kitty Alexander, Dorothy Morley, Doris Philipson, Nancy Sadler and Agnes Gillender. For there to be six Newcastle War Resisters out of the 37 objectors identified, i.e. 17%, is a further indication of the significance of the organisation within the region. It is also significant that all 6 defied the authorities by non-compliance with the regulations.

Constance Bolam was charged with failing to comply with two notices from the Ministry of Labour directing her to take up work as a dining room maid at Newcastle Eye Hospital. She had written to the NSO stating: 'I am not in any circumstances prepared to take up any work of national importance,' and, 'I entirely disbelieve in war as a method of settling disputes and believe war to be futile.'[43] In court she added:

> Conscription means I will be forced to do it by the Government. If you are conscripted to do a job, it shows it is to help the war effort, and I do not intend to take up any work

---

[41] Brock, *Twentieth-Century Pacifism*, p. 160.
[42] Hayes, *Challenge of Conscience*, p.266.
[43] 'Girl Defies Ministry', *Morpeth Herald*, 9 January 1942. P. 3.

of that kind. I would not be offered such work in peace time
so it must be to help the war effort.[44]

The Chairman of the Magistrates, Sir Ralph Mortimer, in expressing the view of many that the nature of this war was beyond conscientious objection, was clearly unimpressed:

By helping people suffering from their eyes, you think that
is helping the war effort? This is a war for civilisation and
not an ordinary war, and not a war to which anyone can
offer any conscientious objection.[45]

He was not the first establishment figure exasperated by Constance. Judge Richardson, whose tribunal had first directed her to land
or hospital work, remarked: 'You must recognise that we on the Tribunal have some common-sense, and you have none. It is no good talking
rubbish like that.'[46]
      The prosecutor had asked the magistrates to make a decision that
would act as a deterrent to others. She was fined 40/-, and when she
intimated that the fine would not be paid it was announced that the
alternative would be one month's imprisonment. As she left the court
there were shouts of, 'all the best Connie.'[47] When it came to her release
the authorities, as Hayes claims, were concerned that there may be
demonstrations so they quietly released her two or three days early to
avoid publicity.[48]
      Being the first woman objector to be jailed brought with it a de-
gree of notoriety in pacifist circles and Constance was interviewed for
the *C.B.C.O. Bulletin*.[49] In this interview she stated: 'I am an absolutist.
If it hadn't been for the war, I should never have been asked to work in
a hospital. I was sent there for the purpose of the war.'[50] Regarding her

[44] Ibid.
[45] Ibid.
[46] Hayes, *Challenge of Conscience*, pages 48-49.
[47] *Morpeth Herald*, 9 January 1942, p. 3.
[48] Hayes, *Challenge of Conscience*, p.267.
[49] 'We Interview Constance Bolam,' *C.B.C.O. Bulletin*, March 1942, p.5.
[50] Ibid.

early release, she said that she did not know if it was to avoid a demon-stration but confirmed she had intended to inform her friends of her release date but she was not allowed to send a letter out as she was only serving 28 days and not one month as per her sentence.[51] Liberal inter-pretations of the definition of one month could benefit the authorities.

She also gave some detail of her time in prison, spending her time working in the laundry or cleaning the prison chapel. She was, however, asked to knit socks for soldiers as her cell task, but declined saying she had not come to do work for the Army. Her main complaints were re-garding the women having to wear blue cotton frocks in cold weather and not being made a 'star' prisoner, as her first offender status entitled her to.[52]

No evidence has been found as to what happened to Constance Bolam after her release. She may have returned to her original employ-ment with Kitty Alexander, another conscientious objector who served time in Durham Prison.

Kitty Alexander

On 11 March 1999, Kitty Hall (nee Alexander) gave an interview which is held in the British Library Sound Archive. She was born 5 November 1906 and was therefore 92 when interviewed. The interview was very clear and lucid and Mrs Hall had a clear recollection of events, speaking with great clarity and intelligence. The following narrative is derived principally from this recording.[53]

She described her background as middle class, although her par-ents were separated. Her mother employed a young housemaid while Kitty worked to earn money, who became, 'the first woman in the world to be sent to prison for being a conscientious objector, for a month.'[54] This was Constance Bolam, but Kitty did not mention her name in the interview, which is perhaps indicative of the different social classes from which the two women came.

---

[51] Ibid.
[52] Ibid.
[53] Interview with Kitty Alice Hall (nee Alexander), British Library Sound Archive.
[54] Ibid.

Kitty worked for an insurance company as a cashier, and could probably have got exemption, but did not: 'perhaps foolishly in hindsight. I believed that I did not have the right to register to save myself going into the Army so I didn't register.'[55] In becoming a conscientious objector, she had been strongly influenced by her father who encouraged her to 'make her own decisions in life and not be co-opted into wars and such like if she did not believe in it':

> I never believed in it. War has never solved anything, has caused more misery than anything else, and I therefore did not want to participate in it. I was asked to take in evacuees but I refused because it was part of the war service. I also refused to do fire-fighting at work and was told that I could get the sack for that. I said that's up to you and not me, and I won't fire-fight and I didn't. I think I was quite respected for it.[56]

When accused at work of being a Russia lover, she denied it saying: 'I was a lover of everyone. I'm a citizen, a person entitled to speak my mind. I have a mind of my own.'[57]

Religion played no part in her decision to be an objector: 'When I got out of prison I wrote to the vicar who had preached a sermon of hate against the Germans and anyone else not on our side. I told him that I was not very religious and if that was preaching God's gospel then I am less so now.'[58]

As she had not registered she did not appear before a tribunal. She appeared before the magistrates, charged with failing to register for National Service. For being the first woman in Britain to be found guilty of this offence she was fined £5, and, on refusing to pay the fine, she went to prison for a month in December 1942.[59] She was also the last women to be charged with this offence as the Ministry of Labour found

---

[55] Ibid.
[56] Ibid.
[57] Ibid.
[58] Ibid.
[59] 'Pacifist Objects to "Bad Laws"', *Morpeth Herald*, 4 December 1942, p. 5.

it legally easier to prosecute for failure to attend an interview.[60] The court heard that she was due to register on 7th March but did not attend, and did not reply to a communication sent to her on 18th March. After ignoring two further letters she was instructed to attend for interview which she did, on 18 September, and gave being a pacifist as the reason for not registering. She admitted to being technically guilty but morally not guilty: 'I am a pacifist and am absolutely opposed to war in any form. Had I registered I should have been admitting willingness to undertake work of national importance and I cannot do that.'[61] On her way to the cells a sympathiser shouted, 'Freedom is in peril, defend it with all your might!'[62] This was reported in the newspaper as, 'This is a land of freedom; defend it with all your strength.'[63]

Kitty recalled that on leaving the court a policeman grabbed her by the arm and said, 'you conscientious objectors,' to which she replied, 'you take your hands off me or I'll have you for assault.'[64] On being sent to prison, she lost the job she had held since 1923. In the Black Maria that took her to prison, a man said to her that she 'was a bloody fool for giving up that good job with its good wage,' to which she replied: 'there were some things that came before that: my way may not be your way.'[65] On leaving prison she worked for an architect who accepted her on her merits and ignored the loss of her green employment card. She continued her active pacifism for a brief period after the war, joining the Campaign for Nuclear Disarmament (CND) when the organisation was founded and going on a couple of marches.[66]

Kitty's description of life in Durham Prison is very revealing and it is given in detail in Chapter 4. Also, as she was one of the first women objectors to be jailed, it is not surprising that she states that there was only one other woman objector in Durham Prison at the time. This objector was a Jehovah's Witness, who she recalled found prison difficult and who worried that she might not make it, but she did. She was, however, aware that there were many male objectors in prison, many of

---

[60] Nicholson, 'Women Conscientious Objectors,' p. 414.
[61] 'Pacifist Objects to "Bad Laws"', *Morpeth Herald*, 4 December 1942, p. 5.
[62] Hayes, *Challenge of Conscience*, p. 267.
[63] 'Pacifist Objects to "Bad Laws"', *Morpeth Herald*, 4 December 1942, p. 5.
[64] Interview with Kitty Alice Hall (nee Alexander), British Library Sound Archive.
[65] Ibid.
[66] Ibid.

whom were also Jehovah's Witnesses, and some of whom were political objectors.[67]

Kitty was not the only conscientious objector in the family. She spoke of two older brothers imprisoned as conscientious objectors, who she claimed escaped and worked in Ireland until the war was finished. No additional evidence was found to identify them, and no evidence that entries on the database for Russell and Russell S. Alexander, are for relatives of Kitty. However, Russell Stanley Alexander, a painter and decorator from Allendale, was given three month's imprisonment for failing to take up agricultural work as directed. He stated that he had served one year for failing to submit to a medical and, on his release, he told the NSO that he intended to do as little as possible to further the prosecution of the war.[68] Kitty also refers to another brother who agreed to work on the land, much to her displeasure, but again there is no additional evidence to identify him.

Juliet Morland

Another woman from a family with a tradition of pacifism was Juliet Morland of Felling, who also gave an interview to the British Library.[69]

As with Kitty Alexander, Juliet came from a middle-class background and was privately educated. She went to the private Dame Allen's Girls School in Newcastle which her sister and mother had also attended. Her father was a teacher and a Felling UDC councillor for one term. He was a member of the CPGB but was nominated by the Co-operative Party as he could not have been elected if he had stood as a Communist. He bought the *Daily Worker* until he became fed up with its negativity. He was a pacifist but thought it politic not to attend pacifist meetings, although he did write anti-war letters to the local press. His own mother had been a keen pacifist and one of the first to sell white poppies. She became President of the Co-operative Congress and a

---

[67] Ibid.

[68] 'Pacifist Returns to Prison', *Evening Chronicle*, 12 June 1944, p. 4.

[69] 'Interview with Juliet Morland', C880/12, British Sound Archive at the British Library, recorded 1998.

member of the Co-operative Women's League, as well as being an activist for contraception.[70]

Juliet's pacifism was therefore influenced by her grandmother and then her father. It was not shared by her siblings. Her sister worked in the offices of an armaments company, Clark Chapman and Co., and was too glad to have a job to be worried about pacifist principles. Her brother was called up for the services but she claimed that he 'diddled his medical' by pretending to be not very intelligent. His motivation was not pacifist, he just did not want to go.[71]

Juliet's pacifism came to the fore after she left school and met Mona Lovell, a librarian, who held classes at Felling library and convinced her fellow librarians to become pacifists. Juliet also became more politically aware and joined the Communist Party 'because of the high level of unemployment.' She was the publicity person for the Young Communist League and sold their organ, *The Challenge*, as well as setting up meetings and organising dances to raise money. Some of the Young Communists were called-up so the group faded away. She found the public meetings exciting, especially a platform shared by Willie Gallagher and Ellen Wilkinson, whom she thought 'charismatic and exhilarating.' 'Labour had done a lot but the Communists were going to put everything else right.'[72] The Communists were not pacifists. She and her father supported the International Brigades in Spain as they considered it a just war. By the time the Second World War came she had come under the influence of the librarian who had taken her to Quaker meetings where they were all absolute pacifists. 'When the war came I was sure it was wrong to fight. When bombs were dropped they did not know who they were killing and without war they may have become friends.'[73] Ultimately her membership of the Quakers led her to the FAU.

On leaving school Juliet got a job training to be a laboratory technician in the Blood Transfusion Service. The Service Head was sympathetic to her pacifism but the Section Head was not and did not like her bringing in pacifist newspapers. 'My work colleagues didn't share my

[70] Ibid.
[71] Ibid.
[72] Ibid.
[73] Ibid.

views but tolerated them.'[74] Whilst in this job she received her call-up for the services and registered as a conscientious objector. Even though a disability from birth would likely have gained her exemption, like many, she wanted to make a statement of her pacifism. She recalled there being a lady member on the tribunal and that they were impressed that she was doing work for the Blood Transfusion Service. She was registered on condition that she stayed in her present job: 'They didn't spend much time on me and I didn't have to make a statement. Nobody spoke in a derogatory way.'[75] The tribunal was therefore, in line with the approach of the Ministry of Labour, content to conditionally register a woman objector already doing work of national importance. Ill-health put her job, and therefore her conscientious objection registration in jeopardy. She learnt shorthand and typing and, helped by her Quaker friends, applied to join the FAU in London. Joining the FAU, even in a clerical capacity, meant the tribunal again accepted her as a conscientious objector.

Like many she faced potential challenges to her pacifist beliefs. She stated that she never thought that a German invasion was ever a possibility and that talk of it was pure propaganda. When she became aware of the Nazi atrocities it did not affect her pacifist beliefs. However, whilst some pacifists wanted to make peace with Germany, she personally did not know what else other than war would have stopped Hitler.[76] Despite her political background and Quaker associates, Juliet's pacifism was not based on dogma. She described it as: 'the horrible waste of life and time. I can't understand why people would be so brutal. It is more humanitarian than religious.'[77]

Marjorie Asquith (Whittles) and Freda Wood

Women objectors who joined the FAU came from different backgrounds, both socially and regarding their pacifism. Two examples are Marjorie Asquith and Freda Wood, who gave interviews to the Imperial War Museum in 1989. For Freda, her objection was on religious

---

[74] Ibid.
[75] 'Interview with Juliet Morland', British Library Sound Archive.
[76] Ibid.
[77] Ibid.

grounds and Marjorie's on moral grounds. What both demonstrate is how much easier it was to get favourable treatment from the tribunals if you were a Quaker or in the FAU.

Marjorie was born in Redcar in 1920, the youngest of four children of a working-class family. Her father worked in a cotton mill in Rochdale, but became a touring theatre musician. He was a left-wing trade unionist who had served in the trenches in the First World War and been mentioned in dispatches. Her youngest brother also belonged to the Left Book Club. The views of her father and brother helped shape her humanitarian views on war, which she expressed in an anti-war essay at the Girl's High School, for which she had obtained a scholarship.

Her route into the FAU, where she volunteered for work in Egypt, Palestine and Greece, was not the traditional Quaker one. Working on defence bonds in Harrogate she met Dorothy Bishop who was going to join the FAU and she decided to do the same. She registered as a conscientious objector on the basis that she objected to the loss of life and the loss of freedom of action. Marjorie, who married the grandson of Prime Minister Herbert Asquith, himself a conscientious objector, was the first woman objector to receive unconditional exemption, attracting Judge Burgis Chairman of the Liverpool Tribunal, to remark: 'Your case forms a marked contrast to the synthetic consciences which come before this tribunal. You threw up safety and comfort to do something for humanity.' The Judges remark was influenced by her decision to join the FAU.[78]

Like many, both during and after the war, she reflected on her pacifism: 'I would probably not have been a pacifist if I had been older and knew what I know now about Hitler.'[79] However, given the forms of work that women were called up for, without her pacifism she would not have been able to give such close assistance to those involved in the fighting. This experience may have helped her form her opinion of the soldiers fighting in the 1985 Falklands War, who she describes as brave, and led her to state pragmatically: 'I don't believe we can do without armies.'

---

[78] *Daily Mirror*, 21 April 1942, quoted in Nicholson, 'Women Conscientious Objectors, p. 420.
[79] 'Interview with Marjorie Asquith', http://www.iwm.org.uk/collections/item/object/80010428.

For Freda Wood the route into the FAU was the traditional Quaker one.[80] She was raised in York by lower middle class parents. Being well educated, she left the local Grammar School at 16 and went into the offices of Rowntree's chocolate factory. The Rowntree family were leading Quaker philanthropists and Tessa Rowntree founded the women's FAU.

She attended Friends meetings from the age of 14. Her pacifism was religious, based on the Quaker ideals: 'In terms of rationalising the threat of Hitler and pacifism it was not something that was greatly thought about at such a young age.'[81] Before the war she was a member of the PPU and sold *Peace News* on the streets. Whilst being a conscious pacifist, she, like many Quakers, was not an absolutist. She was prepared to do nursing help in the ARP but nothing further. She celebrated her 21st birthday in the ARP, along with Eleanora, the mother of actor Judi Dench. Prior to entering the FAU she joined the Friends War Victims Relief Committee. On joining the FAU, which she describes as being a largely middle class organisation with only one-third of its members being from a working-class background, she served time in the Middle East, where she felt a close affinity with the men in the front line, especially as her fiancée, an airman, had been killed, only five months after their engagement.[82]

She felt it was easier being a conscientious objector if you were a Quaker. On applying to be an objector she did not have to attend the tribunal, as she was in the FAU and Philip Rowntree wrote a letter on her behalf. She also thought it was easier for a woman to be a conscientious objector than a man, as she never had any hostility but then she had spent most of her time among pacifists.[83]

---

[80] 'Interview with Freda Wood', http://www.iwm.org.uk/collections/item/object/80010015.
[81] 'Interview with Freda Wood,' Imperial War Museum.
[82] Ibid.
[83] Ibid.

Other Women Objectors

For the remaining women objectors, their registration status resulted from their tribunal appearance. For the majority, there is no further detailed information available. An exception is Amelia Rossi of Bishop Auckland, whose case illustrates the conflict faced by many whose family were considered enemy aliens.

Amelia was born in Britain of Italian parents. Her father having fought for Italy on the side of the Allies in World War I, had been interned for over two years by the time of her tribunal appearance. Her objection on grounds of nationality, supported by her having lived in Italy and only returned to Britain in 1940 because her mother was there, received no sympathy from the tribunal. Judge Richardson commented:

> You don't mind taking what is brought by British seamen at the peril of their lives…You must have known you would have to behave as every other British subject. You had no business to come back to this country unless you intended not only to enjoy its privileges but to share its burdens.

Another tribunal member, Mr Bowman, added: 'Your conscience enables you to run a business protected by the British Navy. You run a café. Don't you think you owe something to the country that gives you that opportunity?' Not surprisingly she was removed from the register of conscientious objectors without qualification.[84] She had, however, not done as many children of Italian parents were alleged to have done in Scotland and adopted her parents' nationality to avoid conscription.[85]

Another who suffered the same fate at the tribunal was Elizabeth Short, one of the principals of a private school near Leyburn. She had been a teacher in Newcastle but resigned when all teachers were required to wear gas-masks. When asked what contribution she was willing to make to the war effort, she said she considered she was doing her best by

---

[84] 'British Birth "Regret" by Woman: Statement at C.O. Tribunal,' *Evening Chronicle*, 28 October 1942, p. 4.
[85] 'Adoption to Avoid Conscription,' *Northern Daily Mail*, 20 April 1940, p. 4.

teaching. Judge Richardson did not agree: 'I think it is about the most poisonous contribution you could make.'[86]

Elizabeth was one of three of the fifteen on the database whose occupations were known who was a teacher. A further six were employed in a clerical capacity and five in a domestic or shop environment, an employment mix in line the analysis undertaken in Chapter 1.

Finally, there is the case of Mary Cockcroft of Sowerby Bridge. Although Sowerby Bridge was not in the North Riding of Yorkshire during the Second World War, as it is today, Cockcroft is included to illustrate that not all Quakers took the same stance on objection as Marjorie Asquith and Freda Wood, and to show the restrictions to applying to a tribunal for those below conscription age (The age limits for compulsion into the military were 22-31, for industrial direction it could be as low as 18). It was also one of the specific cases mentioned by the Duke of Bedford of people who should not be in prison (see Chapter 7).

> Another flagrant case was that of a Quaker girl, Mary Cockcroft, only nineteen years of age, who would not accept industrial conscription on grounds of conscience. She could not go before a tribunal, because only women between the ages of twenty and thirty-one, who are liable for military conscription, are allowed to do so. On July 1, 1942, she was fined £10 and then given another direction, and for maintaining her consistent attitude was prosecuted again on October 14 before the same court, which imposed a fine of £20 and two guineas costs. As she refused to pay the fine she was sent to prison for two months. I have seen this girl. She is a mere child, a simple and sincere person, and again I say that such a persecution, especially of a member of the Society of Friends, is iniquitous.[87]

---

[86] 'British Birth "Regret" by Woman: Statement at C.O. Tribunal,' *Evening Chronicle*, 28 October 1942, p. 4.
[87] The Duke of Bedford, *Hansard*, HL Deb. 02 March 1943 vol. 126 cc358-92.

Probably as a result of the Duke of Bedford's intervention and that of Cecil Wilson MP, Mary was not troubled by the Ministry of Labour again.

Conclusion

Against a background of a registration process which played a major role in understating the potential number of women conscientious objectors portrayed by the official statistics, it is no surprise that only 36 of the 820 objectors on the database were women, of which only 24 were identified as having been before the tribunal. Though small in number they were significant with regard to firsts in women's objection. As with men, they showed that some of the most fervent objection took place outside of the tribunal process. A significant number were prepared to go to prison rather than compromise their beliefs.

Freda Wood asserted that it was easier for a woman to be a conscientious objector.[88] However, the route that her objection took was different to many other women. Those who went to prison would unlikely have shared Freda's assertion. The prison conditions described by Kitty Alexander were equally difficult for both men and women. However, those North-East women objectors who went to prison did so only once, and for a maximum of 3 months, whereas many men were given multiple sentences of up to 2 years. This can be partly explained by women being conscripted later in the war, but also by the fact that, as Nicholson states: 'The Ministry later quietly adopted a policy of leaving women alone after their first prosecution.'[89] The government's principal aim was to present to the public 'the virtual unanimity of Britain's womenfolk making all possible sacrifices in support of their husbands, brothers and sons.' Any contrary views were to be kept in the background, therefore 'the velvet glove was very much in evidence.'[90]

What happened to women after their release from prison is largely unknown, apart from Kitty Alexander who managed to secure some form of employment. Given their determination to state their ob-

---

[88] Interview with Freda Wood', http://www.iwm.org.uk/collections/item/object/80010015
[89] Nicholson, 'Women Conscientious Objectors,' p. 414.
[90] Hayes, *Challenge of Conscience*, p. 275.

jection it would seem unlikely they would merely conform to the requirements of the state. Given the velvet glove approach, their non-conformity was likely to have been ignored.

The procedures for placing women in work of national importance also made it easier for those who were not absolute objectors. Placing them in work acceptable to them thus avoided the ordeal of a tribunal. For those opting to appear before the tribunal the national statistics show a more sympathetic approach to women, however, the statistics for the North-East of England temper this approach.

On balance, it would appear that for some women objectors in the North-East of England it was easier to be an objector than it was for a man. For women absolutists imprisoned the term 'easier' is, however, not appropriate. 'Less extreme' may be the more appropriate description.

Hayes' asserted that, 'women on the whole were less able to express themselves than men…they were also more emotional and more easily upset by tribunal questioning.'[91] On the contrary; the evidence shows they displayed a willingness to state their position and a determination to stand by their principles, no matter the consequences.

---

[91] Hayes, *Challenge of Conscience*, p. 47.

CONSCRIPTION.

A COMMENTARY ON

THE NATIONAL SERVICE (ARMED FORCES) ACT

(With particular reference to
Conscientious Objectors).

_____

Price 2d. Post Free.

Issued by
THE JOINT ADVISORY BUREAU
6 ENDSLEIGH STREET
LONDON
W.C.1

Chapter Seven

'You're in the Army Now'

Stanley Hilton, a Jehovah's Witness from Rochdale, was called up in September 1940 and by December 1943 had been court-martialled five times and sentenced to prison terms aggregating to seven years. During this time, he did not draw a single day's army pay. This treatment, reminiscent of the cat and mouse treatment of the First World War, was ended when he was registered on condition that he undertook underground mining. As the most-imprisoned conscientious objector of the Second World War, his story has been well documented.[1] Not so well documented are cases involving men from the North-East of England who suffered for being conscientious objectors in the Armed Forces, some also facing multiple prison terms.

Conscientious objectors in the Armed Forces fell into a number of categories: those who failed to obtain exemption from the tribunals and were taken into the forces; those who failed to register as objectors and declared their objection after they had been called-up; those who accepted the call-up and subsequently became objectors; and, those registered as conscientious objectors for non-combatant duties in the armed forces. It is the latter group which are considered first.

Non-Combatant Duties

Up to 31 December 1948, 288 in total of the men, or 25.1%, appearing before the Northumberland and Durham Tribunal were registered as liable to be called up for non-combatant duties, compared to 28.1 % or 17,193, nationally.[2] What were the forces going to do with these thousands of men? At the outbreak of war the non-combatant units consisted of the Royal Army Chaplains' Corps, the Royal Army Medical Corps (RAMC), the Royal Army Dental Corps, the Royal Army Pay Corps,

---

[1] Hayes, *Challenge of Conscience*, pp. 106-111; and, Kramer, *Conscientious Objectors of the Second World War*, pp. 135-137.

[2] Ministry of Labour and National Service, PRO, Lab 6, piece 405, National Archives, Kew.

and the Royal Army Veterinary Corps. As the RAMC, in particular, became overloaded the Non-Combatant Corps (NCC) was introduced in April 1940.

Despite the creation of the NCC, the army were concerned that tribunals continued to show a preference to continue recommending objectors to the RAMC. Northern Army Command, whose area included the North-East of England, expressed its concerns:

> That one of the roles of the Royal Army Medical Corps should be the absorption of Conscientious Objectors has not been conducive to its popularity, and it is considered to be an unnecessary slur on a Service which has proved itself to be second to none in the field.
>
> Of late public reaction against the RAMC has been considerable. For instance, during a recent parade in Leeds, a Medical Unit was booed and hissed by the crowds on the footpath, the unit being greeted with "Here come the Conchies". Numerous episodes have taken place at dance halls, public houses, and in trams and trains in the same district, where NCOs and privates have been insulted and referred to as conscientious objectors. The reaction to this treatment has been evidenced by the number of men who have appealed to be transferred to other units; men who have removed their cap badges and shoulder titles; and men who have taken the law into their own hands and reacted against unjustified public abuse.
>
> It is not equitable that Royal Army Medical Corps personnel, consisting of Regular and Pre-Territorials who have volunteered and Army Class Intakes posted to the RAMC… should bear the stigma of conscientious objector.
>
> It would appear that the formation of a Non-Combatant Corps has escaped the notice of the Civil Tribunals……[3]

---

[3] 'Letter from Major General R. W. D. Leslie of Northern Command, 14/10/40 – Conscientious Objectors in the Royal Army Medical Corps,' WO 32/9422 – Posting to the RAMC and RA Dental Corps, National Archives, Kew.

This letter resulted in copious correspondence between the War Office and the Ministry of Labour and National Service, the War Office contending that the RAMC was full and all liable for non-combatant duties should be sent to the NCC. The Ministry of Labour agreed to tell the tribunals that the conscientious objector quota for the RAMC was full and only men possessing special qualifications required by the Corps could be posted there.[4] There were, of course, protests on behalf of men who had been recommended for the RAMC who now had to go to the NCC. One affected was John Richardson of Darlington.[5] The letter to Mr Richardson was agreed as the standard to be sent to men in his position:

> I have to explain that under Section 5(10) of the National Service (Armed Forces) Act, 1939, the Army Council is responsible for making arrangements for securing that, where a person is registered by direction of a tribunal as liable to be called up for service but to be employed only in non-combatant duties, that person shall be so employed during the period of his Army service. The duties of the Non-Combatant Corps have been drawn up so as to be appropriate for such persons.
>
> Where tribunals, in addition to making orders for non-combatant duties, recommend that the person concerned shall, if possible be posted to the RAMC effect is given to such recommendations to the extent that vacancies are available in that corps. The Ministry have been advised by the War Office that there are now no vacancies in the RAMC for conscientious objectors other than those with certain qualifications which you do not appear to possess, e.g. qualified masseur, dispenser or radiographer. It is regretted, therefore, that it will not be possible to post you to the RAMC.[6]

---

[4] 'Letter from Mr Dennys, Ministry of Labour, to Brigadier Pigott, War Office, 28 November 1940,' WO 32/9422 – Posting to the RAMC and RA Dental Corps, National Archives, Kew.
[5] 'Conduct of a Hero,' *Northern Echo*, 18 April 1940, p. 5.
[6] 'Draft Letter (16 December 1940) to J. Richardson, 5 North Lodge Terrace, Darlington,' WO 32/9422 – Posting to the RAMC and RA Dental Corps, National Archives, Kew.

The War Office agreed to 'bear the burden' of dealing with similar enquiries, and 'to combat indignant tribunals, if necessary.'[7] This relieved the situation regarding the RAMC but created a potential for objectors with specialist medical skills to have their expertise wasted in the NCC, a fact recognised by the War Office who agreed to their posting direct to emergency hospitals.[8]

John Richardson was one of 179 objectors on the Database of Conscientious Objectors definitely known to have been recommended for non-combatant duties. Five more were recommended by the Appellate Tribunal. He was also one of 17 known to have been recommended by the tribunal for the RAMC. 14 of these recommendations were prior to the instruction issued to the tribunals, indicating in the main that the Newcastle Tribunal had obeyed the direction given. The remaining referrals were in 1941 and 1943 and it is not known whether these were successful.

Being recommended for non-combatant duties did not satisfy the consciences of at least 30 of those on the database who appealed the decision. 15 had the decision changed to conditional registration, 14 had the tribunal decision upheld, and one was removed from the register. The main problem was that the only non-combatant unit not generally perceived to help the war effort was the Royal Army Chaplains Corps, for which unique entry requirements existed. Therefore, finding tasks which did not significantly assist the war effort was problematic.

In May 1943, Judge Davies of the South-Eastern Tribunal drew the attention of the War Office to a letter sent to Judge Burgis of the North-West Tribunal published in that month's *C.B.C.O. Bulletin*. This letter listed duties objectionable to conscientious objectors, which had been ordered by the NCC:[9]

---

[7] 'Letter from Mr Dennys, Ministry of Labour, to Brigadier Pigott, War Office, 18 December 1940,' WO 32/9422 – Posting to the RAMC and RA Dental Corps, National Archives, Kew.

[8] 'Letter from Mr de Villiers, Ministry of Labour, to Mr Pigott, War Office, 26 June 1941, and reply of 7 July 1941,' WO 32/9422 – Posting to the RAMC and RA Dental Corps, National Archives, Kew.

[9] 'Letter from W. Baxter, Ministry of Labour, to Major Cunningham, War Office, 18 June 1943,' WO 32/15272, C.O.s Right to Non-Combatant Duties, National Archives, Kew.

1. To build blockades and strong points
2. To build machine gun nests
3. To repair runways for bombers of Coastal Command
4. To build sandbag protection for aircraft ammunition
5. To erect barbed wire entanglements around a bomb dump
6. To construct roads on an anti-aircraft site
7. To lay a railway for the supply of an arsenal
8. To supply petrol and oils for the offensive in Africa
9. To improve a siding for a dump containing only tank tracks

To Judge Davies this placed the tribunal in a difficult position in view of assurances repeatedly given to applicants that they would only be required to carry out duties of an appropriate non-combatant nature. Whilst admitting that a small number of applicants would perform any duties that did not involve taking life, even these would object to items 2 and 3, and added:

> Indeed, if an applicant said he had a conscientious objec-
> tion to <u>combatant </u>duties and it appeared that in the course
> of his civilian employment he had been building machine
> gun nests or repairing runways for bombers I think the Tri-
> bunal would be very slow to believe that his objection even
> to <u>combatant</u> duties was genuine.[10]

The Army Council were quick to respond. Whilst pointing out that none of the items on the above list involved the handling of weapons and therefore no legal objection to ordering men of the NCC to perform them, there were practical considerations:

> Taken together, these kinds of work represent a not incon-
> siderable contribution to the aggressive prosecution of the
> war. To order them may result in a conflict with men's con-
> sciences, leading to disobedience, court-martial and punish-
> ment on conviction, with a consequent loss of man power.

---

[10] 'Letter from Judge Davies to the War Office, 25 June 1943,' WO 32/15272, C.O.s Right to Non-Combatant Duties, National Archives, Kew.

Men who are sent to the Non-Combatant Corps are informed by the Tribunals that they will be employed only in non-combatant duties.... It is, therefore, necessary to ensure that they are not ordered to carry out work which may be regarded as falling outside the scope (of that paragraph). If it is ordered, the men are apt to think they have been misled by the Tribunal and that public faith has not been kept.

In view of these considerations, they instructed Commanders-in-Chief to avoid items 1, 2, and 3 on all occasions and only resort to the others when there was no other appropriate work.[11]

The CBCO were concerned that the duties on the list may explain why many men who had complied with their tribunal decision and joined the NCC had afterwards refused orders and gone to prison.[12] Whilst there is no irrefutable evidence of this, five of the 13 North-East objectors on the database ordered to do non-combatant duties who were imprisoned had received their sentences when in the army. All had been sentenced prior to the Army Command instruction: Kenneth Chandler; Albert Foster; W. N. Gibson; James R. Henderson; and, I. Morison. Morison was registered for non-combatant duties while serving a prison sentence imposed by Scarborough Court.[13] The remaining eight received their sentences for refusing to submit to medical examination, a strong indication that they found non-combatant duties problematic.

Violence Towards Conscientious Objectors at Dingle Vale Army Training Camp

Both Barker and Kramer use a case of alleged brutality against non-combatant objectors at Dingle Vale in October 1940 as evidence of ill treatment of objectors by the authorities and inadequate punishment of the

---

[11] 'Letter from the War Office to all General Officers Commanding-in-Chief (Date unknown),' WO 32/15272, C.O.s Right to Non-Combatant Duties, National Archives, Kew.
[12] 'Letter from W. Baxter, Ministry of Labour, to Major Cunningham, War Office, 18 June 1943,' WO 32/15272, C.O.s Right to Non-Combatant Duties, National Archives, Kew.
[13] Hayes, *Challenge of Conscience*, p. 101.

perpetrators. At the centre of the case was Albert Foster, an ILP member and Newcastle War Resister.[14]

Referred to as 'the only organised savagery directly expressed at C.O.s during the war,' by Joseph Brayshaw, the incident attracted protests in Parliament, led to a Court of Enquiry, and ultimately the Court-Martial of an officer and five non-commissioned officers (NCOs).[15] Brayshaw's narrative is the only detailed account of the incident in the secondary literature, and as a CBCO representative it is understandably biased towards the conscientious objectors. There is, however, some evidence in the local newspapers, not mentioned by Brayshaw, which offers some counter-balance to his narrative. There is also some evidence which contradicts some of the evidence surrounding Albert Foster.

Brayshaw provides details of the treatment received by some men prior to the main incident. Men who had been called-up to non-combatant duties and who refused to attend the NCC were arrested and taken to Dingle Vale in Liverpool under escort:

> Once there they were at the mercy of the sergeants; complaints to officers were ignored, and during a period of violence lasting several weeks they either accepted non-combatant duties, like the majority, or suffered extreme punishments....They were half-starved, beaten, kicked. Their heads were shaved that they might be known and recognised as legitimate targets. They were cast into dark cells, and wakened at intervals in the night to do menial tasks or drill on the parade ground. They were cut off from the outside world, to which messages had to be smuggled secretly.[16]

One of these messages referred to Albert Foster being brutally assaulted in the presence of others for refusing to work.

Systematic violence was allegedly directed at five objectors on 26 September 1940. The worst brutality, which led to the complaints in

---

[14] Barker, *Conscience, Government and War*, p. 90, and, Kramer, *Conscientious Objectors*, pp. 112-115.
[15] Joseph A. Brayshaw, 'The Strange Occurrences at Dingle Vale,' in Hayes, *Challenge of Conscience*, pp. 91-92.
[16] Ibid., p. 92.

Parliament, was carried out on 9 October 1940 against eleven objectors, including Albert Foster. The eleven men refused an order to go on parade and when they refused twice more Captain F. K. Wright ordered that they be taken by the NCOs into the rifle range for circuit training. There, one of the objectors, John Radford, later wrote:

> At first, we moved slowly but we were punched and slapped, kicked in the ankle and other places. Bill Jordon had two beautiful black eyes, noses were bleeding, chaps went down here and there, they were hoisted to their feet and kicked off again, bad cases were treated with a bucket of water. Towards the end there were five or six of us down at once......We were mostly finished off with a blow below the belt which winded us; then we were held up by the neck and the officer yelled at us: 'Will you give in?' One by one we gave in.[17]

Two days later 26 conscientious objectors who had either suffered, or witnessed, the treatment were transferred to South Wales. This did not prevent details of the incident from coming to the attention of MPs. Albert Foster sent a letter to a director of a building firm where he was previously employed alleging the ill-treatment, and the director must have passed it to a sympathetic MP. Under pressure from those including John McGovern (ILP), the Parliamentary Secretary to the War Office, Sir Edward Grigg, ordered a Court of Enquiry into alleged ill-treatment.[18] Mr McGovern also alleged that a Colonel came into Foster's cell with a telegram informing him of his mother's death, but told him he could only attend her funeral if he wore a soldier's uniform and agreed to serve. He attended the funeral in uniform.[19]

Despite repeated requests from MPs the results of the enquiry were never published. although this did not prevent Brayshaw claiming that it did not seek out all the available evidence, perhaps on the basis of a statement by Lord Croft, Joint Parliamentary Secretary for War, who reported to the House of Lords: 'If there were any facts to prove that any

---

[17] Brayshaw, 'The Strange Occurrences at Dingle Vale,' in Hayes, *Challenge of Conscience*, p. 94.
[18] 'Alleged Ill-Treatment of C.O.s,' *Northern Echo*, 23 October 1940, p. 5.
[19] '"Kicked C.O.s" Charge,' *Shields Gazette*, 20 October 1940, p. 5.

of the offences, the subject of charges, were condoned by senior officers, such facts will no doubt be brought forward by the accused in their defence by way of a plea in bar of trial. No such facts have so far come to light.'[20] The charges referred to were those faced by Captain Wright and six NCOs in a General Court-Martial which began on 24 March 1941.

During the Court-Martial the claims of brutality were denied by those charged. Many of the denials, given little attention by Brayshaw, concerned the evidence of Albert Foster. Albert Foster alleged he was struck in the stomach and nose, and his head dipped in a bucket of water. When asked by the Judge Advocate in which order he was struck he replied: 'I cannot say, because after that half-hour of purgatory and hell in the hut it was difficult to say which NCO hit me.'[21] One of the accused, Sergeant Cullen, denied hitting any soldier, claiming that it was a conspiracy by four of the men against him. He further claimed that Foster, after his mother's funeral had requested that he be placed in a cell with other men for company and these men, who had previously given no trouble, refused to work.[22]

The Judge Advocate, in summary, said there was a sharp conflict of evidence between the defence witnesses and Private Foster. He referred to the visit of a clergyman, Rev. G E Durham, to Foster on 17 September 1940, and told the Court that the visit was to see if he could help Foster to take a more reasonable attitude. In that discussion he referred to Foster making 'a most ridiculous and stupid allegation against officers and men of H M Forces, that might have the effect of influencing the court against Foster, because one did not like to hear foul and untrue allegations made against the British Army.'[23] Whilst asking the Court not to treat these remarks as a reason to disregard Foster's evidence, he said: 'It was a curious thing that Foster would not help his country when the Germans were threatening invasion and his own mother had been killed by enemy action,' and, 'It was quite clear that Foster had received from his commanding officer and from the accused

---

[20] Hayes, *Challenge of Conscience*, pp. 95-96.
[21] 'Court Martial Allegations,' *Northern Daily Mail*, 29 March 1941, p.3.
[22] 'Objector had wind up,' *Northern Daily Mail*, 2 April 1941, p. 4.
[23] 'Court Martial Charges,' *Northern Daily Mail*, 3 April 1941, p. 4.

sergeant the greatest possible consideration and kindness in his bereavement.'[24] His final observation was that in every case the allegation was not an unprovoked attack, but, at the time of each incident the men were behaving in some way which would cause annoyance to a smart and efficient soldier: 'At the centre was a strange collection of people cast together by the exigencies of war.'[25]

It is therefore no surprise that the majority of charges resulted in a not guilty verdict. Where a guilty verdict was reached, the punishment was minor. One NCO received a reprimand, a Sergeant was reduced to the rank of Corporal, and the Captain was reprimanded for allowing assault and failing to report misconduct. Given that some charges were successfully prosecuted, it is certain that conscientious objectors had been abused, although even Brayshaw conceded that the evidence as presented did not sustain most of the detailed charges. The conflicting evidence surrounding Albert Foster was the clearest indication of this. Nevertheless the enquiry and courts-martial 'were sufficient enough to ensure that throughout four further years of war no planned coercion was attempted by the Army.'[26] One who benefited was Kenneth Chandler who, after serving sentences of 56 and 112 days detention for refusing to lay out his kit, was conditionally discharged from the NCC, despite the unsupportive comment of Captain Gray: 'The line of demarcation between conscience and cowardice in this case is very thin.'[27] What happened to Albert Foster after the Courts-Martial is unknown.

The publicity surrounding the Courts-Martial resulted in some letters to the local press against ill-treatment of objectors. Rose Hall of Byland Abbey in referring to the cruelty meted out to objectors in the First World War, in which her husband was a conscientious objector, expressed the hope that 'we shall be different this time in the handling of such men.'[28] John Wesley Johnson of Morpeth pointed out that things had not been different, quoting directly one conscientious objector:

---

[24] Ibid.
[25] Ibid.
[26] Hayes, *Challenge of Conscience*, p. 100.
[27] 'Appeals Against Service, *Durham County Advertiser*, 9 May 1941, p. 1.
[28] 'Hear All Sides: A Yorkshire Woman on Alleged Treatment of C.O.s,' *Northern Echo*, 28 March 1941, p. 4.

I was put in solitary confinement in a cell less than four feet wide, about ten feet long and ten feet high. No light, save for tiny grating near ceiling and tiled floor. One blanket for covering. Bread and water diet. Roused three times during that night.[29]

and confirmed by a Captain who he quotes: 'there is no doubt at all that the treatment has been most brutal and could hardly be excelled in a German concentration camp.'[30] Perhaps these comments, and a surprising lack of letters in support of the authorities, were also a factor in ensuring there was no further planned coercion undertaken.

Non-Combatants at Work

For those who accepted their fate more readily than Albert Foster, and served in a non-combatant capacity, their experience was varied. Those posted to one of the 14 units of the NCC, or the Pioneers Corps, were likely required to do heavy manual work. Nella Last, in her Mass Observation diary, commented on the presence of a large number of objectors at the Vickers Shipyard. Her initial intolerance towards them evolved into acceptance, an attitude which horrified some of her soldier friends. She described some of the work done by conscientious objectors at Vickers Shipyard in 1944:

> …any C.O. in the Army did their share, and often a dirty and heavy share, on Docks fatigue, unloading cement or heavy oil for the smoke screens – and filling and managing the evil smelling lamps. We would "smell conchies" – we had no need to see their badges or caps! It made me feel we all had our part…[31]

[29] 'Hear All Sides: Treatment of C.O.s,' *Northern Echo*, 1 April 1941, p. 4.
[30] Ibid.
[31] D.R.1061, Nella Last, Barrow-in-Furness, F1922, *Mass Observation on-line*, June 1944.

This work was carried out at all naval installations and shipyards to protect against enemy bombing. Dick Lindrup, No. 8 Company of the NCC, described smokescreen duty in Newcastle:

> We had two types of smoke producers that we had to use – mobile smoke producing machines and small stationary pots the use of which depended upon the weather. These pots were used by local people as a source of fuel with which to light their own fires every morning.
>
> The smokescreens were made when there was an air raid or the prospect of one. We were out on the streets exposed to the dangers of an air raid – sudden flares from the pots or machines had to be dealt with immediately.[32]

The yards on the Tyne were building naval ships, and the smokescreens appeared to have been successful in reducing enemy bombing, certainly in comparison with towns such as Sunderland, Hartlepool and Middlesbrough where the merchant shipbuilding yards did not receive the same degree of protection. This work could have challenged an objector's conscience, however, the subsequent reduction of risk to civilians could have compensated.

Despite the above measures, there remained a risk associated with being located at a military establishment targeted by the enemy. Those objectors who accepted their non-combatant duties were demonstrating that they were not averse to being at risk. This was the case with Vernon Abbott, a Gosforth objector, whose moral objection did not preclude being put in danger.[33] Vernon undertook his duties from 1940 to the end of the war at a military establishment in Wiltshire, his wife and child moving to Catford to be near him.

Unfortunately, not all non-combatant work in military camps was portrayed as positive. A man who appeared at the Bristol tribunal declared that, although employed at a military camp for nine weeks, he did not assist the military programme since he did 'not a stroke of work' the whole time.[34]

---

[32] Goodhall, *We Will Not Go To War: Conscientious Objection During the World Wars*, p. 142.

[33] Interview with Stan Abbott, son of Vernon Abbott, conducted 16 September 2014 at Durham.

[34] 'C.O. Tells Tribunal He Had Camp Job, But No Work To Do,' *News Chronicle*, 7 June 1940.

Conscientious objectors who volunteered for bomb disposal work demonstrated that they were prepared to be put in danger. No evidence was found of any objectors from the North-East undertaking such work, but research has led to the case of John Bridge who was to become Director of Education for Sunderland. Lieutenant-Commander John Bridge was a man of undoubted bravery. He twice received the George Medal for bomb disposal work and was awarded the George Cross for clearing depth charges from Messina Harbour, Sicily, in August 1943. He later explained that he had volunteered for bomb disposal work, before being called-up, because it involved saving lives rather than taking them.[35] John Bridge was not a conscientious objector, but he can be seen as demonstrating what Mass Observation referred to as latent objection. They refer to surveys showing that for every objector there were two latent objectors whose reluctance for war was not strong enough for them to become conscientious objectors. In other words, there was no simple division between whole-hearted war workers and objectors.[36]

For conscientious objectors called-up for non-combatant duties their experiences were varied, depending upon whether they accepted the order as meeting the need of their conscience, or not. For those who could not there was the risk of physical abuse, at least up until the Dingle Vale Courts-Martial. There was also the certainty that a continual refusal would lead to periods of detention. Even for objectors accepting their fate the tasks were likely to be unpleasant and their treatment by the public and fellow workers to be unpleasant or even hostile.

Non-Combatant Corps uniform shoulder badge

[35] 'Obituary: Lieutenant-Commander John Bridge, GC,' *Daily Telegraph*, 29 December 2006.
[36] Mass Observation File Report 312, pp. 89-90.

Objecting Soldiers

Not all conscientious objectors in the Armed Forces were in a non-combatant unit. Up to the end of 1948, 315 men had been removed from the register of conscientious objectors by the Newcastle Tribunal and were liable for call-up to the armed forces.[37] Many did not actually reach the armed forces but a substantial number did. These proved to be a thorn in the side of the War Office and the armed forces. There were also men who had enlisted, or accepted their call-up, who developed a conscientious objection once they were in the forces, and it is this group which are now considered.

One serving soldier did end up in a non-combatant unit. W. N. Gibson of Sunderland had not registered as a conscientious objector as he claimed on registration that Ministry of Labour officials said that he should be put in a non-combatant unit. He was not, and unsuccessfully requested to be transferred. Refusing to pick up a rifle, he was sentenced to 56 day's detention. He served his sentence and again refused to pick up a rifle. He asked for a sentence of at least three months so he could appear before a tribunal, and his request was granted. The tribunal registered him for non-combatant duties, no doubt helped by the statement of Captain Holcombe: 'From my knowledge of this man I am convinced that he is a genuine conscientious objector. We have tried our best to make him parade, but he flatly refuses. He is willing to do any manner of non-combatant duty.'[38]

Raymond V. Cornelius was part way through his Army training when his refusal to continue led to six months in Durham Prison. An officer advised the Appellate Tribunal that he believed his objection was sincere, and he was conditionally registered on the expiry of his sentence and his discharge from the Army. Officers confirming the sincerity of objectors referred to the Appellate Tribunal was not uncommon, as demonstrated by Alexander Smith, a Glasgow objector serving 112 days in Durham Prison for refusing a dental examination. An Army Captain testifying his pacifism was sincere, resulted in his discharge from the Army and conditional registration as a conscientious objector.[39] Another

---

[37] Ministry of Labour and National Service, PRO, Lab 6, piece 405, National Archives, Kew.
[38] 'Refused to pick up a rifle,' *Sunderland Echo*, 16 August 1940, p. 2.
[39] 'Views That Shocked Me – Faith Protects Appellate From Bombs,' *Durham County Advertiser*, 2 May 1941, p. 1.

objector referred to the Appellate Tribunal by a North-East court-martial was Aircraftsman K. John Hollowell, originally a solicitor from Buckingham. Hollowell had originally been conditionally registered by a tribunal but, after a period in the FAU, had volunteered for the RAF as a result of pressure from friends and relatives. Prior to his court-martial he had served two sentences for disobeying a lawful command.[40]

Courts-Martial of men who became objectors whilst in uniform were not restricted to the middle and working classes. The aristocracy was ably represented by Captain the Honourable William Douglas-Home, the son of the Earl of Home and brother of the future Prime Minister, Sir Alec Douglas-Home. When called-up in 1940 he had registered as a conscientious objector, but on being told he must swear that under no circumstances would he kill anybody, withdrew his objection. Captain Home's objection was, whilst he could see no reason for not killing when necessary, he objected to unnecessary killing. In 1944, he defied orders to participate in the attack on Le Havre, fearing thousands of French civilians would be killed. He was Court-Martialed and sentenced to a year's imprisonment, with hard labour, for disobeying an order in the field. Had this offence been committed in the First World war, and considered, 'disobeying in such a manner as to show a wilful defiance of authority, a lawful command given personally by his superior officer', then the punishment would likely have been death. However, after 1930 the death sentence could only be applied for Treason and Murder, as in civilian courts. He thought the attack unnecessary because the German commander offered to send out all civilians if he was given three days.[41] At his Court-Martial he summed up his position:

The future belongs to young men who are dying on the battlefield, not to the old men who had their chance to reform after the last war and did not take it. The future is decided, not at the peace conference, but in the closing stages of the war, and to prolong a war beyond its necessary limit is in my opinion a greater crime than starting one....[42]

[40] 'R.A.F. Court-Martial on C.O. Volunteer,' *North-East Gazette*, 2 February 1942, p. 5.
[41] 'Obituary: William Douglas-Home,' *The Independent*, 30 September 1992.
[42] 'Court-Martial of Earl's Son: "Refused to Attack",' *Shields Gazette*, 17 October 1944, p. 4.

The reasons and forms of objection of men serving were varied and attracted some press attention, but it was men who had been rejected by the tribunal as objectors and taken into the Army who attracted the greatest attention. In the North-East, and indeed nationally, it was Kenneth Makin and Gerald Henderson who made the headlines.

Kenneth Makin of Redcar was a Christadelphian objecting on religious grounds. At the Newcastle tribunal in October 1939 he declared a willingness to do work of national importance but not under military control. He was removed from the register of conscientious objectors, a decision ratified by the Appellate Tribunal in December 1939, and called-up for military training. In February 1940 he was arrested, taken before a magistrate with no press or public present and remanded to be taken by military escort to Scotland for training. It is believed he was the first conscientious objector to be treated this way. The magistrate denied it was a secret court and that proceedings had been carried out as normal for a case of military absence.[43]

In March 1940 Makin was sentenced by Court-Martial to 60 days' detention for wilful denial of orders. Colonel Sprot, Public Relations Officer, Scottish Command was keen to put the record straight:

> It is entirely wrong to say this man is undergoing a prison sentence. He is not in a military prison. Some years ago, in order to remove the stigma of imprisonment, which is one of the sentences which may be given by the army, Parliament decided that another form of punishment should be substituted. This is detention.

It was his alleged treatment in detention which led to Mr McGovern M.P. raising the following question in the Commons to the Minister for War:

> If his attention has been drawn to the arrest of a conscientious objector, Kenneth Makin, who was court-martialled at Dalkeith training centre on March 12th, for refusing to obey orders, was sentenced to 60 days imprisonment, taken

---

[43] 'Redcar C.O. Arrested: "Secret Court" Denial,' *Northern Echo*, 28 February 1940, p. 5.

to Barlinnie prison under the military authorities, where he was formally stripped in his cell on March 17th and offered uniform.

That he was forcibly dressed in uniform on three successive occasions on March 18th held by the neck and nearly choking him.

That he was left from the 21st to the 25th with only his underwear on, given bread and water twice a day from the 18th to 21st March.

Was removed to Edinburgh Castle Hospital on the 26th with nervous trouble, violent pains, and threatened pneumonia, where he was interviewed by the Member for Shettleston on April 8th.

What does the Minister intend to do in this case where the young man has Christian objections to war?[44]

The Secretary for War, Oliver Stanley, replied that Makin had stripped voluntarily for medical examination and at no time was violence used for dressing or undressing. As his hospital admittance was for lumbago and a slight chill, he saw no need to intervene.[45] This version of events drew a sarcastic response from fellow objector W. J. Holbrough of Darlington, who used Makin's experience to counter accusations of cowardice made against objectors: 'Those of your readers who have had army experience will have no difficulty in understanding the explanatory terms used by Mr Oliver Stanley.'[46] It seemed the House of Commons also knew what the correct version of events was. Many, including Herbert Morrison, asked that Makin's case for conscientious objection be reheard. Makin underwent a further Court-Martial where he was sentenced to three months in a civil prison, a sentence which gave him the right to an Appeal Tribunal hearing, where he was granted conditional registration and discharged from the Army to work in agriculture. Ken-

[44] 'Redcar Conchie 'Forcibly Stripped',' *North-East Gazette*, 11 April 1940, p. 5.
[45] 'Treatment of Conscientious Objector,' *Northern Echo*, 17 April 1940, p. 5.
[46] 'Treatment of a Redcar C.O.,' *Northern Echo*, 17 April 1940, p. 5.

neth Makin achieved the double distinction of being the first conscientious objector to be arrested and the first to have a review tribunal after a Court-Martial order under Section 13 of the National Service Act.[47]

Throughout his ordeal, Makin enjoyed the support of his family, his term in prison not attracting any of the stigma referred to by Rachel Barker. His father, William, commented: 'When Kenneth first objected I did not agree, but did not oppose, his views, but after this bloodthirsty and brutal treatment he has my active sympathy.'[48]

Another Redcar objector benefitted from Makin's experiences. William Holness, a Jehovah's Witness, was taken into custody on 26 April 1940. He refused service and, after 14 and 28 days detention, was sentenced to four months imprisonment. This entitled him to a further appearance before the Appellate Tribunal who recommended his discharge from the Army.[49] Unlike Makin, Holness did not take advantage of his release and do civil work of national importance, receiving three-months hard labour in June 1942 for refusing to take up work on the land.[50]

Treatment in Detention Centres

The case of Kenneth Makin occurred before the Dingle Vale scandal. It would therefore appear possible during that period for an uncooperative objector to be liable to some form of abuse, even though Parliament had sought to protect the right to conscientious objection. What should be surprising is that allegations of abuse should continue after Dingle Vale, but they did.

During the Makin case the authorities seemed keen to stress that he had been in detention and not prison. Whilst it may have attracted less stigma the evidence does not suggest that it involved better conditions.

---

[47] Hayes, *Challenge of Conscience*, p. 80.
[48] 'Father Defends Stand of Lazenby Pacifist in Army Hospital,' *North-East Gazette*, 13 April 1940, p. 2.
[49] Hayes, *Challenge of Conscience*, p. 83.
[50] Durham Prison, Index to male prisoners: P/6/3 (Jan '42 – Dec '44); Durham Records Office, County Hall, Durham.

Soldiers sentenced to periods of confinement were likely to serve part of these sentences in military detention barracks, where the conditions were described as being even worse than those in civilian prisons. The CBCO *Prison Routine* pamphlet had warned that: 'The quality of food and the state in which it is served varies from one barracks to another, but on the whole, it is less appetising than that provided in civilian prisons.'[51] The main detention barracks in the North-East was Northallerton. John A. Lindsay was a conscientious objector court-martialled four times. He served two terms of civil imprisonment and two terms of military detention, much of the latter being in Northallerton. His experiences were published in the *New Leader* and some of these are detailed below:

> Although under military law conditions in a detention barracks should not exceed in severity those in any prison, they are in fact considerably worse.
>
> The strictest military discipline with silence must be maintained. Everything is done in a drill movement. There is one rule which must be observed in all circumstances. Communication by talking or signs is not allowed. Soldiers have lost remission for listening even when they themselves are not talking. Remission has to be earned by special industry or conduct whereas in a civilian prison remission is rarely lost.
>
> During the eight weeks I spent at Northallerton I never managed to get hold of any lavatory paper and was forced to use my letters. Also, I never had a mirror, which made shaving very awkward, especially as there was no hot water. We had to wash our own clothes, and often there was not enough soap to go around. But I imagine Northallerton was the exception rather than the rule as elsewhere I obtained cleaning materials in abundance.
>
> One of the greatest evils of DBs is that staff are given almost unlimited rope in handling soldiers under sentence. This seems to result in turning the kindest hearted sergeant

---

[51] C.B.C.O., *Prison Routine*, September 1941.

into a bully and it is rare to come across any member of staff who does not abuse his authority

Until last December books were unknown at Northallerton.

All the main items of food, i.e. bread, porridge, and potatoes are starchy, and stomach trouble is rife.

Sanitary arrangements: chamber pot is provided in each room for use during the night, or, in emergency during the day, but in the daytime you have to use the latrines at one of the four times you are marched out there. In practice the marching out to the latrines is simply a farce. The maximum time allowed in the latrines is about 30 seconds, and all the time the staff are yelling at you to hurry up. The soldier is forced to use the chamber pot in his room, emergency or no emergency.

It is not an unusual occurrence for a soldier under sentence to swallow razor-blades or needles, or even try to cut his throat in an attempt to either be taken out of the DB into hospital or to be discharged from the Army on medical grounds, or to commit suicide. This was particularly prevalent at Northallerton.

If any soldier under sentence is found to be dirty, or lousy, or suspected of having fleas, he is scrubbed by one of the staff with an ordinary floor scrubbing brush and cold water. I have seen men at Hull taken to the hospital so raw and bleeding that they were unable to wear their clothes for days. Many of the staff seemed to have people scrubbed out of sheer dislike when there was nothing wrong with them at all.[52]

The conditions in Northallerton Detention Barracks and Durham Prison appear to be worse than other similar institutions. The North-East Tribunal may have treated its conscientious objectors better than most parts of the country but its institutions of incarceration did not, in terms of basic conditions. The instances of self-harm described are particularly disturbing, but what about the instances of harm inflicted by

---

[52] 'What Soldiers Face in Detention Barracks,' *The New Leader*, 27 June 1942, p. 3.

their jailers? Did these improve after the Dingle Vale allegations? The above extract suggests there remained cause for concern.

Following widespread criticism in the press over conditions in detention barracks, most notably following the sentencing in June 1942 of two sergeants for the manslaughter of a private, a committee was set up in 1943 by the Prime Minister, 'to enquire into and report on the treatment of men under sentence in Naval and Military Detention Barracks in the United Kingdom.' The chairman was Sir Roland Oliver, MC, KC.[53] The committee's report was considered by the War Cabinet on 5 July 1943. It included a summary of the complaints heard, which included those of three conscientious objectors:[54]

No.37 was a conscientious objector in detention from March –October 1940 for refusing to obey orders. He described having been assaulted on his arrival by two members of the Staff, one of whom told him that he had been specially sent to "deal with the likes of him". He was then forcibly undressed (as he refused to undress himself), during the process of which he was repeatedly struck in the stomach and when he fell was lifted up by his hair and struck again until his clothes were off. Later in the day his arm was twisted. He also said he saw the injured condition of the witness next to be referred to (No. 36) after the latter had arrived. He further said that on another occasion two Staff Sergeants pushed a soldier into his (witness's) cell, turned him out of it, and when soon they came out the witness went back to find the soldier lolling in a corner weeping.

No. 36 was a conscientious objector who was sent to detention in June 1940 and for a time was there with witness 37. He said that when he arrived, because he refused to pick up a rifle and equipment he was struck and his head was violently and repeatedly knocked against the wall, and that, as he still refused to obey, he was assaulted and

[53] Minutes of the War Cabinet 5 July 1943, Item 8 'Detention Barracks: Proposed Enquiry into Conditions', National Archives.
[54] 'Report of the Prime Minister's Committee of Enquiry into Detention Barracks,' HMSO, 11 October 1943, War Cabinet, 4 November 1943, Item 4.

punched about the face and body by a number of the Staff and actually kicked in the eye. He said that the medical officer refused to assist him against the N.C.O.s concerned and that he was eventually paraded before the Assistant Commandant and charged with attempted violence against an N.C.O. and, after the evidence had been heard, was punished. The Committee has by enquiry found support, other than No. 37, for the fact that he made the allegations at once and that his face and head bore marks of violence.

(NOTE – The demeanour of the above two witnesses very favourably impressed the Committee)

No. 13 was a conscientious objector who had served 28 days in detention during April-May 1941 for refusing to obey orders. He said that after being chased upstairs by members of the Staff, another member of the Staff opened a cell door and the witness, not knowing what he was expected to do, stood still. He was then pushed violently into the cell, but did not actually fall. He said he warned the N.C.O. that he would report him if he broke King's Regulations, and that the N.C.O., after blustering, became reasonable and intimated he did not like the sort of work he had to do. The witness said that was the only instance of physical violence he had seen or experienced.

The committee concluded: 'there is not now nor has there been for some time past any violence or physical ill-treatment practiced upon men in detention.' In support of this conclusion they referred to no less than five conscientious objectors who had been at various detention barracks between November 1942 and July 1943, none of whom said they had experienced or seen any violence towards prisoners by staff anywhere, adding:

the force of this testimony is threefold. In the first place, these were men all of good character, education and intelligence. In the second place, it is in the nature of things that a conscientious objector is fearless about expressing his opinions, and, therefore, would not hesitate to make a complaint. Finally, it would be difficult to imagine a type of man more calculated to arouse the fury of a brutal N.C.O. than a conscientious objector who refuses to obey orders and sometimes to dress...

    With regard to shouting, chasing and bad language, the Committee feel sure that a certain amount of this does go on. In any body of men in authority, such as N.C.O.s, amounting to many hundreds, as is the case with the Staff under consideration, a few bullies will almost inevitably be found.

The committee were, however, 'less satisfied about the conditions prevailing the early part of the war.'[55] This was a clear indication that the testimony of objectors 36, 37 and 13 had been believed. They also serve to confirm the belief that ill-treatment of conscientious objectors in military establishments was rife prior to Dingle Vale. The committee were also concerned with improving physical conditions, and made a number of recommendations regarding sanitation, staff numbers and staff training. The Secretary of State for War, Mr J. J. Lawson, confirmed in Parliament that the recommendations had been implemented successfully.[56] No further testimony was found as to how far conditions had actually improved, but the lack of any CBCO concerns reported after the Oliver Enquiry by Hayes suggests that the worst of the conditions had been removed. Also, the number of objectors subjected to detention was significantly reduced as concerns over 'cat and mouse' treatment led to changes in the rules for the military treatment of objectors.

    No matter how much conditions improved the comment in *Prison Routine* is likely to have been accurate: 'You will probably leave the barracks without escort, or probably, any overwhelming sense of regret.'[57]

'Cat and Mouse'

---

[55] 'Hereford and Mosley,' *The Spectator*, 26 November 1943, p. 3.

[56] 'Conditions in Military Detention Barracks', *Hansard*, HC Deb, 07 November 1945, Vol. 415, cc1390-6.

[57] C.B.C.O., *Prison Routine*, September 1941.

The phrase 'cat and mouse' originated with the suffragettes, but was more commonly used during the First World War to describe the repeated cycle of men refusing an order, being imprisoned, refusing the order again on release to be then further imprisoned.[58] During that war 655 objectors were court-martialled twice, 521 three times, 319 four times, 50 five times, and, 3 six times.[59] This was regarded as a scandal and attempts were made, unsuccessfully, to include a clause in the Military Training Bill to eliminate the practice. The government were willing to be pragmatic and during the Bill's introduction in the House of Lords introduced a clause allowing a man serving a minimum three-month court-martial sentence for an offence claimed to have been committed on conscience grounds, to apply to the Appellate Tribunal. This became the previously mentioned Section 13 of the National Service (Armed Forces) Act, 1939, Backed up by Regulation 13(3) of the National Service (Armed Forces) (Miscellaneous Conditions) Act, 1939, with regard to procedures to apply.

There were four main problems associated with Section 13: there was no compulsion for courts-martial to give a sentence of three months minimum; there was no compulsion to give a prison sentence instead of a detention which, no matter how long, was not subject to the clause; there was no guarantee that the Appellate Tribunal would register them as conscientious objectors, and, Section 13 only applied to men who had registered as conscientious objectors and called-up, but not to men who developed an objection after enlisting. The last stipulation was to prevent non- bona fide objections being raised with the prospect of a three-month prison sentence followed by discharge being preferable to serving in the field.[60] The Army Council were quick to rectify this anomaly and issued the following instruction:

> ...Presidents of Courts-martial, before whom a plea of conscience has been raised should bear in mind that a sentence of penal servitude or three or more month's imprisonment

---

[58] Barker, *Conscience, Government and War*, p. 85.

[59] Ibid.

[60] 'Letter from G. W. Lambert, War Office to the Ministry of Labour and National Service, 18 December 1939,' WO 32/14529 – Policy for Officers who became Conscientious Objectors, National Archives, Kew.

will in future enable soldiers who did not register themselves as conscientious objectors or appear before a Tribunal
when called up under the National Services Act 1939 to
apply to have their cases considered by the Advisory Tribunal whilst undergoing such sentence.[61]

Nevertheless, by the end of June 1941 the CBCO records showed
that almost 47% of sentences given by courts-martial did not qualify
objectors for new tribunal hearings, the majority being the result of varying levels of military detention. There were a few cases of insufficient
sentences ranging from 84 to 90 days when 91 to 93 days would have
entitled the objector to a tribunal appearance. To the CBCO this was
deliberate 'cat and mouse' by the Courts.[62] However, ongoing pressure
from MPs such as Cecil Wilson and the CBCO meant the practice declined. There still remained the other problems concerning Section 13,
and, despite the government's intentions, 'cat and mouse' crept back in,
epitomised by the case of Gerald Henderson of West Hartlepool, which
ultimately led to reforms which eliminated the practice.

The problems faced by Gerald Henderson, a Jehovah's Witness,
began with his tribunal appearance on 18 January 1940, where ex-Ser-
geant Major Robinson said on oath that Henderson, formerly an engineer, told him he was 'joining some religious cult so that he could become a conscientious objector.' He said he was a 'foul mouthed person
whose language had shocked even him.'[63] He had known Henderson
for 6 or 7 years and 'before the war his religion was virtually nil.'[64] Henderson admitted he gave up his job to be a full-time Jehovah's Witness
preacher but denied joining the organisation to escape military service,
claiming he joined 3 years earlier. His application was supported by
James Woodburn, a Jehovah's Witness representative, who said he had
never heard Henderson use foul language in the 8 or 9 years he had
known him, and he had approached Henderson about entering the organisation full time and he had not done so to avoid military service.

---

[61] 'Letter from G. W. Lambert, War Office to all General Officers Commanding, 18 April 1940,' WO
32/14529 – Policy for Officers who became Conscientious Objectors, National Archives, Kew.
[62] Hayes, *Challenge of Conscience*, p. 101.
[63] '"Jehovah's Witness" Liable for Service', *Sunderland Echo*, 18 January 1940, p.1.
[64] Ibid.

The tribunal removed Henderson from the list of conscientious objectors, without qualification, Judge Richardson commenting: 'There was never a more honest man than Robinson and he should have left the court without any interruption from so-called pacifists.'[65]

Given the comments of Judge Richardson and the attitude of tribunals to Jehovah's Witnesses, it was no surprise that his appeal was rejected by the Appellate Tribunal. He was called for medical examination on a number of occasions, which he ignored, and was remanded in custody by Newcastle Magistrates on 27 November 1940. He submitted to an examination and was posted to the Royal Engineers. Henderson's penal history in the Royal Engineers was summarised in a letter sent to the *New Statesman and Nation* by Fenner Brockway of the CBCO. In this letter Brockway, referring to Henderson, stated:

He was court-martialled in April 1941 for refusing to obey orders and sentenced to 28 days' detention. In June 1941, he was sentenced to 4 months' imprisonment with hard labour. He made his first application to the Appellate Tribunal under Section 13 of the 1939 Act which was considered by the Northern Division of the Appellate Tribunal on 23rd July 1941, when the Tribunal decided not to recommend that he should be discharged from the Forces. A second application under Section 13 followed a sentence of 6 months with hard labour and was considered by the Northern Division of the Appellate Tribunal on 16th October 1941 with the same remit. On completion of this sentence he was transferred to a unit in the South of England.

Following a third sentence of 7 months with hard labour, his third Section 13 application was considered by the South of England Division of the Appellate Tribunal on 1st April 1942, but with the same result, the Tribunal finding that his offence was not committed by reason of his conscientious objecting to perform military service. He has since been sentenced to a further term of 15 months' imprisonment which he is serving in Leeds prison and the fourth

[65] 'Objector's Language Shocked Me, Says ex-Sergt. Major,' *Northern Echo*, 19 January 1940, p. 5.

application under Section 13 has recently been sent to the North of England Division of the Appellate Tribunal for consideration.'[66]

He continued to protest to the ongoing process of 'cat and mouse':

> When compulsory military service was introduced on the eve of the war the promise was given that the persecution of conscientious objectors which took place in the last war would not be renewed, and I wish to acknowledge that, as a whole, objectors have now been treated more liberally.
>   ….. Despite pledges to the contrary, "cat and mouse" treatment has recurred. May I draw your attention to the two severest cases? (Gerald Henderson, of West Hartlepool, and Stanley Hilton)..Have not these boys proved their sincerity? It is of no benefit to the Army to keep on sending them back to prison and it is a blot on the administration of the conscience clause of the National Service Acts.'[67]

Brockway's letter prompted a flurry of activity within the Ministry of Labour and National Service and the War Office. This activity is not recorded by either Hayes or Barker as, certainly in the case of Hayes, the archive would not have been open. It is therefore quoted here in some detail.

Responding to the note, and a request from Cecil Wilson MP for the Secretary of State for War, P. J. Grigg, to receive a deputation, Mr Hardman wrote to his superior, Mr de Villiers:

> The War Office would welcome an excuse to get rid of these two men, but, in face of the Tribunal's decisions, has felt bound to keep them although it is well recognised that they will never become efficient soldiers. If, however, the Ministry of Labour were to suggest to the War Office that

---

[66] Extracts from letter from Fenner Brockway to the *New Statesman*, 'Note to Mr Hardman,' dated 9 October 1942 re Gerald Henderson and Stanley Hilton,' LAB 6/14, National Archives, Kew.
[67] Ibid.

discharge from the Army would not be inappropriate I think that the War Office would be very pleased...[68]

Mr de Villiers, on the same note, whilst stating that the Appellate Tribunal had continuously held the view that the men are not conscientious objectors, was of the view that their position was not very different from the man imprisoned for refusing to be medically examined. He further added: 'court-martialled soldiers are ex-hypothesis pretty bad cases in view of their repeated rejection of their applications by the Appellate Tribunals and they are hardly likely to make themselves useful in civilian employment.' He therefore suggested that after the expiry of the second of two long court-martial sentences a soldier be discharged from the forces and be directed to appropriate civilian work with prosecution to follow if non-compliance.[69]

The suggestion was met with support from Mr G. W. Lambert of the War Office. Acknowledging that it might undermine the position of the Appellate Tribunal he nevertheless was of the opinion that: 'this must be faced if we do not wish the cat and mouse treatment to continue indefinitely.'[70] Mr Grigg was now in a position to appease Mr Wilson to whom he wrote on 8 December 1942:

> It seems to me that it is contrary to the public interest that an individual conscientious objector should again and again be sent back to the Army with little prospect that he will change his mind or that the Appellate Tribunal will change its mind...The Army gets no benefit from a man of the kind we are here considering, and his trial and punishment consume a great deal of valuable time.
>
> On the other hand, it is quite obvious that the conditions under which an escape can be allowed from the chain of offence and punishment must be sufficiently severe to act as an effective check on the mere skrimshankers.

---

[68] 'Note from Mr Hardman to Mr de Villiers, 19 October 1942,' LAB 6/14 – Discharge of Prisoners Claiming to be Conscientious Objectors, National Archives, Kew.

[69] Comments of Mr de Villiers on 'Note from Mr Hardman to Mr de Villiers, 19 October 1942,' LAB 6/14 – Discharge of Prisoners Claiming to be Conscientious Objectors, National Archives, Kew.

[70] Comments of Mr G. W. Lambert on 'Note from Mr Hardman to Mr de Villiers, 20 October 1942,' LAB 6/14 – Discharge of Prisoners Claiming to be Conscientious Objectors, National Archives, Kew.

After balancing these considerations, I have decided that in future when a man has served two sentences of three or more months' imprisonment and has twice had his appeal rejected by the Appellate Tribunal, he shall, on receiving a third such sentence for an offence of the same character as before, be immediately discharged from the Army "Services no longer required".

I do not think this arrangement will affect more than a handful of men at present or in the near future, but I cannot regard that as a disadvantage. It does, however, represent a serious attempt to try and find a way out of indefinite 'cat and mouse' treatment, and I hope that you and your friends will accept it, without pressing me to receive a deputation. For the moment, I would ask you to treat what I have said as confidential information for the members of your Parliamentary Committee, as I see no reason to make a public announcement on the subject.[71]

This brought an effective end to 'cat and mouse' treatment which was a relief, not only to the objectors, but to the Army Council who regarded conscientious objectors as: 'useless, and their periodic terms of imprisonment, besides costing public money, prevent them from being directed to work which will be of benefit to the State, and to that extent represent a loss of man-power.'[72] It was also kept low key. The CBCO were informed of the decision, and again asked not to make it public, but were unaware of the discussions which led to it. Hayes could only speculate that it was James Grigg's tolerance of unusual views which had led to the decision.[73] Barker referred to it only as 'an administrative concession.'[74]

---

[71] 'Letter from P J Grigg to Mr Wilson, M.P., 8 December 1942,' LAB 6/14 – Discharge of Prisoners Claiming to be Conscientious Objectors, National Archives, Kew.
[72] 'Letter from G. W. Lambert of the War Office, 22 December 1942, to the Secretary, Ministry of Labour and National Service,' LAB 6/14 – Discharge of Prisoners Claiming to be Conscientious Objectors, National Archives, Kew.
[73] Hayes, *Challenge of Conscience*, p. 112.
[74] Barker, *Conscience, Government and War*, p. 88.

Resulting from this decision some 30 objectors were discharged 'whose release could not be explained as being within any known category,' according to Hayes.[75] Ironically Gerald Henderson, whose case was one of the prime reasons for initiating the process which resulted in the change in procedure, was not one of them. His fourth appearance before the Appellate Tribunal, his sixth before a tribunal of any type, resulted in him being conditionally registered as a conscientious objector. This was described by Hayes as 'a striking tribute to his persistence.'[76] The Duke of Bedford saw it as more, and afforded him the opportunity to further attack Judge Richardson:

> If the original tribunal who first heard Henderson's case had realised the genuineness of his conscientious objection, Henderson could have been doing useful work all the months that he has spent in prison.[77]

By the end of 1946 the CBCO had record of 1,050 conscientious objectors who had been court-martialled. 635 had registered as such at the outset and 415 had reached a conscientious objection while in the Forces. The total number of times these were court-martialled were: Once 716; Twice 210; Three Times 106; Four Times 15; Five Times 2; and, Six Times 1.[78] Without the change in procedure it can only be speculated as to how many of those 1,050 would have progressed to further courts martial.

The cases of 'cat and mouse' referred to here and in the secondary literature do not relate to officers. As officers were often from the upper-middle or upper classes, it is possible to conclude that class distinction was being practiced in the treatment of conscientious objectors by the Army. When the Army agreed a firm policy in April 1940 that officers who develop conscientious objection should be called upon to resign their commissions, they were conscious that they may appear to be receiving more favourable treatment than other ranks. One North-East officer allowed to resign his commission was Lieutenant Tim Miles of

---

[75] Hayes, *Challenge of Conscience*, p. 112.
[76] Ibid.
[77] Duke of Bedford, *Hansard*, HL Deb. 2 March 1943, Vol. 126 cc358-92.
[78] Hayes, *Challenge of Conscience*, p. 118.

Darlington, who, in an interview stated that he came from a conventional middle-class background of unreligious parents.[79] As a student at Oxford University he had, despite his pre-determination not to fight, joined the Officer Training Corps and at the end of 1942 went to train as an army officer. As he was in an anti-aircraft unit he convinced himself that this was alright as it was a defensive role, but this changed when he was posted to the Middle East and had to give orders to men to fire on aircraft. On being transferred to an infantry unit in 1944, with the involvement in direct fighting, he became increasingly concerned with what he saw as the unnecessary policy of unconditional surrender. As he had not refused to obey an order his commanding officer granted his request to resign his commission and, after being granted exemption by a tribunal, was allowed to return to University. The army took the view that conscientious objection was incompatible with commissioned status as the officer was vested with powers of command over all ranks, and that their continued presence in a unit was a menace to the other soldiers.[80] Therefore it is concluded that although class may have played a role in the appointment of officers it was not a factor in the treatment of those who were objectors.

Conclusion

There were many ways in which conscientious objectors could find themselves in the army. Some went there voluntarily, some by accident and others, such as Kenneth Makin, by the employment of methods of forcible removal not completely dissimilar to the Press Gangs of the Napoleonic period. By far the largest proportion were sent by the tribunals for non-combatant duties. Non-combatant status caused problem for both the Army and the objectors. Seen by the government as an acceptable alternative to armed service, there were simply too many of them. Finding duties to satisfy the consciences of over 17,000 was always going to be impossible, particularly once the RAMC could absorb no more.

---

[79] Goodhall, *We Will Not Go to War: Conscientious Objection during the World Wars*, p.227.
[80] 'O.S. 56 (revised), 19 April 1940,' WO 32/14529 – Policy for Officers who became Conscientious Objectors, National Archives, Kew.

Many, including some from the North-East, were to continue their objection by failing to obey orders.

Therefore, when conscientious objectors from the North-East of England found themselves in the armed forces, they could not be blamed for thinking that the experiences of the First World War were going to be repeated. Some experienced brutal treatment whilst in the hands of the authorities, although there were contradictions regarding the evidence given by Albert Foster as to the exact details of this abuse. Fortunately, in this war both the army and the government saw publicity regarding such brutality as counter-productive to the war effort and it was largely eliminated. Others were subjected to 'cat and mouse' treatment combined with appalling conditions in detention barracks such as Northallerton. One notable example was Gerald Henderson whose case led to the practice being eliminated. North–East objectors and facilities therefore figured prominently in these events.

It is perhaps no coincidence that the worst conditions were experienced at the time when the country was in greatest peril. As the country's military prospects improved, so did conditions experienced by soldier conscientious objectors and the worst excesses of the First World War were not repeated. The government's desire that objectors should have their conscientious objection respected was certainly challenged and it was only due to the pragmatism of government officials and politicians that this desire was generally realised. There was also a recognition by the authorities that to attempt to change the mind of a determined objector was counter-productive to the war effort in terms of time and cost. Britain did in the end show it was different from Nazi Germany in how it treated its dissenters. Nevertheless, many did suffer, notably Kenneth Makin and Gerald Henderson, before their conscientious objection was recognised. This suffering should not be underestimated because of the later improvements achieved, some as a result of their suffering.

Summary

This book set out to enhance the scant coverage of conscientious objectors in the North-East of England during the Second World War. It has sought to establish the extent of objection and to place it within the narrative of the War, both regionally and nationally. The result has been to place North-East conscientious objectors at the forefront of many developments regarding the treatment of objectors nationally. This, however, has not been its main contribution. The regional case study, and, in particular, the compilation of a database of over 800 known objectors, which as approximately 1% of the national figure is the largest database prepared for analysis, has advanced the general understanding of conscientious objection in the Second World War by providing a detailed analysis of those who objected. By studying the North-East, the bigger picture of objection nationally has been enhanced. It has also, through its examination of political objection in the region, enhanced the understanding of wartime politics in Britain.

Determining how conscientious objectors in the region were treated required that it be determined who they were. Establishing this, and the extent of conscientious objection in the region, was not made easy by the destruction of the records of the Northumberland and Durham Tribunal. The only official figure of conscientious objectors in the North-East of 1,148 appearing before the tribunals has been shown to be undoubtedly understated. In terms of the number of officially recorded objectors, the region had one of the lowest rates of objection in the country. This was less an indication of greater patriotism, as the local press asserted, but a reflection of the region's population demographics. Compiling a database from other available sources allowed a number of statistically viable analyses to be conducted. They included demographic analyses of who the objectors were, their occupations and the reasons for their objection, which allowed for comparison with available national data collected by Mass Observation. Such a comparison also provided evidence to support the findings of Mass Observation. It also provided explanations as to why the highest proportion of objection in the region was to be found in Newcastle, Darlington and Scarborough. Most importantly the sources provided biographical details and experiences of individual objectors, such as Kenneth Makin, James Kirkup and Douglas Hardy, which provided insight of their experiences. It also identified many women objectors, such as Kitty Alexander, who, because of the different way the authorities dealt with their objection, would otherwise have not appeared in official records of conscientious objectors.

Whatever the actual number of conscientious objectors, it was not insignificant and represented an administrative burden to the authorities at a time when the country's resources were required for the war effort. That they were prepared to bear this burden indicates how seriously the government regarded the right to conscientious objection and, also, how important it was that this objection was tested thoroughly. It was also important that the instructions of the state were carried out, and the courts found themselves dealing with cases of refusals, often involving repeated appearances before them by the same individuals. The prison authorities also found the number of their inmates swelled by objectors who had committed no criminal offence. It was certainly more than 'minimal', as described by Armstrong, especially when the numbers involved in Newcastle War Resisters are taken into account.

One thread which runs throughout this book is the contention that this was, in comparison to the First World War, a 'good war,' of democracy versus fascism, and a war for national survival. It was the concept of the 'good war' which led many objectors from the First World War becoming ardent supporters of the Second World War, particularly within the Labour Party, as shown in the North-East by Ellen Wilkinson and Will Lawther. It nevertheless resulted in conflicting views as to how conscientious objectors were treated. Those who objected were seen by some as not pulling their weight and to many it was offensive that they were not fighting for their country's survival. To others in a war of democracy versus fascism conscientious objection was the embodiment of the freedoms that the country was fighting for. This conflict was evident in the discussions which took place within local authorities when they were deciding whether or not to dismiss their objectors, and in the letters to the regional press, both for and against objectors. However, in a state of total war, when a political truce was declared, opposition from trade unions was minimal and a raft of Defence Regulations restricted freedoms, democracy had in effect been put on hold. In respect of the First World War, André Keil refers to this as 'a system of constitutional dictatorship.'[81]

Objection, common in the First World War, on the grounds of it being an imperialist war did not, however, disappear. As long as the Soviet Union was not a war belligerent then many, though not all, members of the CPGB were to convey this view of the war, as were the members of the declining ILP, which has been shown, retained a strong base of support in Newcastle and formed the core of the Newcastle War Resisters. Their form of political objection, counter to the majority view of the war, was shown to have resulted in harsh treatment by the authorities, epitomised by the experiences of the Morley family.

The significant increase in both the number of, and the proportion of, those registering as conscientious objectors was confirmation that the government had learned many of the lessons of the First World War, at least with regard to recognising conscientious objection. It also soon learned that the legislation they introduced was not going to address the complexity of such objection. This was total war, and with it came a number of complicating factors which extended conscientious objection beyond that relating to military service. Such factors brought many of the objectors from the First World War, such as Jack and Mark Sadler, back into the frame, and it was their belligerence which presented the authorities in the region with many of their greatest difficulties. The greatest difficulty was presented by Jehovah's Witnesses whose exponential growth had taken place after the First World War. They represented the largest number of religious objectors, which itself was the most common reason for objection. Nowhere was this more evident than at the Northumberland and Durham Conscientious Objectors' Tribunal.

The book has also examined the inference by historians that the notoriety of Judge Richardson, Chairman of the Newcastle Tribunal, equated to a harsh treatment of objectors. He lived up to his reputation with his unjudicial comments and his bias against Jehovah's Witnesses, in which he was not alone amongst tribunal chairmen, yet the analysis of his tribunal decisions showed that the decisions of his tribunal were

---

[81] André Keil, 'States of Exception: Emergency Government and 'Enemies Within' in Britain and Germany in the First World War,' (Unpublished PhD thesis: Northumbria University, 2014), p.115.

not the least reasonable. Whether the same degree of reasonableness could be applied to other organisations in the region is debatable.

Treatment of objectors by local authorities in the region did not vary much from the position nationally. Many of the major authorities, notably Northumberland, North Yorkshire, York City, Darlington and Middlesbrough, displayed an intolerance which led to the dismissal of objectors, and they employed a variety of ways of doing so. Teachers, as potential influencers of the young, were the main target. Yet this intolerance was not total. Despite intense pressure the majority of the councillors of Newcastle and South Shields, for example, saw the right to object as a fundamental feature of a democracy. For those whose objection led to dismissal from their local authority jobs the support of their trade union was minimal.

The pressure on local authorities and other employers came in the main from the local press which showed a clear intolerance of conscientious objectors through their sensational headlines, and their often-vitriolic features and editorial comments. They also provided through their letters pages a vehicle for the expression of the more extreme degrees of intolerance. This suited the authorities so long as things did not go too far. However, being aware that the right to conscientious objection was an example of the freedoms for which the country was fighting, they did not go as far as arousing hatred. In fact, their intolerance was partially balanced by allowing the publication of pro-objector letters and reporting the good work done by the FAU and others. Pressure was also exerted by certain members of the clergy, such as the Rev. Pickering, through their utterances from the pulpit and in the local press. However, they generally managed well the delicate balancing act, between supporting the majority of their congregations who had family members in the armed forces and ministering to conscientious objectors.

Objectors appearing before the courts, though often receiving sympathy, were dealt with in accordance with a rigid legal framework. This, if repeated, invariably, for a significant number in the region, led to incarceration in Durham Prison where conditions, vividly described by Kitty Alexander, were on a par with the worst in the country. This low standard was maintained for any objector in the forces incarcerated in the region's main detention centre at Northallerton. Such discomforts could be expected to be avoided if an objector complied with the conditions imposed by the tribunal. As James Kirkup graphically illustrates, this was often not the case for those directed to work on the land.

Pacifism in the North-East had been significant before the war. This, combined with the residual support for the ILP, led to a number of firsts in the region when conscription was extended to women for the first time: the first to be unconditionally registered; the first to be prosecuted for refusing to fire-watch; the first, and last, to be prosecuted for failing to register for National Service, and, the first, Constance Bolam, to be sent to prison.

The significant contributions of these individuals contributed ultimately to a more humane treatment of conscientious objectors as the war progressed, and beyond. Much has been written about the suffering of objectors in the First World War, yet it was during the Second World War that a significant transition was made towards the United Nations recognising conscientious objection to military service as a derivative human right, derived from an interpretation of the right to freedom of thought, conscience and religion.[82] The North-East of England played a significant role in this transition. No more so than the changes resulting from the experiences of serving soldiers Kenneth Makin, Albert Foster and Gerald Henderson, regarding the end of 'cat and mouse' and improved treatment in detention centres. By 1946 even Jehovah's Witnesses were being released from conditions imposed by tribunals. Yet the treatment of objectors in the Second World War, through the pragmatism of the authorities, was to be less severe than in the previous war. This may have been partly due to the considerably larger numbers of objectors but was more likely the view that the war was being fought to protect freedom.

This book complicates the perceived view of the North-East of England in wartime of everyone stoically pulling together through adversity. It has shown that there was no simple definition of what constituted a conscientious objection. Be it moral, religious or political, or a

---

[82] United Nations, *Conscientious Objection to Military Service* (New York: OHCHR, 2012) p. 7.

combination of these factors, there were a significant number who re-fused to fight the 'good war' and suffered discrimination as a conse-quence.

Appendix A: Local Statistics of Conscientious Objectors

Date	Ashington Registered	CO	Darling-ton Reg.	CO	Durham Reg.	CO	M/Boro Reg.	CO	N/castle Reg.	CO	Scarbor' Reg.	CO	S/land Reg.	CO	Source	Total	CO	%	GB %
11.12.39	1027	11	829	12	2535	16	2417	10	5733	34	480	4	1775	8	NE	14796	95	0.64	2.1
11.03.40	1407	3	1444	13	2799	3	3288	9	6837	38	641	7	2370	7	NE	18786	80	0.43	1.6
07.04.40	1331	5	1347	7	2731	4	3131	24	6277	32	588	5	2171	7	SS	17576	84	0.48	1.4
29.04.40	1361	5	1270	5	2465	8	2994	4	6010	21	618	9	2078	6	NE	16796	58	0.35	1.2
26.05.40	1442	5	1423	3	2782	8	3177	15	6178	23	690	5	2157	8	SS	17849	67	0.38	1.04
16.06.40	1219	1	1180	4	2361	2	2351	13	5562	18	583	2	1876	2	SS	15132	42	0.28	0.77
23.06.40	1404	4	1420	4	2755	2	3147	7	6371	17	698	3	2172	7	SS	17967	44	0.24	0.69
14.07.40	1333	0	1408	3	2666	2	3160	9	6043	16	679	3	2136	6	SS	17425	39	0.22	0.51
22.07.40			1268	1	2416	1	2932	9			627	0			EG	7243	11		
28.07.40	1453	3	1503	2	2860	3	3323	5	6500	21	688	2	2339	4	SS	18666	40	0.21	0.57
14.01.41	778	0	809	1	1307	2	1850	3	3675	6	358	1	1252	1	EC	10029	14	0.14	0.45
27.02.41	1177	1	1132	4	2602	3	2945	1	6430	9	535	2	2307	3	EC	17128	23	0.13	0.57
Totals	13392	38	15033	59	30279	54	34715	109	65616	235	7185	43	22633	59			597		
% COs	0.27		0.39		0.18		0.31		0.36		0.6		0.26					0.32	

Appendix B: Occupations of Conscientious Objectors

	Total	Managerial	Skilled	Semi-Skilled	Unskilled
Local Government					
Local Government Professionals	5		5		
Local Government Clerical	6			6	
Local Government Manual	7				7
Teachers/Lecturers	26		26		
	44	0	31	6	7
White Collar Occupations					
Clerical	37			37	
Law - Barristers and Articled Clerks	8		8		
Advertising Agent	1		1		
Insurance Agents and Reps	9			9	
Accountants	5		5		
Journalists	2		2		
Canvassers	2			2	
Central Government	1		1		
Credit Manager	1		1		
Salesmen	8			8	
Draughtsmen	4		4		
Bank Clerk/Cashier	3			3	
Son of Ship Owner	1	1			
Estimator	1		1		
Estate Agent	1		1		
MD Retail Concern	1	1			
Tax Inspector	1		1		
MD Shipyard	1	1			
Own Business	2	2			
	89	5	25	59	0

Health and Welfare

Nurses	2			2	
Chemists	3		3		
Social Workers	1			1	
Dental Mechanic	1		1		
Optician	1		1		
Doctor	1		1		
Natureopath	1		1		
	10	**0**	**7**	**3**	**0**

Agriculture and Horticulture

Farm Workers	12				12
Gardener	1				1
Market Gardener	2		2		
Forestry	2				2
Farmer	6		6		
Blacksmith	2		2		
Blacksmith's Striker	1			1	
	26	**0**	**10**	**1**	**15**

Manufacturing

Engineers	14		14		
Electrical Engineer	1		1		
Steel Workers/Slingers	7			7	
Electricians	6		6		
Munitions Worker	1			1	
Chemicals	2			2	
Machinists/Machine Operators	1			1	
Master Repairer	1		1		
Coke Oven Workers	3			3	
Ship Repairer	1		1		
Ship Painter	1		1		
Tent Maker	1		1		
Maintenance Fitter	3		3		
Capp Fitter	1		1		
Pattern Maker	1		1		
Welder	1		1		
Plater's Helper	1			1	
	46	**0**	**31**	**15**	**0**

Building

Bricklayer	7		7		
Joiners/Carpenters/Cabinet Makers	10		10		
Plumbers	3		3		
Plasterers	2		2		
Slater	1		1		
Painters and Decorators	7		7		

30	**0**	**30**		**0**
Transport				
Signalman	1			1	
Bus Conductor	1			1	
Motor Mechanic	2		2		
Motor Driver	2			2	
Cellulose Sprayer	1		1		
Coach Builder	1		1		
Train Driver	2			2	
Bus Driver	3			3	
	13	**0**	**4**	**9**	**0**
Services				
Post Office Worker	1		1		
Photographer	1		1		
Printing	6		6		
Shop Assistants	16				16
Water Workers	2			2	
Retail Managers/Grocers/Distributors	5		5		
Furniture Veneerer	1		1		
Milk Roundsman	1				1
Tailor	1		1		
Confectioner	1		1		
Canteen Assistants/Café Workers	1				2
Sweet Manufacturer	1	1			
Window Cleaners	3				3
Butchers	2		2		
Warden	1			1	
Newspaper Distributors	1				1
Boot Repairers	2			2	
Switchboard Operator	1			1	
Baker's Van Man	1				1
Radio Engineer	1		1		
Overhead Linesman	2			2	
Shoe Maker	1		1		
Baker	1		1		
Wireless Operator	1			1	
Watchmaker	1		1		
	56	**1**	**22**	**9**	**24**
Mining				
Miners	12				12
Quarrymen	3				3
	15	**0**	**0**	**0**	**15**
Arts and Entertainment				
Artist	2		2		
Instrument Maker	1		1		

Actors/Writers/Musicians	2		2		
Cinema Operators	3			3	
Entertainer	1				1
	9	0	5	3	1
General Workers					
Students	18		18		
Labourers	23				23
Storemen/Warehousemen	5				5
Steward	1				1
Watchman	1				1
Housemaid/Kitchen Maid	3				3
	51	0	18	0	33
	389	6	183	105	95

Appendix C – Biographies of Members of the Newcastle Tribunal

The main members were: Alderman F. Nicholson CBE, JP; Professor James F. Duff M.A.M. Ed.; Sir Luke Thompson; J. Bowman; and, the chairman, Judge Thomas Richardson, OBE. In 1943 Dr E. L. Allen a lecturer at Durham University accepted an invitation to become a member of the tribunal.

Professor Duff

Professor Duff was Warden of the Durham Colleges in the University of Durham. He was also formerly a lecturer in Education at Armstrong College in Newcastle and education superintendent of the Northumberland County Council.

Mr. J. Bowman

Little is known of Mr. Bowman except that he was a representative of the trade unions.[1]

He may have been James Bowman who in 1935 was elected general secretary of the Northumberland Miners' Association, and in 1936 was elected to the executive committee of the Mineworkers' Federation of Great Britain (MFGB). In 1939 he was elected vice-president of the MFGB. Throughout the 1940s Bowman shared power within the MFGB with William Lawther.

In 1955 Bowman was appointed deputy chairman of the NCB and in 1956 was appointed chairman. He was also knighted in 1957.

Dr Allen

Dr Allen was a well-known pacifist and he had made his position clear before accepting the position.[2]

Alderman Nicolson

Knighted in 1943, was a native of Sunderland and grandson of the famous Chartist and pioneer of improved sanitation, James Williams.

He joined Vaux Brewery as an accountant and became Managing Director and later Chairman of the controlling company.

He married the daughter of Mr. John Storey Vaux and they had one son, Major F Douglas Nicholson and two daughters.[3]

He had also been Chair of Sunderland Finance Committee, Chair of the Wear Commission, and was at this time Chair of Durham County War Agricultural Committee. In 1939 he was High Sheriff of Durham County and in 1940 Deputy Lieutenant, and had been awarded the CBE in 1937.

Sir Luke Thompson

[1] 'Tribunal for Conscientious Objectors', *Durham County Advertiser*, 11 August 1939, p. 6. ; and, 'File Report No. 312, Conscientious Objectors', *Mass Observation*, June 1940, p. 208.
[2] 'Pacifist on Tribunal,' *Central Board for Conscientious Objectors Bulletin*, No. 39, May 1943, p. 2.
[3] 'Honours for Wearsiders', *Sunderland Echo*, 1 January 1943, p. 4.

Sir Luke Thompson was a director of John Thompson and Sons, Sunderland coal merchants, and had represented Sunderland in the House of Commons, from 1922 to1929 and 1931 to1935. He was knighted in 1934 for his public and political services.

He was Chairman of the Durham and North Yorkshire Coal Merchants Association, a vice-president of the Sunderland Guild of Help and took a deep interest in the Council of Social Service. He was also Chairman of the North of England Building Society and since 1932 he had been the representative of the Minister of Transport on the Wear Commissioners. He was a life-long Methodist and lay preacher.[4]

In 1941, he was killed in an accident at his business premises, prompting Judge Richardson to remark: 'I don't think I ever met a man in my life for whom I had a better regard.'[5]

Judge Thomas Richardson

The son of Sir Thomas Richardson, former MP for the Hartlepools.

He was educated at Rossall School and Clare College, Cambridge, where he obtained a Second Class Honours degree in History and Law. He was called to the Bar in 1905 and became a County Court Judge in 1927. He unsuccessfully contested the parliamentary seat of Houghton-le-Spring for the Conservative Party in 1913 and served as a Captain in the First World War.

His interests were shooting, golf, gardening, sketching, music and fishing, and he lived at Corbridge, Northumberland.[6] He was married to the daughter of Judge Templar and had three children. His daughter served in a military hospital and her husband was a major in the Royal Artillery. His son was a Lieutenant in the North Africa campaign. His eldest son, Thomas, an officer in the County of Durham Auxiliary Air Force Squadron, was killed in a flying accident in 1937.[7]

He lost five brothers in the First World War. He and his six brothers all served in the First World War, bar one who was lost in a submarine disaster before war began.[8] One of those brothers received a Victoria Cross at the Battle of the Somme.[9]

Appendix D: Article by AUGER in the *Ripon Gazette*
15 February 1940 – 'A Conchie Talks to Me'

It happened in the waiting room of the dentist. Tired of looking at the comic journals which have lain on the table since the last war, I began taking stock of the other people in the room. Not far from me sat a handsome young man. He, too, had been looking at the comic cartoons. He, too, had had enough of them. To start the conversation going I said to him politely:

"This endless waiting for the dentist reminds me of occasions when I waited to go over the top."

"Excuse me," said the handsome young man, "what do you mean?"

"Well," I said, "waiting for the invitation to sit in the dentist's chair reminds me of the feeling one has before going over the top in wartime."

---

[4] 'Tributes to Sir Luke Thompson', *Sunderland Echo*, 16 January 1941, p. 2.

[5] 'Tribunal Tribute', *Sunderland Echo*, 11 March 1943, p.3.

[6] *Who's Who, 1940* (London: Adam and Charles Black, 1940), p. 2863.

[7] 'Judge's Son Wins M.C. Emulates Godfather', *Hexham Courant*, 26 September 1942, p. 1.

[8] 'Judge's Son and Five Brothers', *Manchester Guardian*, 6 December 1939, p. 8.

[9] *Hexham Courant*, 26 September 1942, p. 1.

"Oh, I see," he said with a disgusted air, "you are making comparisons with war conditions, I did not understand you at first, because my mind does not work that way."

I suppose my face registered surprise, because the young fellow added with a condescending smile, "I am a conscientious objector, you see."

I woke up. I was immensely interested. I had read and read so much about those people who object to war that to meet one in the flesh was an exciting experience. I put to the fellow a question which I confess was stupid:

"How do you do it?"

"What do you mean?" he said, "How do I do what?"

"Oh well, how do you become a conscientious objector?"

"Oh, we refuse to accept war as a part of our existence. War is evil, and we will have nothing to do with it. Least of all can we agree to take part in a war, whether actively or in a passive form."

"I see," I exclaimed, "how interesting. Tell me more about this please." The handsome young man was perfectly ready to oblige. Indeed, he began to display an apostolic fervour, which made it quite plain that he hoped to make me a conscientious objector himself. He told me a long and beautiful story about his cross examination by the specially instituted tribunal. "I told them finally," he exclaimed, "that my principles absolutely forbade me to touch a weapon, even in self-defence. But then," he added as a magnificent afterthought, "these war-mongers speak much utter nonsense that it is childishly easy to defeat them in debate."

"May I be permitted," I put in, "to put to you a few questions arising out of the problem you have raised?"

"Fire away," the fellow said charitably, "it will do you good for once to hear the truth about these wars."

"You understand," I insisted, "that my questions are those which come to the mind of a man ignorant of the dangers you mention. I have a simple mind, of course, but I do not mind to be instructed."

"Fire away," he repeated with magnanimity, "I will do my best to make you see the truth."

"My first question," I said, "Is this: Do you consider that we are at war?"

He laughed. "What a funny question to ask. Or perhaps," he added as an after-thought, "you are cleverer than you make out. My reply is that for us conscientious objectors the war simply does not exist. Let those who make it give their thoughts to the war. We conscientious objectors want to ignore the fact of its existence altogether."

"But," I broke in, "although you are not of it, still you know that a war is on?" the fellow grudgingly agreed.

"In that case," I went on, "may I ask whether you wish the Germans to win?"

"That question does not arise," he said angrily, "because I tell you that we do not acknowledge war's existence."

Still I came back on the attack: "Do you wish the Germans to win?"

Annoyed, he replied: "Of course not." Then he added curiously: "But I do not want to see the Russians beaten."

"How's that," I inquired. "What has Russia specially to do with your conscientious objection to war in any form?"

He looked at me with suspicion. "What are you leading up to?"

"To nothing, I assure you," I said innocently. "but I want to understand your principles."

"Well," he said, "I agree to answer one question more, but it must be the last."

I collected my wits and fired at him my last broadside. "Tell me," I said, "admitting for the sake of argument that the Germans can win this war, and admitting also that Hitler sends his gauleiters to rule us, what will you do if such a gaulitier sends his orderly to request the company of your wife for the night?"

"He would not dare," he blurted out. Then seeing my quizzing expression, he abruptly walked out of the room without even glancing in my direction.

Now I have not invented this incident. To me it was a real revelation of the addled condition of the mind of a fellow like that. I felt no anger, only a great pity. Those fine gentlemen, who speak fine words about their anti-war attitude based on high moral principles, they lose their balance when you suddenly confront them with a stark fact. My advice to readers is to try out my recipe. Put these questions to a high stepping conchie: (1) Is there a war on? (2) If there is, which side do you wish to win? (3) If the Germans win, what will you do? (4) If the Germans come here and try to use the methods they apply to the Poles, for example, what would you do? (5) The last question is the one about the gauleiter and the wife or sister I put to my handsome friend at the dentist's.

The French are a practical and democratic people. They treat their conscientious objectors as cranks. If the misguided fellows persist in their error, they are treated as ordinary criminals. But, in France there are remarkably few conscientious objectors. Few young men will agree to be branded as cowards. I am certain that the legalised existence in Great Britain of a class of conscientious objectors is the source of continuous wonderment to our allies across the Channel. Some Frenchmen ask me about that. My advice to them is to leave the question alone for a time. The nation has only begun to find its stride. As the war develops and its aspect becomes more terrible the conscientious cranks will disappear and the conscientious criminals will be dealt with as they deserve.

Archives

British Library, Euston Road, London

Interview with Kitty Alice Hall, C900/11093, Sound Archives.
Interview with Maurice Scurr, C900/01645, Sound Archive.
Interview with Miles Peter Richmond, C466/263, Sound Archive.
Interview with Juliet Morland, C880/12, Sound Archive.

Durham County Records Office, County Hall, Durham

Nominal Register of Male Prisoners, Durham Prison, P/1/27.
UD/BB/25-31, Minutes of Brandon and Byshottles U.D.C.
CC/A1/1/37, Minutes of Durham County Council.
RD/Ea/21, Minutes of Easington R.D.C.
UD/Sta/81, Minutes of Stanley U.D.C.

Imperial War Museum, Interviews, www.iwm.org.uk/collections/object/.

8994, Alan Brian Davey.
10235, Freda Wood.
4746, Alexander Bryan.
4686, Stanley Iveson.
10650, Marjorie Asquith.

National Archives, Kew, London

CAB/23/99/5, Cabinet 3 May 1939.
CAB/65/8/32, War Cabinet, 6 August 1940.
CAB/65/36/20, War Cabinet, 10 November 1943.
CAB 66/14, Papers of the War Cabinet.
CAB/66/16/30, War Cabinet, May 1941 and 7 July 1943.
CAB/66/57/24, War Cabinet, 6 November 1944.
CAB 67/6/16, War Cabinet, 30 April 1940.
CAB/68/4/19, Cabinet, January 1940.
CAB/68/5/52, Cabinet March 1940.
CAB/128/1/14, Cabinet, 13 September 1945.
CAB/129/1 39, Cabinet, 13 August 1945.
LAB 6/14, Discharge of Prisoners Claiming to be Conscientious Objectors.
LAB 6/183, National Service (No. 2) Bill 1941, General Procedure for dealing with Women Conscientious Objectors.
LAB 6/405, Papers of the Ministry of Labour and National Service, Statistics of Conscientious Objectors.
WO 32/15272, C.O.s Right to Non-Combatant Duties.
WO 32/9422, Posting to the RAMC and RA Dental Corps.

WO 32/14529, Policy for Officers who become Conscientious Objectors.
National Archives Website, discovery.nationalarchives.gov.uk/details/r/C14432.

Northumberland County Records Office, Woodhorn, Ashington, Northumberland

CC/CM/CC/50-52Minutes of Northumberland County Council.

North Yorkshire County Records, Northallerton, North Yorkshire

Minutes of North Riding of Yorkshire County Council.
Minutes of Skipton U.D.C.

Teesside Archives, Middlesbrough

Minutes of Middlesbrough County Borough Council, CB/M/C1/100.

Tyne and Wear Archives, Discovery Museum, Newcastle-upon-Tyne

Ref. 5336, Papers of Grigor McClelland.
UD/BO/2/18, Minutes of Boldon U.D.C.

Local Studies Sections - Other Local Authority Minutes

Minutes of Darlington Corporation, Central Library, Darlington.
Minutes of Gateshead Borough Council, Central Library, Gateshead.
Minutes of Jarrow Council, Central Library, South Shields.
Minutes of Newcastle Corporation, City Library, Newcastle-upon-Tyne.
Minutes of the County Borough of Sunderland, City Library, Sunderland.
Minutes of the Borough of West Hartlepool, Central Library, Hartlepool.
Minutes of the Borough of Hartlepools, Central Library, Hartlepool.
Minutes of the City of York Corporation, Central Library, York.

Other Archives

Record of Debates of the House of Commons and The House of Lords, *Hansard,* www.mill-banksystems.co.uk.
Mass Observation Online (Reference TC6), www.massobservation.amdigital.co.uk.

Primary Sources – Newspapers

Alnwick County Gazette and Guardian, 1939 – 1945, Branch Library, Alnwick.
Darlington and Stockton Times, 1939 – 1945, Local Studies, Central Library, Darlington.
Durham County Advertiser, 1939 – 1945, Local Studies, Clayport Library, Durham City.
Evening Despatch, 1942 – 1945, Local Studies, Central Library, Darlington.
Evening Chronicle, 1939 – 1945, Research Section, City Library, Newcastle-upon-Tyne.
Friend's Ambulance Chronicle, 1939 – 1945, Personal Papers of Stan Abbott, Durham.
Globe and Mail (Toronto, Canada), 1939 – 1945, ProQuest Historical Newspapers, Northumbria University Library.

Hexham Courant, 1939 - 1945, Branch Library, Hexham.
Manchester Guardian, 1939 – 1945, www.britishnewspaperarchive.co.uk/.
Morpeth Herald, 1939 – 1945, Branch Library, Morpeth.
North-East Gazette, 1939 – 1945, Local Studies, Central Library, Middlesbrough.
Northern Daily Mail, 1939 – 1945, Local Studies, Central Library, Hartlepool.
Northern Echo, 1939 – 1942, Local Studies, Central Library, Darlington.
Northern Echo, 7 May 2013, www.northernecho.co.uk/news/10402990.print/.
Peace News, 1939 – 1945, Library, Friends House, Euston Road, London.
Ripon Gazette, 1939 – 1945, Branch Library, Ripon.
Shields Gazette, 1939 – 1945, Local Studies, Central Library, South Shields.
Sunday Sun, 1939 – 1945, Research Section, City Library, Newcastle-upon-Tyne.
Sunderland Echo, 1939 – 1945, Local Studies, City Library, Sunderland.
Teesdale Mercury, 1939 – 1945, www.teesdalemercuryarchive.org.uk/.
The Friend, 1939 – 1945, Library, Friends House, Euston Road, London.
The New Leader, 1939 – 1945, People's History Museum, Manchester.
The Spectator, 1939 – 1945, archive.spectator.co.uk/.
The Word, Some Editions, 1938 – 1945, MSS.15B/7/36, Modern Records Centre, Warwick University, Coventry.
The Word, L908.09, Newspaper Cuttings, Local Studies, Central Library, Gateshead.
Yorkshire Evening Post, May 1939 – May 1945, www.britishnewspaperarchive.co.uk/.

Central Board for Conscientious Objectors Publications

Bulletin, Numbers 25 (March 1942), 39 (May 1943), 41 (July 1943) and 49 (March 1944).
Murry, John Middleton, *The Economics of Peace*, December 1943.
The Case for Stanley Hilton, September 1943.
Questions to C.O.s, January 1944.
Civil and Military Prison Routine, September 1941.

Other Primary Sources

Pamphlet - Various contributors, *All About Pacifism and Armaments* (London: No More War Movement, 1928).
A Declaration from the Harmles & Innocent people of God called Quakers..., submitted to King Charles II on 21 November 1660, full text available on www.quakers.org.uk/350.
BBC Peoples' War, www.bbc.co.uk/history/ww2peopleswar/.
Letters from Ellen Wilkinson to wife of Albert Cocks (Cox), held in the private papers of the Cocks family, Nunthorpe, Middlesbrough.
Peace Pledge Union Website, www.ppu.org.uk/cosnew/co_sadler1.html.
Peace Pledge Union Website, www.ppu.org.uk/coproject/guide.html.
Norman Gaudie Papers, Liddle Collection, Leeds University Library.
Who's Who, 1940 (London: Adam and Charles Black, 1940)

Autobiographical Studies

Broad, Richard and Fleming, Suzie, eds., *Nella Last's War: The Second World War Diaries of Housewife, 49* (London: Profile Books Ltd., 2006).

Brockway, Fenner, *Inside the Left: Thirty Years of Platform, Press, Prison and Parliament* (London: George Allen and Unwin, 1942).

Churchill, Winston S., *The Second World War: Part 1, The Gathering Storm* (London: Cassell, 1948).

Kirkup, James, *I, Of All People* (New York: St. Martin's Press, 1988).

Kirkup, James, *Me All Over* (London: Peter Owen, 1993).

Mellanby, Kenneth, *Human Guinea Pigs* (London: Victor Gollanz Ltd., 1946).

Oral Interviews Conducted

Telephone interview with Wendy Acres of Darlington, conducted 28 October 2013.

Telephone interview with Paul Ronchetti, conducted 1 November 2013.

Interview with Steve Ronchetti, son of Louis Ronchetti, conducted 30 October 2013.

Telephone interview with Sheila Ross, conducted 23 October 2013.

Interview with Robert Faldon, at his home in Gateshead, conducted 8 November 2013.

Secondary Sources – Books

Addison, Paul and Crang, Jeremy A., *Listening to Britain: Home Intelligence Reports on Britain's Finest Hour – May to September 1940* (London: Vintage Books, 2010).

Alston, Charlotte, *Tolstoy and his Disciples: The History of a Radical International Movement* (London: I. B. Taurus Ltd., 2014).

Armstrong, Craig, *Tyneside in the Second World War* (Chichester: Phillimore and Co. Ltd., 2007).

Attfield, John and Williams, Stephen, eds., *1939: The Communist Party and War* (London: Lawrence and Wishart, 1984).

Balfour, Michael, *Propaganda and War: Organisations, Policies and Publics in Britain and Germany* (London: Routledge, 1979).

Barker, Rachel, *Conscience, Government and War* (London: Routledge, 1982).

Bartley, Paula, *Ellen Wilkinson: From Red Suffragist to Government Minister* (London: Pluto Press, 2014).

Bibbings, Lois, S., *Telling tales About Men: Conceptions of conscientious objectors to military service during the First World War* (Manchester: MUP, 2011).

Branson, Noreen, *History of the Communist Party of Great Britain 1927-1941* (London: Lawrence and Wishart, 1985).

Branson, Noreen, *History of the Communist Party of Great Britain 1941-1951* (London: Lawrence and Wishart, 1997).

Brayshaw, A. Joseph, 'The Strange Occurrences at Dingle Vale,' in Hayes, *Challenge of Conscience* (London: George Allen and Unwin, 1947).

Brittain, Vera, *England's Hour* (New York: Continuum, 2005).

Brittain, Vera, *Humiliation With Honour* (London: A. Dakers Ltd., 1942).

Brittain, Vera, *Testament of Youth* (London: Virago press, 1978).

Brock, Peter, *Against the Draft: Essays on conscientious objection from the Radical Reformation to the Second World War* (Toronto: Toronto University Press, 2006).

Brock, Peter, *Pacifism in Europe to 1914* (Princeton: Princeton University Press, 1972).

Brock, Peter, *Twentieth-Century Pacifism* (New York: Van Nostrand Reinhold, 1970).

Brock, Peter, ed., *These Strange Criminals: An Anthology of Prison Memoirs by Conscientious Objectors from the Great War to the Cold War* (Toronto: Toronto University Press, 2004).

Brock, Peter and Nigel Young, *Pacifism in the Twentieth Century* (New York: Syracuse University Press, 1999).

Brockway, Fenner and Stephen Hobhouse, eds., *English Prisons Today: Being the Report of the Prison System* Committee (London: Longmans Green and Co., 1922).

Brooke, Steven, *Labour's War: The Labour Party during the Second World War* (Oxford: Clarendon, 1992).

Brown, Callum, G., *Religion and Society in 20th Century Britain* (Harlow: Pearson, 2006).

Burns, Alan, *Sunderland's War Diary* (Sunderland: Otterburn Publications, 2007).

Caedel, Martin, *Pacifism in Britain 1914-1945: The defining of a Faith* (Oxford: Clarendon Press, 1980).

Ceadel, Martin, *Thinking About Peace and War* (Oxford: Oxford University Press, 1987).

Ceadel, Martin, *Semi-Detached Idealists: The British Peace Movement and International Politics, 1854-1945* (Oxford: Clarendon, 1996).

Calder, Angus, *The Myth of the Blitz* (London: Pimlico, 1969).

Calder, Angus, *The Peoples War* (London: Jonathan Cape, 1969).

Chrisp, Peter, *Conscientious Objectors: 1916 to the Present Day* (Brighton: Tressell, 1988).

Curran, James, and Seaton, Jean, *Power Without Responsibility: The Press and Broadcasting in Britain* (London: Routledge, 1997).

Davies, Arfor, Tegla, *Friends Ambulance Unit, the story of the FAU in the Second World War* (London: George Allen and Unwin, 1947).

Sam Davies, R G Morley, Bob Morley *County Borough Elections in England and Wales 1919-1938: A Comparative Analysis, Volume 3* (Farnham, Surrey: Ashgate Publishing, 2006).

Eller, Cynthia, *Conscientious Objectors and the Second World War: Moral and Religious Arguments in Support of Pacifism* (New York: Praeger, 1991).

Ellsworth-Jones, Will, *We Will Not Fight: The untold story of World War One's conscientious objectors* (London: Aurum Press, 2008).

Field, G. C., *Pacifism and Conscientious Objection* (Cambridge: Cambridge University Press, 1945).

Freedman, Jean, *Whistling in the Dark: Memory and Culture in Wartime London* (Lexington: University Press of Kentucky, 2015).

Gardiner, J., *Wartime Britain 1939-1945* (London: Headline, 2004).

Gardiner, J., *The Blitz* (London: Harper Press, 2010).

Goodall, Felicity, *We Will Not Go To War: Conscientious Objection during the World Wars* (London: The History Press, 2010).

Goodall, Felicity, *A Question of Conscience: Conscientious Objection in the Two World Wars* (Stroud: Sutton Publishing, 1997).

Gregory, James, *Of Victorians and Vegetarians* (London: Taurus Academic Studies, 2007).

Hayes, Denis, *Challenge of Conscience* (London: George Allen and Unwin, 1947).

Hayes, Denis, *Conscription Conflict: The conflict of ideas in the struggle for and against military conscription in Britain between 1901 and 1939* (London: Shepherd Press, 1949).

Hinton, James, *Nine Wartime Lives: Mass Observation and the making of the modern self* (Oxford: Oxford University Press, 2010).

Hughes, Michael, *Conscience and Conflict: Methodism, Peace and War in the Twentieth Century* (Peterborough: Epworth, 2008).

Hylton, Stuart, *Reporting the Blitz* (Stroud: The History Press, 2012).

Hylton, Stuart, *Their Darkest Hour: The Hidden History of the Home Front 1939-1945* (Stroud: Sutton Publishing, 2003).

Implay, Talbot C., *Facing the Second World War: strategy, politics and economics in Britain and France, 1938-1940* (Oxford: Oxford University Press, 2003).

James, David and Tony Jowitt, *The Centennial History of the Independent Labour Party* (Edinburgh: Edinburgh University Press, 1992).

Jappy, M. J., *Danger UXB: The Remarkable Story of the Disposal of Unexploded Bombs during the Second World War* (London: Channel 4 Books, 2003).

Kirkup, James, *White Shadows, Black Shadows: Poems of Peace and War* (London: J. M. Dent & Sons, 1970).

Kramer, Ann, *Conscientious Objectors of the Second World War* (Barnsley: Pen and Sword, 2013).

Laybourn, Keith, *A Century of Labour: A History of the Labour Party 1900-2000* (Stroud: Sutton Publishing, 2000).

Lowe, Roy, ed., *Education and the Second World War* (London: Routledge, 1982).

MacKay, R., *Half the Battle: Civilian Morale in Britain during the Second World War* (Manchester: Manchester University Press, 2002).

Martin, David, A., *Pacifism: An Historical and Sociological Study* (London: Routledge & Kegan Paul, 1965).

Marwick, A., *The Home Front: The British and the Second World War* (London: Thames and Hudson, 1976).

Milburn, Geoffrey and Miller, Stuart, *Sunderland – River, Town and People* (Sunderland: Borough of Sunderland, 1988).

Moorehead, Caroline, *Troublesome People: Enemies of War 1916-1986* (London: Hamish Hamilton, 1987).

Morgan, David, and Evans, Mary, *The Battle for Britain: Citizenship and Ideology in the Second World War* (London: Routledge, 1993).

Morrison, Sybil, *I Renounce War: The Story of the Peace Pledge Union* (London: Sheppard Press, 1962).

Nicholson, Virginia, *Millions Like Us: Women's Lives During The Second World War* (London: Penguin, 2012).

Noakes, Lucy and Pattinson, Juliette, eds., *British Cultural Memory and the Second World War* (London, Bloomsbury Publishing, 2014).

Norman, Bill, *Wartime Teesside* (Lancaster: Dalesman Books, 1989).

Overy, Richard, *Britain in the Second World War 1939-1945* (London: Sevenoaks, 2014).

Pearson, Arthur & George, *Friends Ambulance Unit in World War I and World War II: Experiences of Two Generations of a Dublin Quaker Family* (Dublin: Friends Historical Library, 2015).

Penton, James, M., *Apocalypse Delayed: The Story of Jehovah's Witnesses* Toronto: Toronto University Press, 2015).

Perry, Matt, *'Red Ellen' Wilkinson: Her Ideas, Movements and World* (Manchester: Manchester University Press, 2015).

Pois, Anne Marie, 'Practical and Absolute Pacifism in the Early Years of the U.S. Women's International League for Peace and Freedom,' in Brock, Peter and Socknet, Thomas Paul, *Challenge to Mars: Essays on Pacifism from 1918 to 1945* (Toronto: University of Toronto Press, 1999).

Rae, John, *Conscience and Politics: The British government and the conscientious objector to military service 1916-1919* (London: Oxford University Press, 1970).

Reynaud, Michel and Sylvie Graffard, *Jehovah's Witnesses and the Nazis 1933-1945* (New York: First Cooper Square Press, 2001).

Rose, Sonya, O., *Which People's War? National Identity and Citizenship in Wartime Britain* (Oxford: Oxford University Press, 2003).

Schott, L. K., *Reconstructing women's thoughts: The Women's International League for Peace and Freedom before World War II* (Palo Alto, CA: Stanford University Press,1997).

Smith, Lyn, *Voices Against War: A Century of Protest* (London: Mainstream Publishing, 2010).

Smithies, Edward, *Crime in Wartime: A Social History of Crime in World War II* (London: George Allen & Unwin, 1982).

Stevenson, John, *British Society 1914-45* (Harmondsworth: Penguin, 1984).

Stridiron, Gordon, *Blackshirts in Geordieland* (London: Black Horse, 2013).

Storey, Neil, R. and Housego, Molly, *Women in the Second World War* (Oxford: Shire Publications, 2011).

Taylor, Anthony, *The Prison System and its Effects: Wherefrom, Whereto, and Why?*, (New York: Nova Science Publications).

Taylor, Richard, K., S. and Young, Nigel, *Campaigns for Peace: British peace movements in the twentieth century* (Manchester: Manchester University Press, 1987).

Thomas, Donald, *An Underworld at War: Spivs, Deserters, Racketeers and Civilians in the Second World War* (London: John Murray, 2003).

Thorpe, Andrew, *A History of the Labour Party* (London: Palgrave Macmillan, 2015).

Thorpe, Andrew, *Parties at War: British Peace Movements in the Twentieth Century* (Oxford: Oxford University Press, 2009).

Todd, Nigel, *In Excited Times: The People Against The Blackshirts* (Whitley Bay: Bewick Press, 1995).

Trow, M., J., *War Crimes: Underworld Britain in the Second World War* (Barnsley: Pen & Sword, 2008).

Tulloch, John, 'The Return of the 'Conchie': Newspaper Representations of Conscientious Objectors and Pacifists in World War II,' in Gibson, Stephen and Mullen, Simon, *Representations of Peace and Conflict* (Basingstoke: Palgrave Macmillan, 2012).

Wilkinson, Alan, *Dissent or Conform?: War. Peace and the English Churches 1900-1945* (London: SCM Press, 1986).

Wills, Claire, *That Neutral Ireland: A Cultural History of Ireland during the Second World War* (London: Faber and Faber, 2007).

Wing, Sandra, Kos, ed., *Our Longest Days: A People's History of the Second World War* (London: Profile Books, 2007).

Yin, Robert, *Case Study Research: Design and Method* (London: Sage, 1994).

Secondary Sources – Journal Articles

Armstrong, Craig, 'Wartime Industrial Action on the Tyne 1939-1945,' *North-East* History, Vol 36, 2005, pp. 50-78.

Bales, Mitzi, 'They Said "No" to War: British Women Conscientious Objectors in World War II', www.wri-irg.org/node/11902.

Bourke, Joanna, 'Remembering War', *Journal of Contemporary History,* 39, 4 (2004), 473-485.

Brown, Matthew, *ILP History 4: War and After*, 22 January 2012, www.independentlabour.org,uk/main/2012/01/22/ilp-history-4-war-and-after.

Dekar, Paul, 'The "Good War" and Baptists who refused to fight in it,' *Peace and Change*, Vol. 32, 2 (April 2007), pp. 186-202.

Eller, Cynthia, 'Oral History as Moral Discourse: Conscientious Objectors and the Second World War,' *Oral History Review*, 18, 1 (Spring 1990), pp. 45-75.

Feld, Rena, 'From the Interviewer's Perspective: Interviewing Women Conscientious Objectors,' *Oral History Review*, 31, 1 (Spring 2003), pp. 29-37.

Gardiner, Juliet, 'Prisoners of Conscience', *History Today*, November 2004, pp. 32-39.

Gilbert, Mark, 'Pacifist Attitudes to Nazi Germany, 1936-45', *Journal of Contemporary History*, Vol. 27, No. 3, July 1992, pp. 493-511.

Girvin, Brian and Roberts, Geoffrey, 'The Forgotten Volunteers of World War II', *History Ireland*, 6, 1 (1998), 46-51.

Griffiths, Richard, 'A Note on Mosely, the 'Jewish War' and Conscientious Objection,' *Journal of Contemporary History*, Vol. 40, 4 (Oct. 2005), pp. 675-688.

Jefferys, Kevin, 'British Politics and Social Policy During The Second World War,' *The Historical Journal*, 30, 1 (1987), pp. 123-144.

Kelly, Tobias, 'Citizenship, Cowardice, and Freedom of Conscience: British Pacifists in the Second World War,' *Comparative Studies in Society and History* 57(3), 2015, pp. 1-29.

Mates, Lewis, 'A Most Fruitful Period? The North-East District Communist Party and the Popular Front, 1935-9', *North-East History*, 36, 2004, pp. 54-98.

McClean, Patricia, 'Catholic Conscientious Objection During World War II,' *The Catholic Historical Review*, Vol. 61, No. 2 (April 1975), pp. 222-242.

Nicholson, Hazel, 'A Disputed Identity: Women Conscientious Objectors in Second World War Britain', *Twentieth Century British History*, Vol. 18, No. 4, 2007, pp. 409-428.

Overy, Richard, 'Pacifism and the Blitz 1940-1941', *Past and Present* No. 219, May 2013, pp. 201-236.

Pemberton, John, 'Medical Experiments carried out in Sheffield on Conscientious Objectors to military service during the 1939-45 war', *International Journal of Epidemiology*, No. 35, 2006, pp. 556-560.

Pugh, Michael, 'Pacifism and Politics in Britain, 1931-1935,' *The Historical Journal*, Vol. 23, 3 (Sept. 1980), pp. 641-656.

Rempel, Richard A., 'The Dilemmas of British Pacifists During World War II', *The Journal of Modern History*, Vol. 50, No. 4, December 1978, pp. 213-229.

Rhoton, Nicole, 'World War II Resisters: Creating Communities of Resistance in Prison,' *Peace and Change*, October 2007, pp. 191-217.

Van den Dungen, Peter and Wittner, Lawrence S., 'Peace History: An Introduction,' *Journal of Peace Research*, Vol. 40, 4 (July 2003), pp. 363-375.

Wallace, R. G., 'The Origins and Authorship of the 1944 Education Act,' *History of Education*, 10, 4 (December) 1981, pp. 283-290.

Secondary Sources – PhD Theses

Anderson, Stuart, Unpublished PhD thesis: 'Refusing to fight the "Good War": Conscientious Objectors in the North-East of England during the Second World War,' (Northumbria University, November 2016).

Keil, André, Unpublished PhD thesis: 'States of Exception: Emergency Government and 'Enemies Within' in Britain and Germany in the First World War,' (Northumbria University, 2014).

Upham, Martin, 'Appendix F: Trotskyism and the ILP,' The History of British Trotskyism to 1949 (unpublished PhD Thesis, University of Hull, September 1980).

Secondary Sources – Television Fiction

Dad's Army, 'Branded', BBC Television, 1969.

Foyle's War, 'A Lesson in Murder', ITV Television, 2002.

Secondary Sources – Obituaries

www.telegraph.co.uk/news/obituaries/1538032/Lieutenant-Commander-John-Bridge-GC.html,
'Obituary: Lieutenant-Commander John Bridge, GC,' *Daily Telegraph*, 29 December 2006.
www.theguardian.com/artanddesign/2010/oct/13/maurice-bloomfield-obituary, 'Obituary:
Maurice Broomfield,' *The Guardian*, 13 October 2010.
www.independent.co.uk/news/people/obituary-william-douglashome-1554492.html, 'Obituary:
William Douglas-Home,' *The Independent*, 30 September 1992.
www.theguardian.com/education/2013/nov/14/grigor-mcclelland, 'Obituary: Grigor McClelland,' *The Guardian*, 14 November 2013.
www.scarboroughfieldnats.co.uk, 'Obituary: Athol Johnson Wallis (1919-2002),' *Scarborough Field Naturalists*.

Secondary Sources – Other

British Religion in Numbers, www.brin.ac.uk.
www.footbballand the firstworld war.com/norman-gaudie/, 'Norman Gaudie – Footballer and Conscientious Objector.
Moral Re-Armament, www.britannica.com/print/topic/391743.
Grace's Guide, www.gracesguide.co.uk/BartramandSons.
Audit Bureau of Circulations, www.abc.org.uk/.

A

Abbott, Vernon: 274

Absolutism: 28-29, 31, 42, 58-59, 60, 176-177

Adams, David MP: 90-91

Alexander, Kitty: 60, 212-214, 217, 248, 250-253, 260, 296, 298

Allen, Rev. Dr E. L.: 81

Almond, Amos & H: 66

Alnwick Gazette: 171

Appellate tribunal for Conscientious Objectors: 27, 47, 51, 210, 278, 288, 290, 292

Archbold, Edward: 60-62

Asquith (Whittles), Marjorie: 41, 255-256, 259

Assembly of God: 43, 105

Astor, Lady: 46

Aveling, Alderman (Member, North-West CO Tribunal): 105-106

B

Bailee, Sir James (Member, London CO Tribunal): 105

Bailey, Douglas: 52

Baines, Joseph: 52

Baldwin, Stanley PM: 26

Barnes, Ernest (Bishop of Birmingham): 192

Bartram, George Hylton: 16, 33-35, 71-72

BBC People's War Project: 22,

Bedford, Duke of: 27, 79-80, 106, 210-211, 259-260, 292

Bell, George (Bishop of Chichester): 192

Bell, James: 43

Bevin, Ernest MP (Minister of Labour): 30, 124,

Biagioni, John: 54

Bishop, Dorothy: 256

Blishen, Edward: 225-226

Boggon, John Robert: 101

Bohenna, Raymond: 99-100

Bolam, Constance: 35, 60, 248-250, 299

Boldon UDC: 113

Bowman, J.: 81, 258

Braithwaite, Arthur, Gregory: 52

Braithwaite, Isaac W.: 179-180

Bridge, John: 275

British Library (BL): 11, 22, 250

British Union of Fascists (BUF): 54

Brittain, Vera: 237-238

Brockway, Fenner: 45, 48, 206, 207, 208-209, 288-289

Brough, William: 41

Brown, Ernest MP (Minister of Labour / Minister of Health): 86-87, 131, 232

Brown, George: 215

Bryan, Alexander: 207, 214-215, 217-218

Burgis, Judge (Chair, North-West CO Tribunal): 81, 83, 256

C

Carden, Rev P. S.: 16

Carrick, T. R .: 70, 102

Carter, Frank: 52

'Cat and Mouse': 285-293, 294, 299

CBCO Bulletin: 249-250, 266

Central Board for Conscientious Objectors (CBCO): 11, 30, 92, 205-206, 208-209, 241, 268, 269, 281, 285, 287, 291, 292

Challenge, The: 254

Chamberlain, Neville PM: 26, 47

Chandler, Kenneth: 268, 272

Charlton, Clarence: 43

Charlton, Dorothy: 43, 244-245

Christadelphians: 43-44, 102, 278

Christian Pacifist Forestry Land Units: 222

Church of England: 44, 190

Church Times: 190-191

Churchill, Winston, S. PM: 124, 160
Civil Defence Direction (including fire-watching): 27-28, 60
Civilian Service Corps: 66
Cockcroft, Mary: 259-260
Communist Party of Great Britain (CPGB): 47, 49-51, 55, 160, 253, 254, 297
Conservative Party: 46
Cornelius, Raymond V.: 276
Council of Christian Pacifist Groups: 15, 16,
Cox, Alfred Peter: 132
Curry, George: 66
Curry, Leonard:66
D
Daily Mirror: 102, 160, 162
Daily Worker: 50, 160, 253
Dalston (Cumberland): 181-182
Darlington and Stockton Times: 128
Darlington Borough Council: 128-131, 153
Darlington Memorial Hospital: 151-152
Database of Conscientious Objectors: 10, 22, 23, 33, 35, 81, 144, 203-204, 228, 243-244, 259, 266, 268
Davey, William: 16, 68,
Davies, Rhys J. MP: 89
Davis, Judge (South-Eastern Conscientious Objectors Tribunal): 81, 266-267
Denny, Thomas & William: 66
Dickinson, Alan: 41
Dingle Vale Army Training Camp (Abuse allegations): 59, 268-273, 275, 280, 285
Distance, Leonard: 53
Dixon, Joseph: 100, 144
Dodds, Ruth: 46
Dodsworth, Joan: 246-247

Douglas-Home, Captain the Honourable: 277
Dover, Oswald: 144
Duff, Prof. James F.: 81
Durham County Advertiser: 115, 162,
Durham Prison: 29, 41, 61, 67, 203, 205, 207, 211-214, 215, 236, 250, 252, 276, 282, 298
Durham RDC: 144
Durham, City of, Corporation: 115-116
E
Earnshaw, Angus: 40, 41
Easington RDC: 143
Ede, Chuter MP: 90
Edwards, Alfred MP: 98-99
Elder, Jim: 227
Elton, Lord: 124-125, 156
Evening Chronicle: 127, 137, 146, 148, 153, 161, 162, 171, 241
F
Faldon, Bob: 230-231
Featherstone, Raymond: 51, 90
Fellowship of Reconciliation (FoR): 15, 16, 17, 33, 41
First World War: 18, 22, 25-26, 28, 29, 33, 45, 48, 49, 55-56, 60, 63-64, 66, 74, 75, 78, 86, 94, 154, 190, 207, 256, 258, 263, 272, 286, 294, 296, 297, 299
Fisher, Dorothy: 247
Foster, Albert: 49, 268, 269-272, 294, 299
Franklin, Judge (Chair of Manchester Tribunal): 98, 100
Friend, The: 85, 95, 100, 125, 190
Friends Ambulance Unit (FAU): 21, 40-41, 64-66, 96, 144, 151, 171, 180, 201, 231, 254, 255, 256-257, 277, 298

Friends War Victims Relief Committee: 257

G

Gale, James A. B.: 41, 133

Gaudie, Martin: 63, 64

Gaudie, Norman: 63-64

Gibson, W. N.: 268, 276

Gillender, Alma / Agnes: 60, 248

Gillender, Frank: 60

Gollan, John: 50

Goom, Kenneth: 41

Goulden, Thomas: 210

Grant, K. E.: 144

Griffiths, Prof. MP: 124

H

Handyside, Robert: 139

Harbottle, Robert: 72

Hardy, Douglas: 21, 41, 65-66, 296

Hargreaves, Judge (Chair, London CO Tribunal):104

Hartlepools Borough Council: 121-122

Harvey, T. Edmund MP: 78-79

Hayley, Muriel: 247

Hazel, H. M.: 66

Hazel, J. P.: 66

Heddon, Doreen: 247

Hemmings, Alfred: 210

Henderson, Gerald: 278, 287-289, 292, 294, 299

Henderson, James R.: 268

Henson, Bishop (retired) of Durham, Henley

Henson, Donald: 62, 208

Hepple, Mr: 53-54

Hexham Courant: 169

Hicken, Bernard: 232

Hillary, Edith: 247

Hilton, Stanley: 191-192, 263

Hobhouse, Stephen: 207

Hodgson, William: 44

Holbrough, W. J.: 179, 279

Holloway Prison: 207

Hollowell, K. John: 277

Holroyd, J. G.: 120, 123

Hunt, Elsie: 242

I

Imperial War Museum (IWM): 11, 22, 207, 255

Independent Labour Party (ILP): 15, 45, 47-49, 55, 269, 297, 299

J

Jarrow Housing Committee: 144-145

Jehovah's Witnesses: 20, 39-40, 42-43, 45, 74, 96-101, 102, 106-107, 109, 176, 204, 210, 217, 244-247, 252-253, 263, 287-288, 297, 299

Johnson, Matthew: 41

Jones, R. C. H.: 147-148

Jones, Royston: 44, 100

Judaism: 190

Jupp, Kathleen: 244-246

K

Kerr, Hazel: 101

Kilmourn, Basil, Alfred: 69-70

Kirkup, James: 9, 68-69, 79, 223-225, 226, 296, 299

L

Labour Party: 45-46, 296

Lamb, George: 85

Lang, Cosmo (Archbishop of Canterbury): 191

Lansbury, George MP: 15, 45, 78, 136, 226

Lawson, J. J. (Secretary of State for War): 285

Lawther, Steve: 227

Lawther, Will: 45, 227,296

Lazarsohn, Theo: 190

Leaf, J.: 120

League of Nations Union: 15,

Leeds Conscientious Objectors Tribunal: 47, 53

Leslie, J. R. MP: 219
Leyland, Peter: 21, 41, 66
Lindsay, John A.: 281
Liverpool City Council: 128
Long, Major Lawrence: 70
M
Maitland, Gordon: 60
Makin, Kenneth: 43, 49, 278-280, 293, 294, 296, 299
Marshall, Hilda: 242
Marshall, Mr: 52
Mass Observation: 9, 11, 22, 23, 31-32, 35-36, 38, 39, 50-51, 67-68, 70, 74, 104-105, 115, 149, 181-190, 201, 216-217, 222, 225, 227-228, 229-230, 273, 275, 295-296
McClelland, William, Grigor: 41, 43, 64-65
McGovern, John MP: 49, 105, 270, 278-279
Medical Experiments: 231-235
Mellanby, Dr Kenneth: 231, 233-235
Methodist Church: 44, 65, 101, 190, 195, 197-198
Middlesbrough Borough Council: 131-135, 153
Miles, Lieutenant Tim:292-293
Military Training Bill, 1939: 26-27, 51, 78
Ministry of Information: 160, 161, 162, 163-164
Ministry of Labour and National Service: 27, 33,
Morison, I: 268
Morland, Juliet: 40, 41, 253-255
Morley, Alan: 56, 57, 210
Morley, Dorothy: 248
Morley, John: 55, 56-57, 58-59, 210
Morley, Robert: 56, 57, 208, 210
Morpeth Herald: 141-142
Morris, Canon S. D.: 16,

Morrison, Herbert (Home Secretary): 45, 50, 203, 279
Mosley, Sir Oswald: 54
Mounsey, Ernest: 52-53
Mounsey, Michael: 41
Musgrave, Ray: 70
N
National Archives: 22,
National Association of Local Government Officers (NALGO): 144, 148-150
National Farmers Union (NFU): 219, 221-222
National Services (Armed Forces) Act (1939): 27, 94, 286
National Services Act (1941): 27, 94, 204-205, 209-210, 239, 241
National Union of Agricultural Workers: 218
National Union of General and Municipal Workers: 146, 150
National Union of Public Employees: 150
Neil, Thomas: 72
New Leader: 172, 203, 207
Newby, Thomas: 41
Newcastle City Council: 111, 135-139, 156
Newcastle Journal: 104
Newcastle War Resisters: 55-62, 75, 216, 248, 269, 296
Nicholson, Alderman F.: 81, 106, 247
No More War Movement: 15,
Noble, James Cecil: 72
No-Conscription Fellowship (N-CF): 15,
No-Conscription League: 50-51
Non-Combatant Corps (NCC) / Duties: 27, 243, 264-268, 269, 273-275
North Yorkshire County Council: 118-121, 153, 156

Northallerton Detention Barracks: 281-282, 294

North-East Gazette: 120, 153, 161, 162, 164, 172

Northern Daily Mail: 72, 124-125, 153, 162, 166, 168, 172

Northern Echo: 21, 127, 128, 151, 153,162

Northern Ireland: 36

Northumberland and Durham (Newcastle) CO Tribunal: 22, 31, 77-110, 263, 276, 278, 282, 288, 295, 297

Northumberland County Council: 114

Northumberland Miners Association: 151

Nunn, G. W. C.: 178

O

O'Neill, Denis: 51

Oglesby, T. W.: 122

Oxley, Albert: 60

P

Pacifist Service Units: 234

Parry, D. P.: 83-84

Peace News: 58-59, 60, 85, 91, 92, 103, 105, 155, 162, 172-173, 189, 191-192, 198, 229, 237, 239, 257

Peace Pledge Union (PPU): 15, 16, 17, 20, 22, 41, 59, 71-72, 239, 257

Pearce, R. D. W. H.: 247

Pearson, George: 120

Pedley, Robert: 41

People's War: 12-13,

Pethick-Lawrence, Kenneth MP: 80, 89, 104

Phelps, Rev Lloyd: 16

Philipson, Doris: 60, 248

Phipps, Sir Edmund (London Tribunal): 104

Pickering, Rev F. H.: 193-196, 201, 298

Pitt, Alfred: 43

Plymouth Brethren: 43, 101

Pollitt, Harry: 49-50

Ponsonby, Lord: 15, 45

Poole, C. C. MP: 78-79

Potter, Percy: 105

Presbyterian Church: 196-197

Q

Quakers (Society of Friends): 13, 14, 31, 37, 39-42, 63-66, 74, 96, 105, 107, 126, 171, 177, 254, 256, 257, 259

R

Radford, John: 270Ramsay, Charles: 44

Ramsbotham, Mr (President of Board of Trade): 123-124

Reeve, Dorothy: 99, 244

Reeves, Martha: 246, 247

Revolutionary Communist Party: 47-48

Richardson, John: 66, 265, 266

Richardson, Judge Thomas (Chair, Newcastle CO Tribunal): 54, 77-110, 244, 249, 258, 259, 297

Richardson, Sydney: 66

Richmond, Miles, Peter: 69

Ripon Gazette: 163, 169, 172

Robinson, Fred: 66

Robinson, James: 66

Robson, John Harvey: 34

Roman Catholic Church: 44, 190

Ronchetti, Louis: 67, 189, 226

Ronchetti, Paul, 67, 189, 212, 217, 226

Rossi, Amelia: 54, 258

Rowntree, Maurice: 41-42, 174

Royal Army Medical Corps (RAMC): 14, 21, 25, 44, 64, 99, 100, 263-266, 293

Rutherford, Walter: 138, 216

Rutter, Matthew: 52

S

Sadler, Cornelius & Dorothy: 56
Sadler, John (Jack): 55-56, 297
Sadler, Mark: 55, 56, 297
Sadler, Nancy: 56, 242, 248
Sadler, Robert: 56
Salkeld, John & Robert: 66
Seventh Day Adventists: 139
Shanklin, Frederick, John & Robert: 67
Sharp, Alf: 60
Sheffield Telegraph: 232-233
Shepherd, Dick: 15,
Shiel, Patrick: 141
Shields Gazette: 140-141
Short, Elizabeth: 120, 258-259
Shrimplin, Christopher: 205
Silverman, Mr MP: 86-87
Skipton UDC: 147-148
Smith, Alexander: 276
Smithson, George D.: 70-71
South Shields County Borough Council: 140-142
Sowerbutts, Geoffrey Lloyd: 128
Sowerby, George: 71
Spectator, The: 127-128, 154, 220-221
Stanley UDC: 145
Stanley, Oliver (Secretary of State for War): 279
Stewart, Judge (Chair of Leeds CO Tribunal): 98, 105, 122-123, 128, 168
Strangeways Prison: 214
Strauss, G. MP: 155
Sunday Sun: 77, 102-103, 161
Sunderland and District Peace Council: 17
Sunderland Borough Council: 155
Sunderland Echo: 109-110, 161, 164-166, 171, 172, 219-220
Sunderland Transport Committee: 145-146

T - V
Taylor, Dennis: 41, 72
Taylor, Norman: 41
Temple, Dr William (Archbishop of York / Canterbury): 127, 191-192
Thompson, Sir Luke: 81, 83, 103-104
Tomblin, Jack: 101-102
Torre, R. G. C.: 54
Trade Union Congress (TUC): 45-46
Troyte, Lieutenant-Colonel Acland MP: 123
Turner, A.: 72
Tyneside Apprentices Strike: 47
W - X
Walker, Edward: 131
Wallis, Athol, Johnson: 41,42
Walton Prison: 207
Walton, Jack: 60
War Cabinet: 124, 283-285 (treatment of men in detention barracks)
War Resisters International (WRI): 15, 17, 226
Ward, Cyril: 42-43
Waring, Cecil, Kathleen & Thomas: 67
Watson, Clarence L.: 231
Webb, William: 101
West Hartlepool Borough Council: 122, 142-143, 156
Wethered, Judge (Chair, South West CO Tribunal): 40, 80-81, 98
Whipp, Rev C. W.: 192
Whitby, Bishop of:132-134
White, Joseph Horton: 102
Wilkinson, Ellen MP: 15, 28, 49, 296
Willan, Joseph B.: 72
Wilson, Cecil MP: 155, 289, 290
Wilson, Fred: 41, 144
Wilson, John: 43
Wilson, Sir Arnold MP: 78
Wodeman, Richard: 235

Women Objectors: 30, 43, 237-261
Women's International League for
Peace and Freedom (WILPF): 238-
239
Wood (Smith), Freda: 41, 255, 257,
259, 260
Wood, Constance: 60
Wood, Harry: 60

Word, The: 58
Work Direction: 27
Wormwood Scrubs Prison: 211
Y - Z
York City Council: 125-128
Yorkshire Evening Post: 87, 152, 168,
170-171
Yorkshire Observer: 148

This project required the establishment of a database of objectors. In the absence of tribunal records this information was drawn together from prison records, regional and national newspapers, information held by the BBC *People's War Project*; the Mass Observation Archive; Imperial War Museum and British Library sound recordings; government records in the National Archives; the Peace Pledge Union objectors' database; and references to objectors in the secondary literature. A database of 820 conscientious objectors in the region was created, a valuable resource for future research, which can be found at https://sa-book.co.uk/